IMAGES
of America

ASSUMPTION PARISH

ON THE COVER: John "Sonny" Thibaut supervises plowing to prepare the field for planting with longtime employee Henry in 1949. Henry "Hank" was the only employee on the Thibaut farm trusted with the much-coveted Aliss-Chalmer tractor; he was also the only person capable of using it. (Courtesy of the John "Sonny" and Carolyn W. "Tini" Thibaut estate.)

IMAGES
of America

ASSUMPTION PARISH

Vivian Achee Solar

ARCADIA
PUBLISHING

ISBN 978-0-7385-9195-7

Published by Arcadia Publishing
Charleston, South Carolina

Printed in the United States of America

Library of Congress Control Number: 2012933018

For all general information, please contact Arcadia Publishing:
Telephone 843-853-2070
Fax 843-853-0044
E-mail sales@arcadiapublishing.com
For customer service and orders:
Toll-Free 1-888-313-2665

Visit us on the Internet at www.arcadiapublishing.com

Dedicated to Gerald and Olivia Chenevert: photographers, teachers, community leaders, and devoted parents whose contributions to Assumption Parish and this book are deeply appreciated.

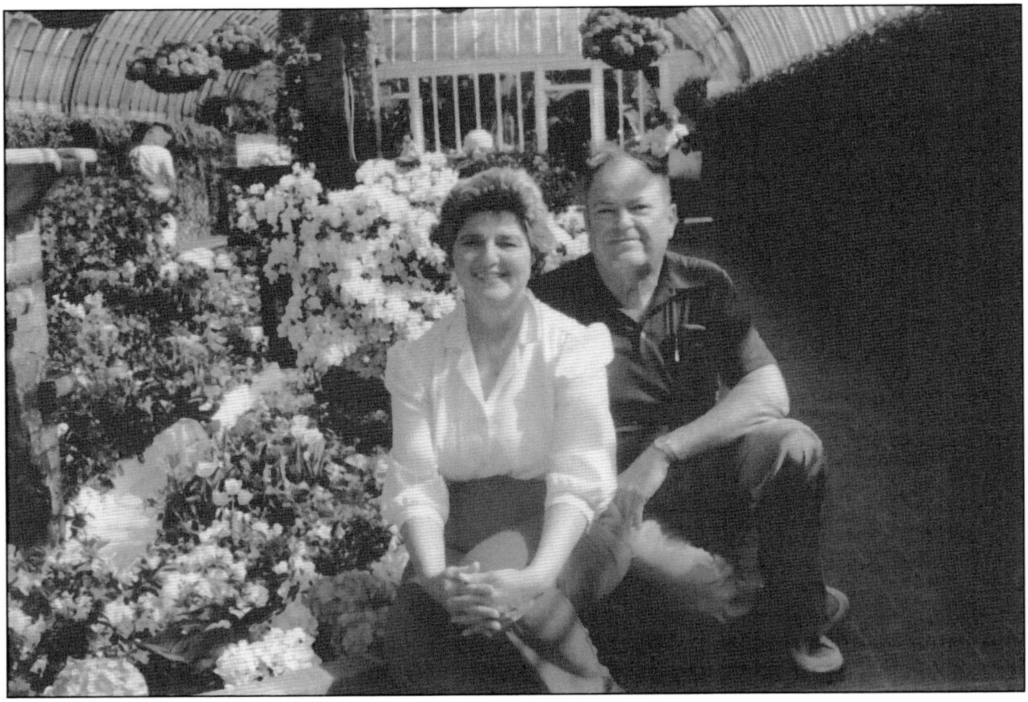

(Courtesy of the Gerald and Olivia Chenevert family.)

Contents

Foreword

As a person who was born and raised in the Midwestern small town of Paris, Illinois, and having been transplanted to this wonderful part of south central Louisiana, I have a perspective of this place, its people, and its customs that is unique to that of others whose families have lived here for generations. In addition to being a "converted Cajun," my perspective also comes from marrying a young lady in the late 1960s whose ancestors lived here for generations. The people have more than welcomed me. It has been my honor and privilege to serve on the parish school board for over 30 years. It has been a way to give back to this community. This is truly home.

This book is written by one of Assumption's native daughters, herself a descendant of several generations of this land. I have known Vivian Achee Solar since she was a child; however, I really began to see her talents for writing and storytelling when she was a student worker of mine at Nicholls State University in the computer science department. Her attention to detail was very evident, as was her demonstrated love of this area. Vivian Solar's pictorial history conveys Assumption's rich past and current success. Some things have not changed much since the 1800s. Beautiful plantation homes, among those pictured in this book, still stand in Assumption Parish. The cane fields are also as abundant as they were many years ago, altered by modern advances in harvesting and transportation. Several churches in the area have stood the test of time; some built over 100 years ago are still in use as places of worship for this community, which has strong religious roots.

Assumption is a proud parish, a place that many notable people have called home. Its citizens, past and present, have made great contributions in several different fields. Many physicians and lawyers were born, raised, and educated here. The mere mention of the names of educators, too numerous to list, can spark a conversation about the impact that they have had on the lives of their students. This parish is the birthplace of many public servants, from US congressman to federal judges, state supreme court justices, state senators, and representatives. Currently, it is the home of a federal judge, two state representatives, and a state senator. An Olympic medal winner and two consecutive Super Bowl winners have also called Assumption home. Even with these accomplished people, the true strength of Assumption Parish is indeed its everyday people: the hardworking, community-minded, and extremely friendly residents.

—Lawrence "Larry" Howell
Executive Vice President
Nicholls State University

ACKNOWLEDGMENTS

I offer a heartfelt thank-you to the people who contributed to Arcadia Publishing's Images of America: *Assumption Parish*. Robbie Solar's research and support made this project possible. Jacob Winston's insights assisted in the development of the text. I thank my former mentor and boss, Larry Howell, for his foreword. Betty Lott and Meredith Miceli supported me during the writing. Thanks to Joe Daigle for office space. I thank friends, family, and neighbors who shared their stories, photographs, and support.

Dr. Teri Maggio, director of the Assumption Parish Library, provided contact information and sources. Special thanks to Clare Chenevert Acosta for taking the time to share her parents' body of work and to the Chenevert family, who shared in this contribution. Thanks to David Mitchell, Phillip Gianelloni, and the *Assumption Pioneer* for providing background information for captions. Grateful appreciation is offered to Ellender Memorial Library director Robert J. Bremer, archives director Clifton Theriot, and associate Emilie P. Pitre for historical assistance as well as technical support.

Several vintage photographs were utilized from the John "Sonny" and Carolyn "Tini" Thibaut estate. Thanks to Linda Cooke, who made photographs available from the Gerald and Olivia Chenevert collection of the historical committee of the friends of the Assumption Parish Library. Carolyn Talbot Maloney offered cherished family photographs. Thank-you to Mildred Sylvester, who graciously welcomed me into her home, offered photographs, and shared stories. Thanks to Jerilyn Williams, Catherine B. Moore, and Albert Steib, who provided photographs, information, and contacts on behalf of St. Benedict the Moor Catholic Church.

Thanks to Carol Guillot, Cheryl Arboneaux, Rev. Joel LaBauve, St. Anne Church, Fr. Joseph Van Baast, SSJ St. Jules Church, St. Elizabeth Church, Cathy Albarado, Rev. Andrew Merrick, Diane LeBlanc, Martha Newchurch, Kent Templet, Yvette Winston, Henry and Gene Adolph, Don and Diane Bergeron, Amy Roth, Mignon Gillen, Raymond and Marlene LaBarre Folse, Larry and Tina Howell, Caroline Klotz Masur, Martin Triche, Jane Triche-Milazzo, Joey and Kim B. Comeaux, Renee B. Richard, Johnny Meads, Nick and Loretta Carier, and Donald, Billie, and Nikki Blanchard.

Introduction

French explorers first came through Assumption Parish in the early 1700s, finding a variety of Native American tribes. The largest of these was the Chitimacha Tribe, which is thought to have been one of the leading Louisiana tribes in 1700. Assumption Parish was established under both French and Spanish rule as part of the Lafourche Settlement during the middle 1700s. Acadians exiled from Nova Scotia between 1755 and 1765 greatly increased the area's population, clearing land and settling in the Pierre Part. Valenzuela was one of the four communities in south Louisiana founded and inhabited primarily by settlers from the Canary Islands, imported in family units around 1778 by the Spanish government. It served as military post, located on Bayou Lafourche near the later site of Belle Alliance Plantation, the 841-acre grant to Don Juan Vives, an early Spanish physician and officer in the Galvez Expedition. In 1785, Assumption had a population of 646. Assumption Parish became the eighth parish of Lafourche Settlement on March 31, 1807, five years before Louisiana entered the Union. It was named for the Festival of the Assumption of the Blessed Virgin Mary.

Assumption Parish has always been agriculturally based, beginning with Indian inhabitation. Historical records indicate that the first settlers to come to the region were likely trappers and traders, but farmers soon followed. In 1861, sugarcane was the principal crop grown in Assumption Parish. In 1879, the steamboat *Assumption* traveled up and down Bayou Lafourche. Crevasses from the bayou would flood the surrounding land; so in 1904, the bayou was damned up where it meets the Mississippi River, and steamboat travel was no longer a part of Bayou Lafourche. Since then, most soils in the parish that are not prone to flooding produce sugarcane. Today, Assumption Parish remains an important sugarcane-producing parish. Large farms or plantations have kept sugar in production for generations.

Napoleonville, situated on Bayou Lafourche, at about the center of the parish, is the parish seat. Assumption Parish is bordered on the north by Iberville and Ascension Parishes, on the east by St. James and Lafourche Parishes, on the south by Terrebonne and St. Mary Parishes, and on the west by St. Martin and Iberia Parishes.

One

Early

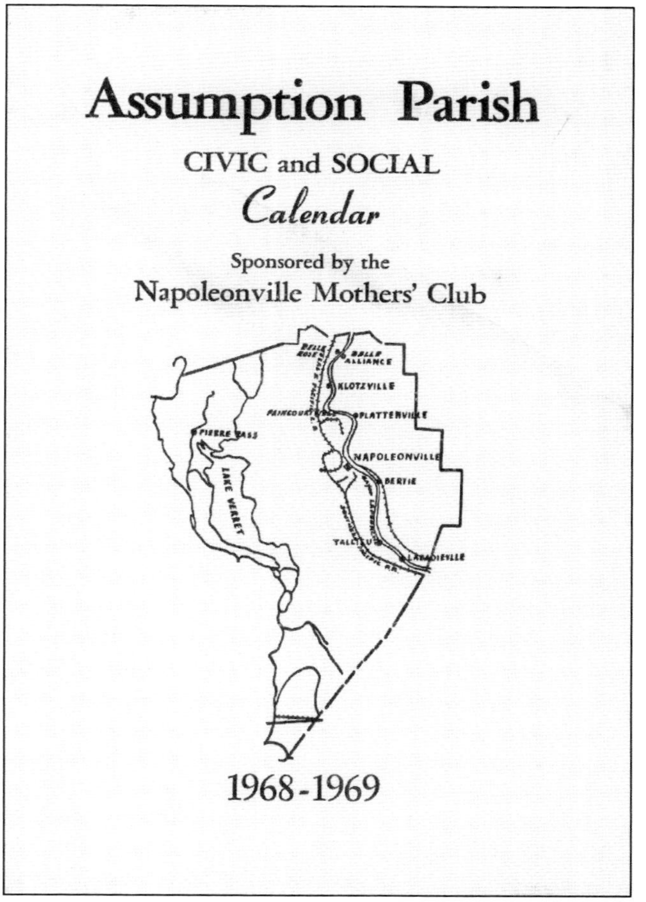

The 1968–1969 Napoleonville Mother's Club civic and social calendar is adorned with a parish map.

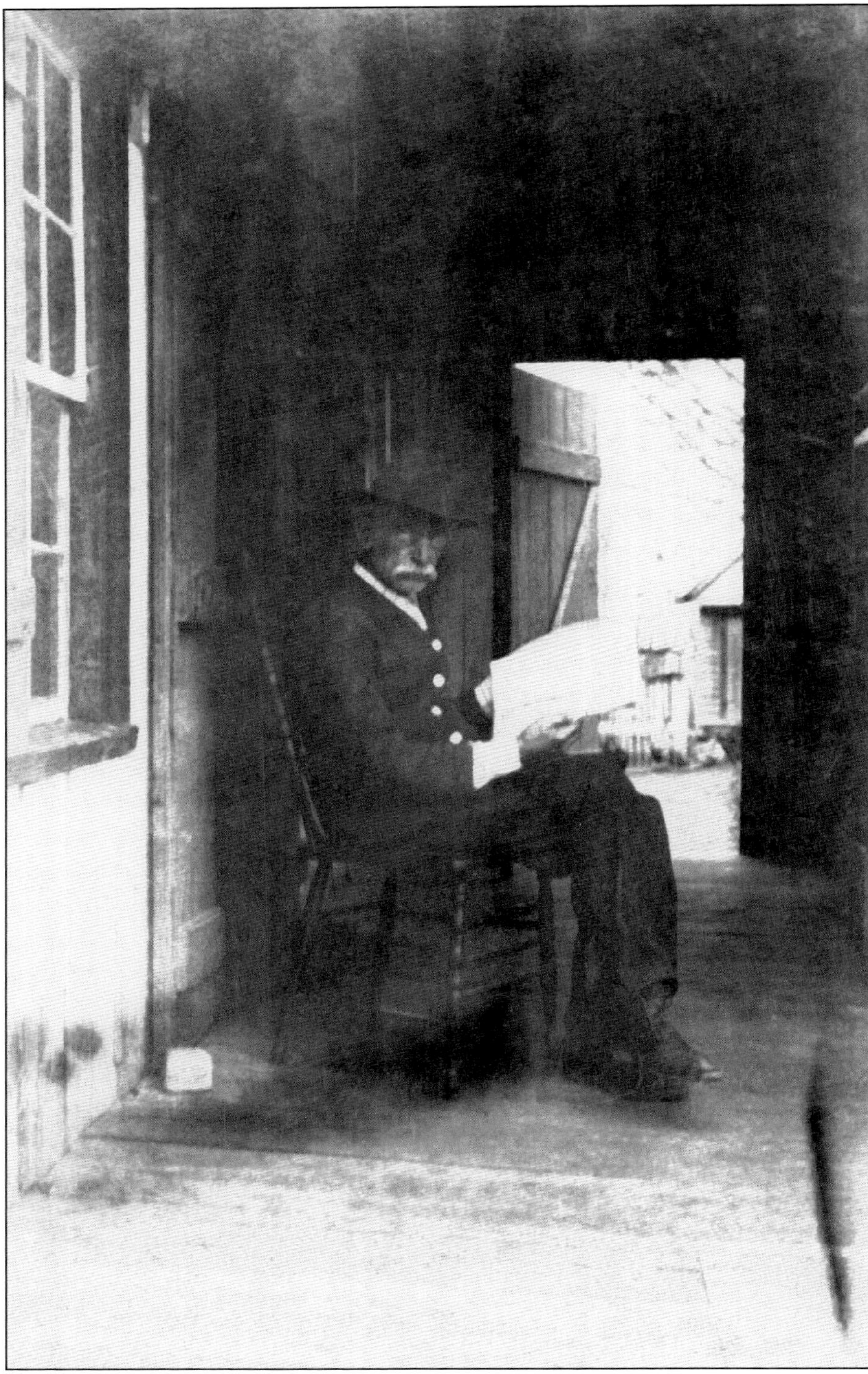

Emile Adolph sits on the porch of his family home. He was born in 1848 and was married to Lelia Marie Templet. They were parents to 11 children; many of his descendents remain in Assumption Parish. (Courtesy of the Adolph family.)

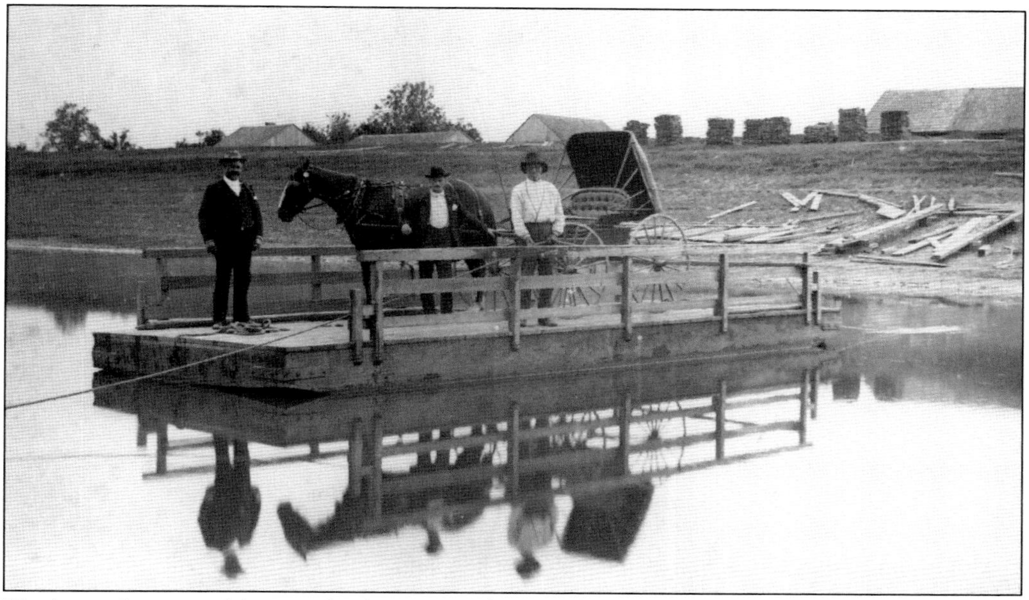

The horse, buggy, and ferry in this late-1800s photograph from Labadieville are the three common forms of transportation of the day. The ferry was privately owned by Philibert Gauthe, caretaker of St. Philomena Church and son of Jean Marie Gauthe. The elder Gauthe, a veteran of the Louisiana 17th Infantry at Vicksburg, died in 1878 of the epidemic contracted through caring for victims of yellow fever. (Courtesy of William Littlejohn Martin Collection, Archives and Special Collections, Nicholls State University, Thibodaux, Louisiana.)

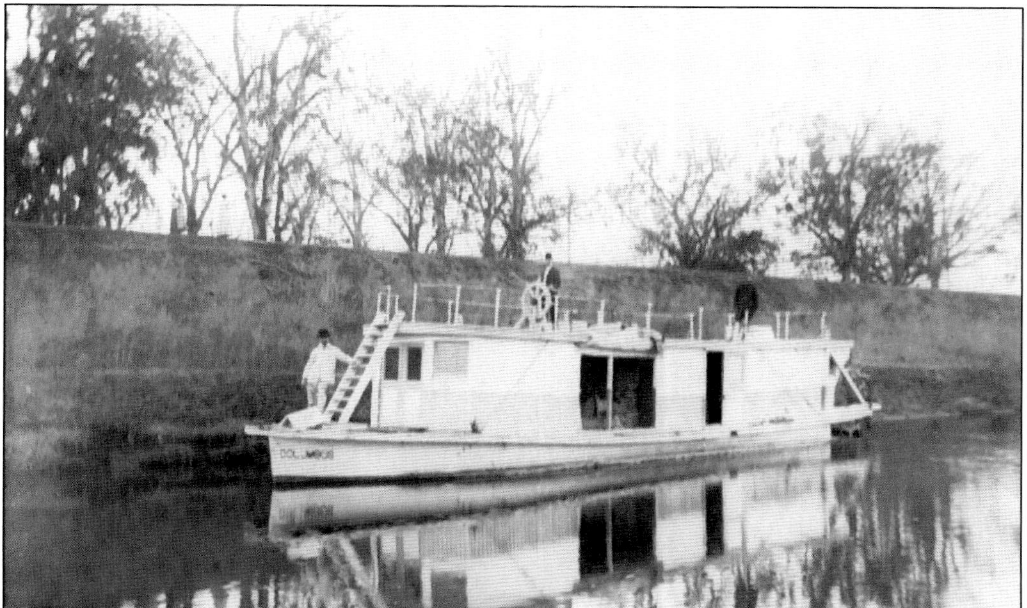

The *Columbus* paddle wheeler was one of many types of boats common along Bayou Lafourche in the 1890s. Many goods and services made their way to the bayou-side communities, making them efficient places to dock and conduct business. (Courtesy of Donald and Billie Eris Blanchard.)

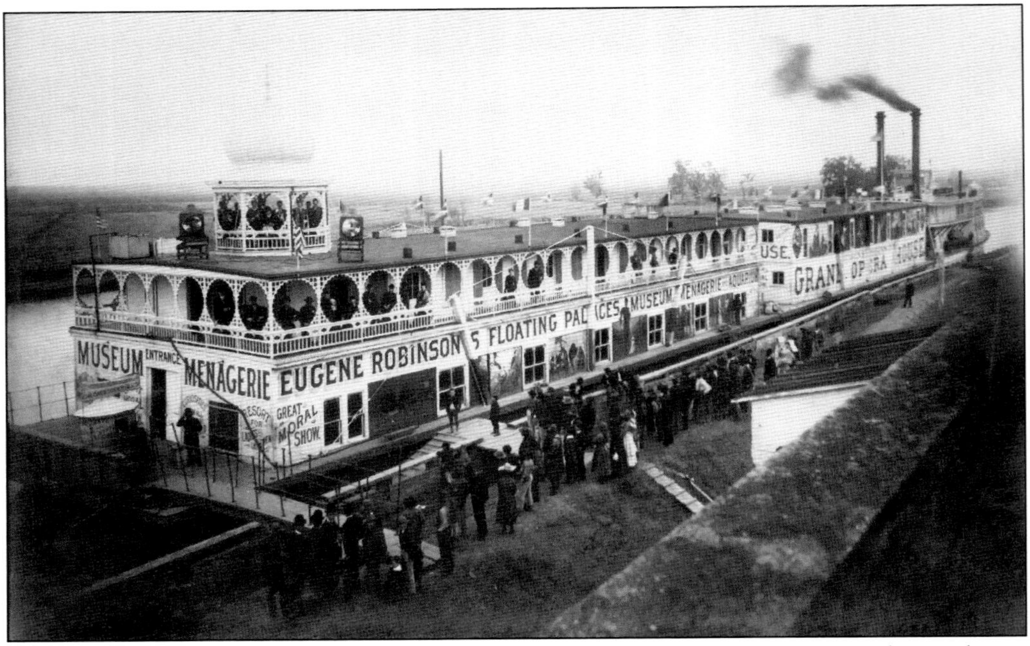

The 1890s steamship *Eugene Robinson* was an entertainment barge, menagerie, and opera house that served as a leading portable venue. Its namesake and promoter ran multiple enterprises in New Orleans and was a promoter of the P.T. Barnum School of Entertainment. (Courtesy of William Littlejohn Martin Collection, Archives and Special Collections, Nicholls State University, Thibodaux, Louisiana.)

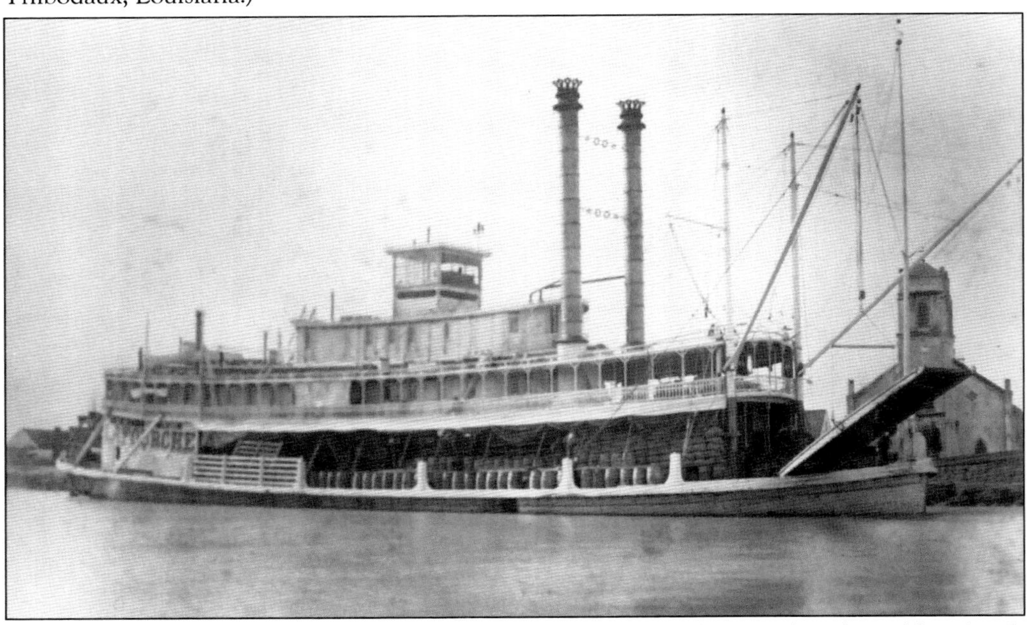

This photograph of *Lafourche* was taken in Labadieville. Loaded down with sacks and hogsheads of sugar on the lower deck, the steamboat was owned and piloted by Pierre Charlet. (Courtesy of William Littlejohn Martin Collection, Archives and Special Collections, Nicholls State University, Thibodaux, Louisiana.)

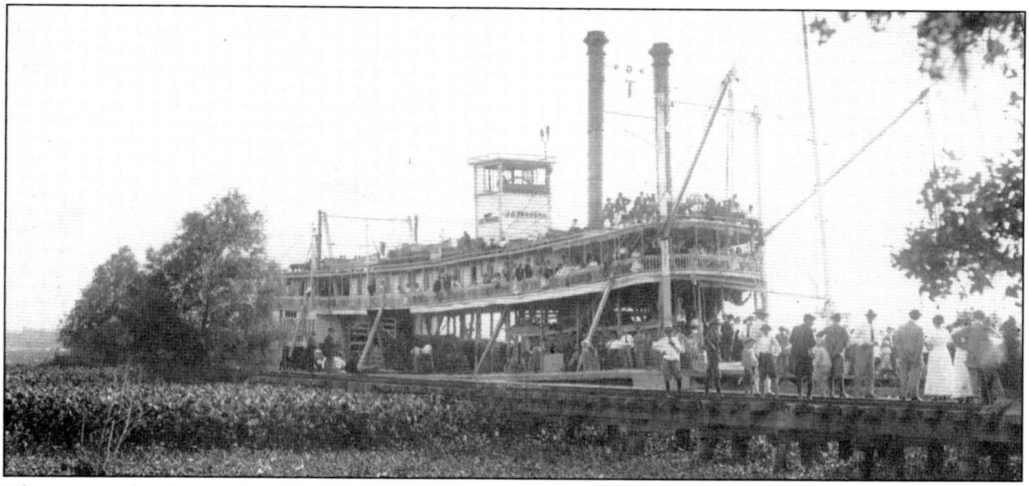

The stern-wheeler packet *The Trudeau*, built in 1889 and owned by New Orleans & Washington Packet Co., operated in the New Orleans and Atchafalaya area. She burned at Belle River, Louisiana, on February 29, 1912. (Courtesy of William Littlejohn Martin Collection, Archives and Special Collections, Nicholls State University, Thibodaux, Louisiana.)

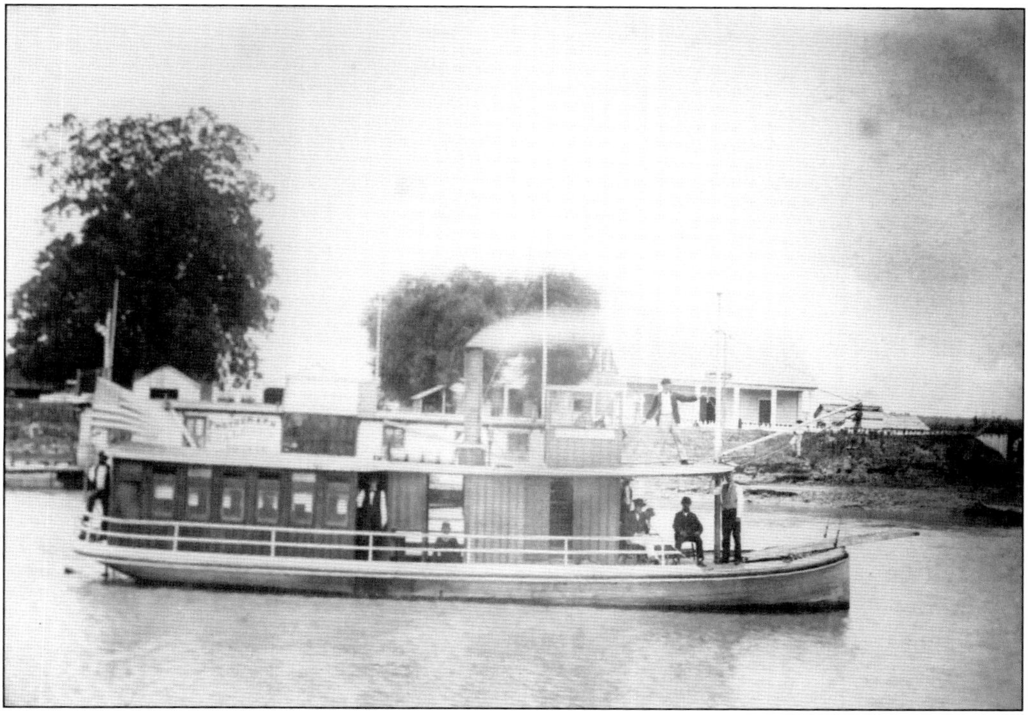

Photograph boats like this one, *Success*, were so common in the mid-1880s that Assumption levied a special license tax on them. The vessels were a way for photography studios to serve the outlying communities. This one was owned by a New Orleans photography studio on Canal Street and made periodic trips to Bayou Lafourche. An example of the onboard studios can be seen at the bottom of page 21. (Courtesy of William Littlejohn Martin Collection, Archives and Special Collections, Nicholls State University, Thibodaux, Louisiana.)

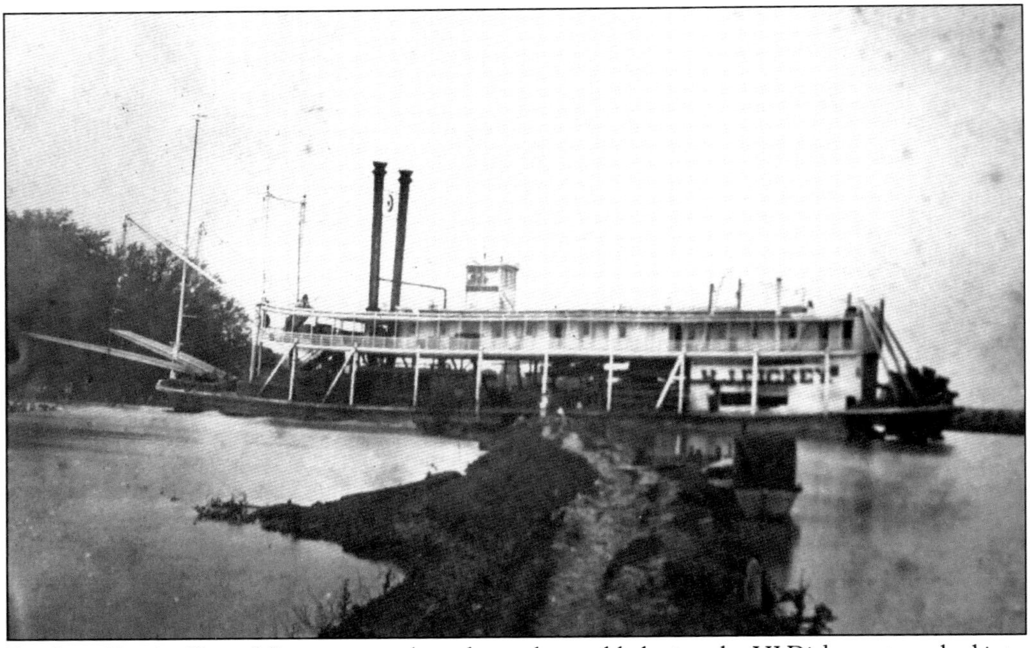

Employed by the United States to supply and patrol unstable levies, the *HJ Dickey* gets sucked into Jones Crevasse in 1883 at Melrose Plantation above Labadieville while unloading sacks to plug the breach. (Courtesy of William Littlejohn Martin Collection, Archives and Special Collections, Nicholls State University, Thibodaux, Louisiana.)

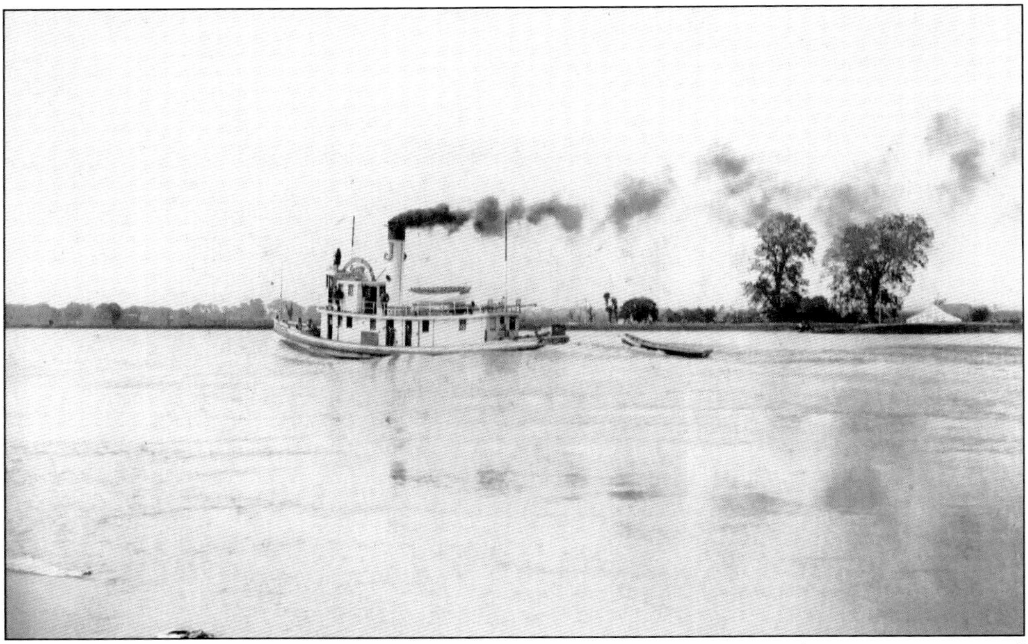

Tugboats work on waterways assisting vessels, transporting cargo, and providing services essential to commerce and recreation. This late-1890s tugboat pulls a skiff along a swelling Bayou Lafourche. Conditions along levees were precarious, with common breaching and threat of seasonal flooding. (Courtesy of Nick and Loretta Carrier.)

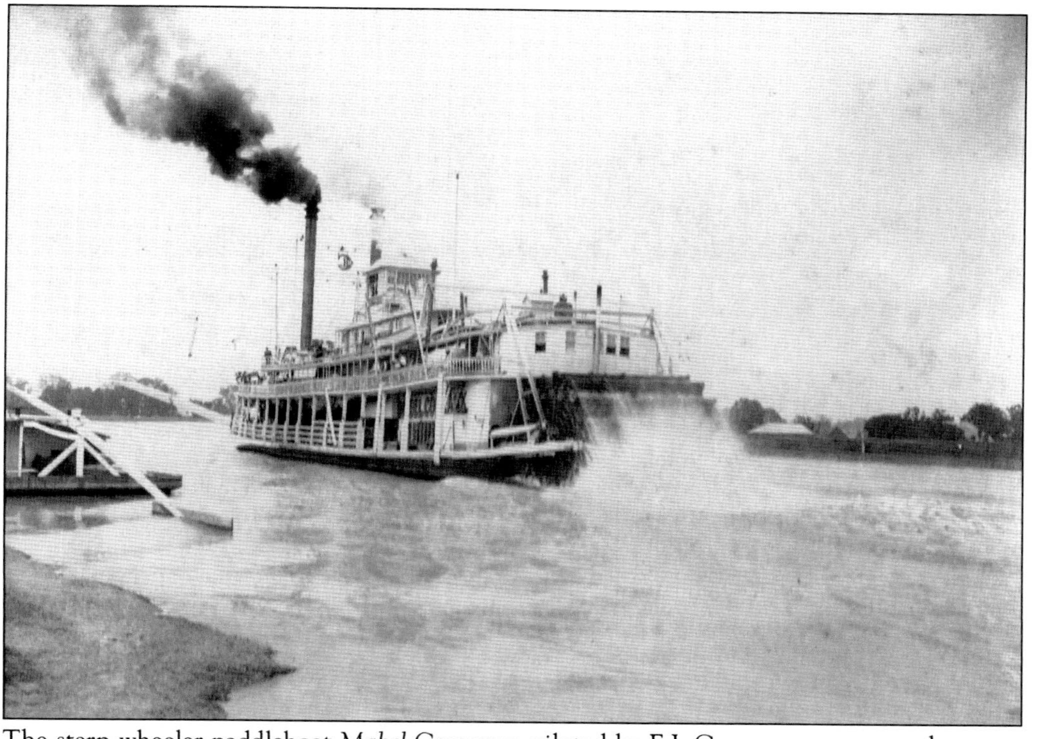

The stern-wheeler paddleboat *Mabel Comeaux*, piloted by E.J. Comeaux, ran a regular route from New Orleans to Donaldsonville and down Bayou Lafourche in 1902. In 1897, John Duffy, known as the "Terrible Swede," matched Joe Green in a clandestine boxing match aboard *Mable Comeaux*; about 100 men paid $5 to watch the fight. The paddleboat was dismantled in 1909 in Donaldsonville. (Courtesy of Nick and Loretta Carrier.)

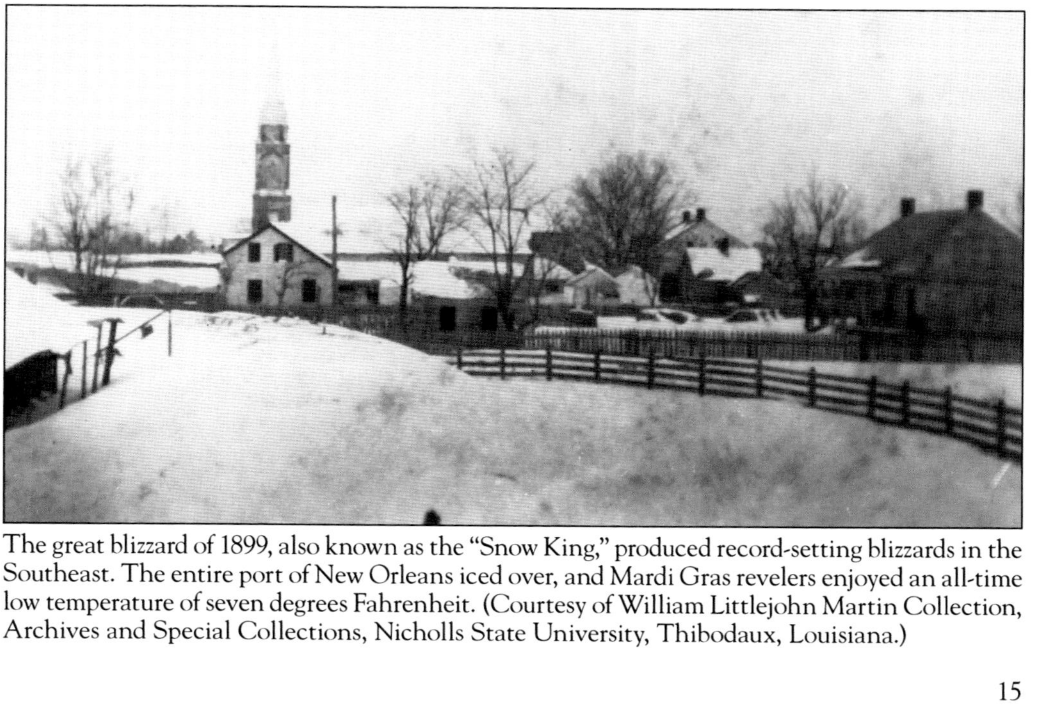

The great blizzard of 1899, also known as the "Snow King," produced record-setting blizzards in the Southeast. The entire port of New Orleans iced over, and Mardi Gras revelers enjoyed an all-time low temperature of seven degrees Fahrenheit. (Courtesy of William Littlejohn Martin Collection, Archives and Special Collections, Nicholls State University, Thibodaux, Louisiana.)

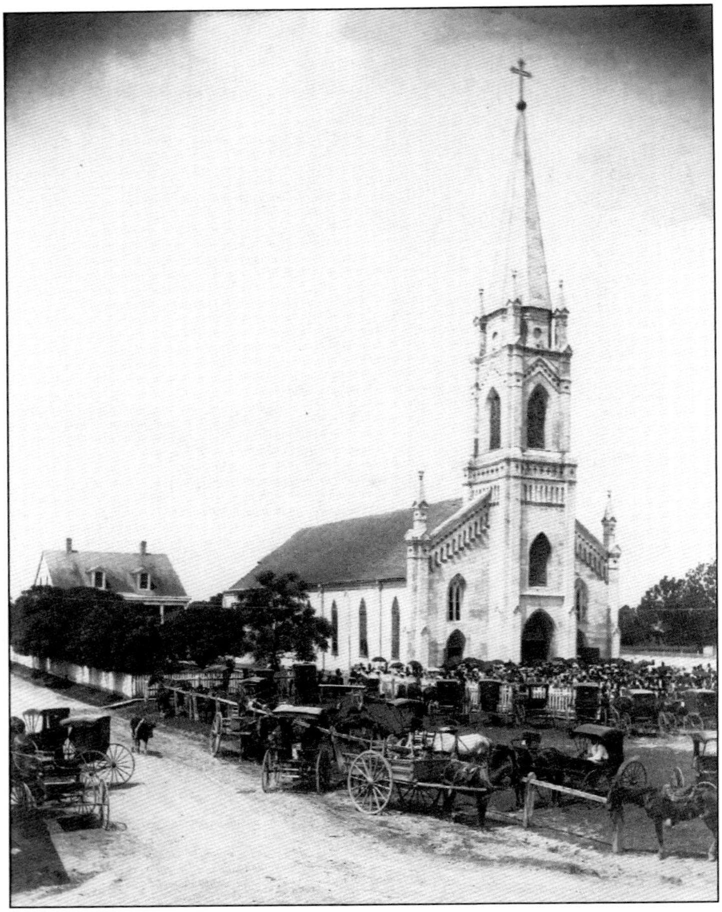

This late-1890s photograph depicts a typical church gathering in Labadieville. Horses and buggies wait along the road and in the churchyard for the services to end. (Courtesy of Nick and Loretta Carrier.)

Cancienne Plantation Train Station was on the Southern Pacific line. Train lines were frequently used to transport sugarcane to mills. They were the single largest boon to the industry at the time. (Courtesy of the Adolph family.)

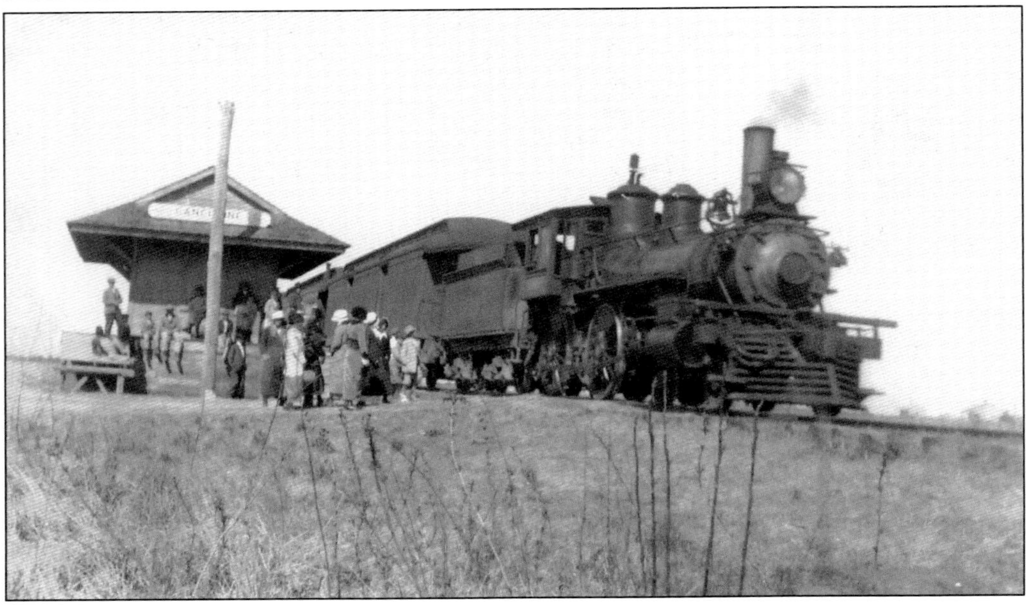

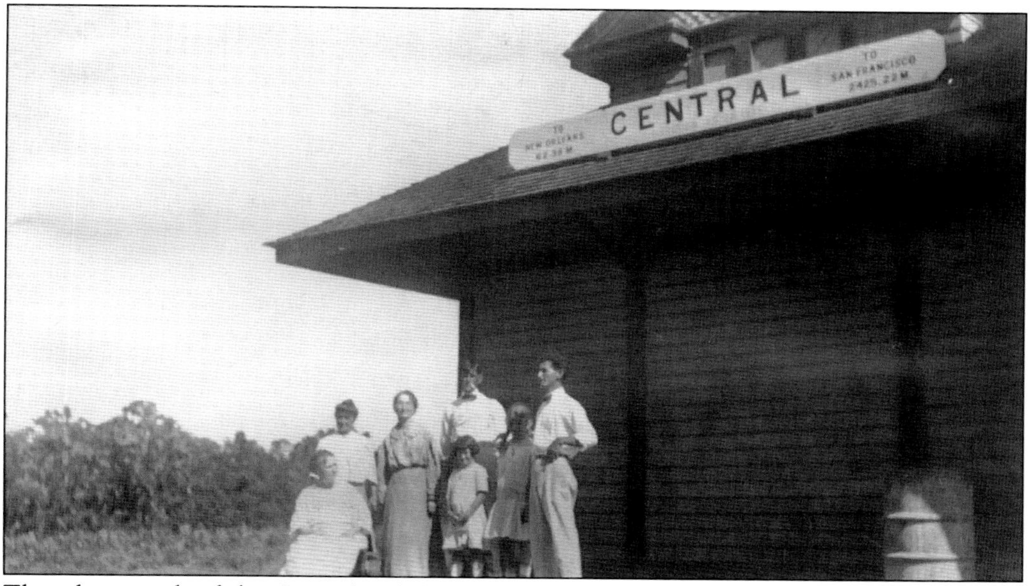

This photograph of the Central rail depot shows the Singer family with John (in the back) and Rita Cancienne. Rita was the third daughter of Emile and Lelia Adolph. (Courtesy of the Adolph family.)

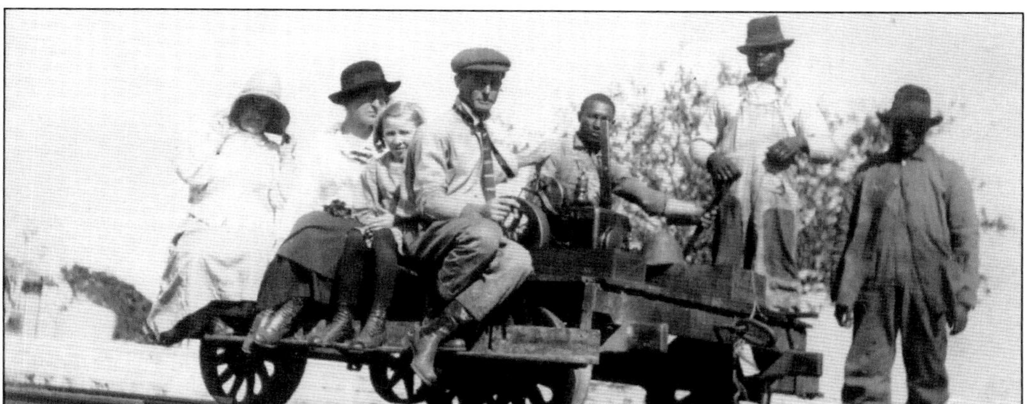

Handcars, like the one in this photograph, made regular railroad inspection and maintenance easier. Here, line man Arthur Singer takes a group for a leisure ride. (Courtesy of the Adolph family.)

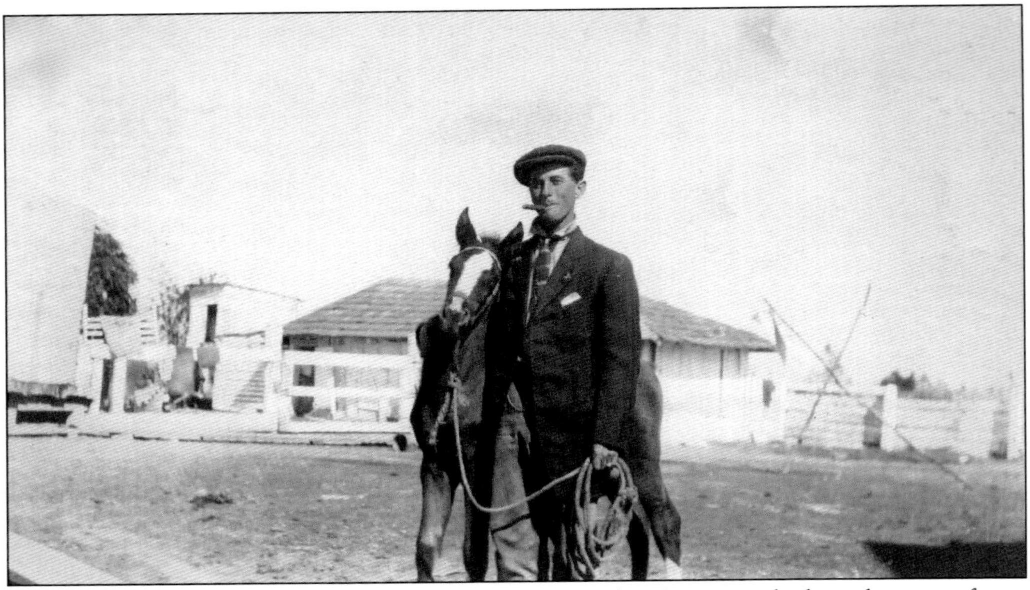

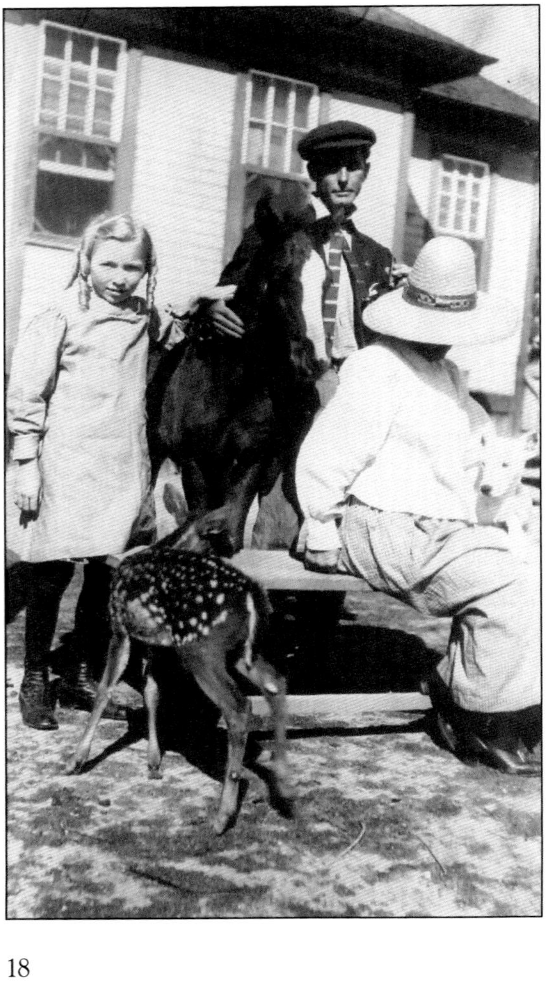

Arthur Singer worked as a line man for Southern Pacific. His responsibilities included inspection, maintenance, and repair of railroad tracks that ran through the Cancienne Plantation Train Station. (Courtesy of the Adolph family.)

The Singer family is shown here with service animals and pets. Although the line men worked for the railroad company, they lived in communities where they were stationed. (Courtesy of the Adolph family.)

Here, the daughter of Arthur Singer poses with her pet fawn. In rural communities, animals that would be considered exotic pets by today's standards were commonplace. (Courtesy of the Adolph family.)

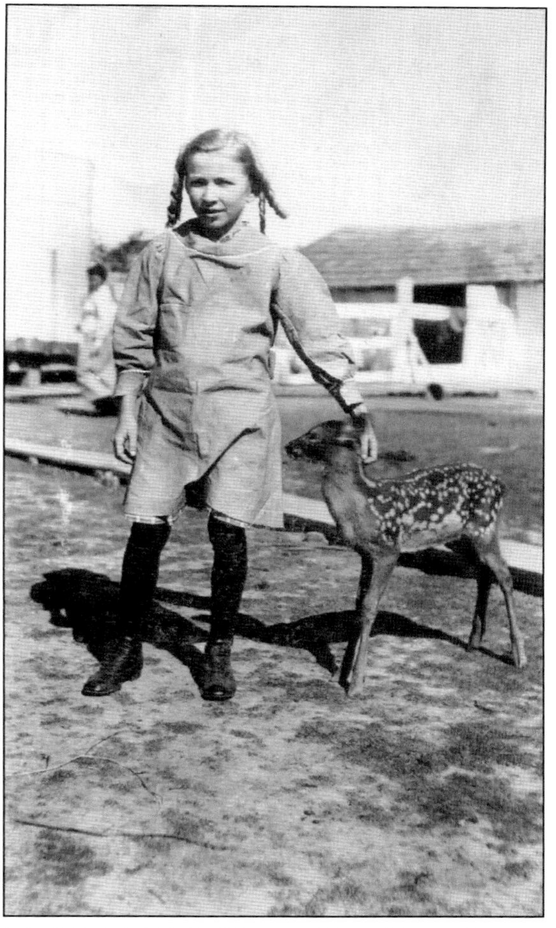

Horse-and-buggy travel was the primary form of local and regional transportation. Dirt roads made only the nicest weather practical for daily rides. (Courtesy of the Adolph family.)

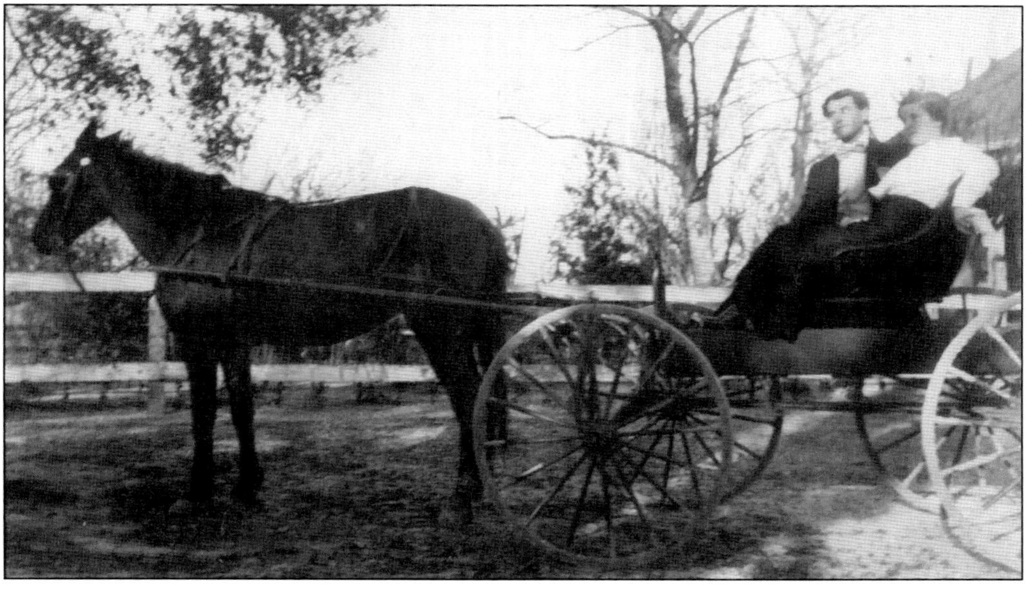

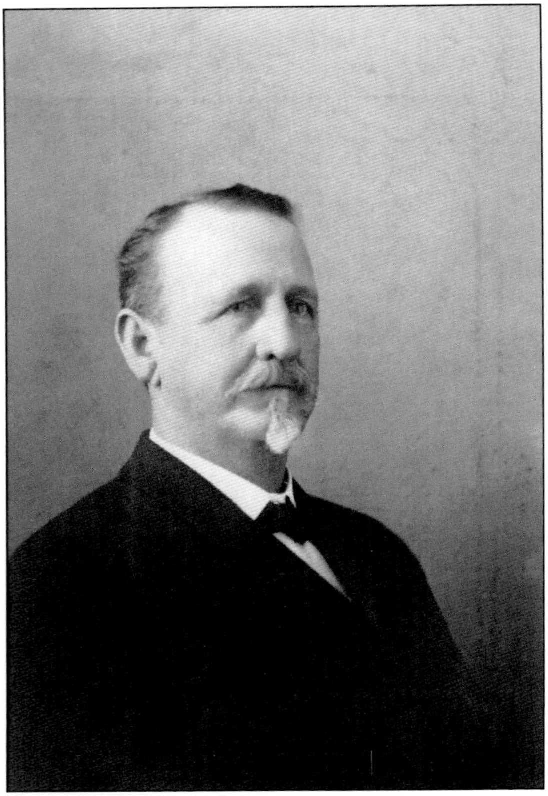

Capt. Pierre Charlet was a pioneer steamboat man and Confederate veteran who served with the 2nd Louisiana regiment during the war. He ran the steamboats *Lizzie Hopkins*, *Belle of the Coast*, *Assumption*, *Lafourche*, *Gem*, and *Mabel Coumeaux*. He transported a great part of the sugar from Lafourche to New Orleans and was also part owner of the Lafourche line. He died in 1911. (Courtesy of the John "Sonny" and Carolyn W. "Tini" Thibaut estate.)

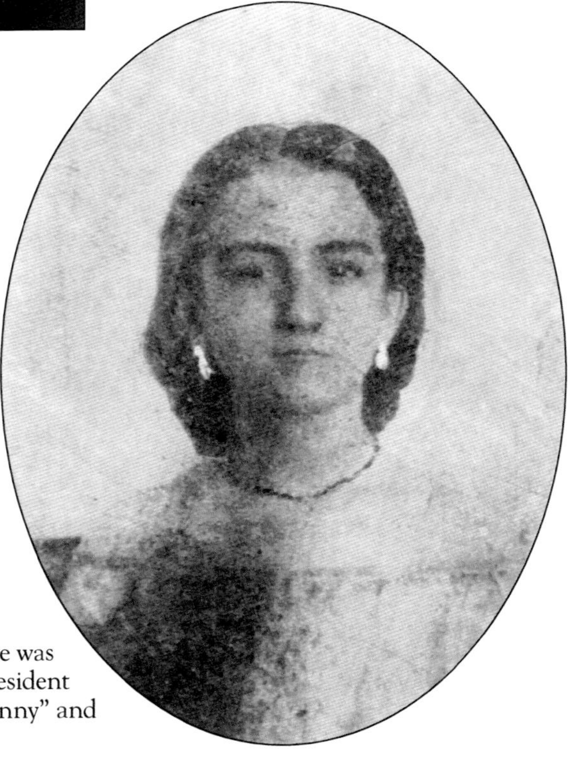

Pictured here is Eulalie Pintado Charlet. She was the wife of Pierre Charlet and a lifetime resident of Assumption. (Courtesy of the John "Sonny" and Carolyn W. "Tini" Thibaut estate.)

Alcee M. Charlet practiced medicine in Assumption Parish after graduating from Tulane University in 1891. He was the son of Pierre and Eulalie Pintado Charlet. (Courtesy of the John "Sonny" and Carolyn W. "Tini" Thibaut estate.)

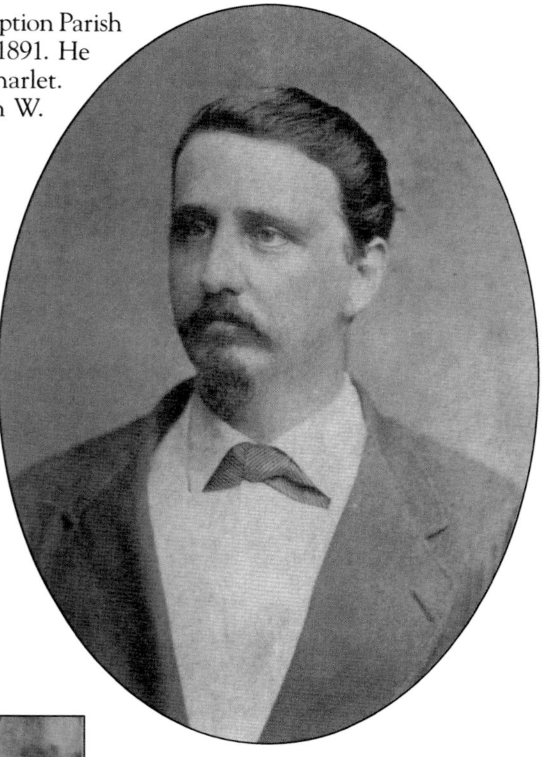

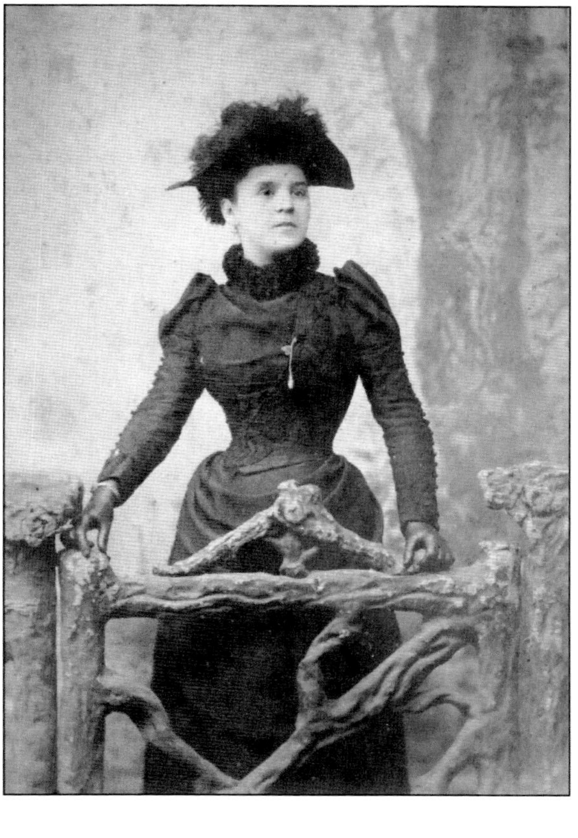

Lillia Dugas Charlet is seen here in this 1880s portrait. She was the daughter of Honore Dugas and married Elphage Charlet, son of Capt. Pierre Charlet and Eulalie Pintado Charlet. (Courtesy of the John "Sonny" and Carolyn W. "Tini" Thibaut estate.)

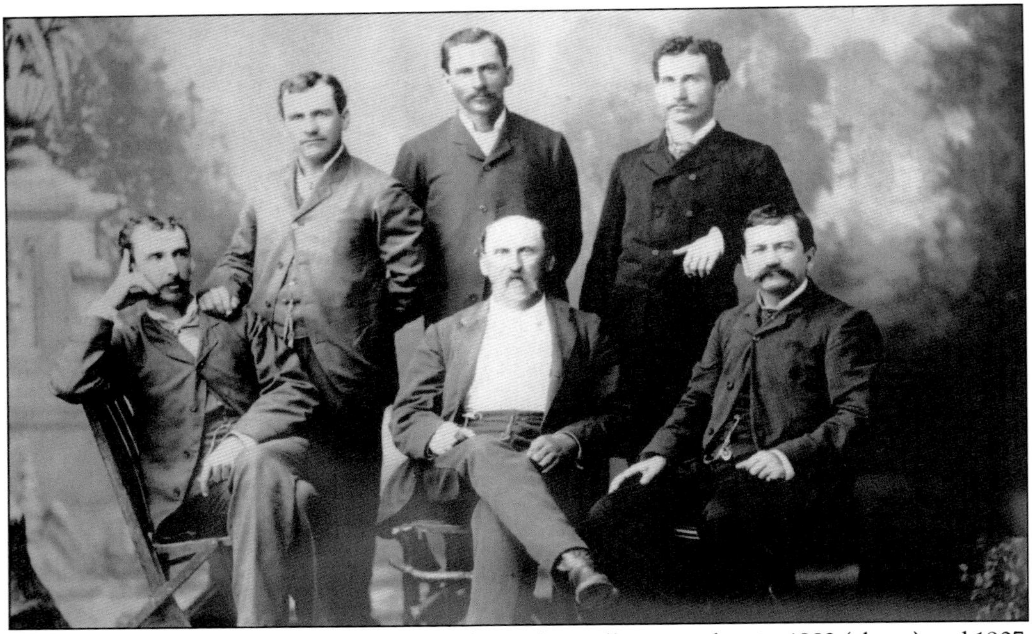

These photographs of the Dugas brothers of Napoleonville were taken in 1882 (above) and 1907. The brothers include Claiborne, Felix, Ulysse B., Dr. Elphege T., Honore, and Xavier. They had notable careers in the Assumption area. Ulysse B. was a planter and co-owner of Nottoway. Both Claiborne and Xavier served as parish clerks of court. After Xavier's death, his wife, Minta Joffrion, continued his tenure, subsequently becoming the first female clerk of court to serve in the parish. Dr. Elphage Dugas formed a successful insurance partnership with Solomon Klotz; his daughter Elizabeth married Tulane-educated attorney Aubert L. Talbot, whose legacy would figure into the history of Assumption politics over the next 100 years. (Both, courtesy of the John "Sonny" and Carolyn W. "Tini" Thibaut estate.)

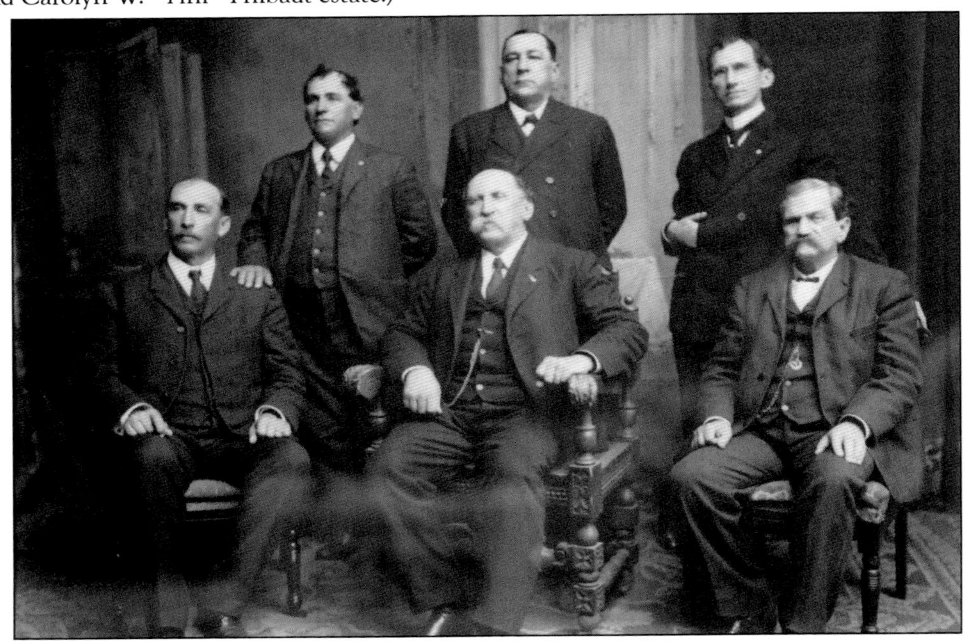

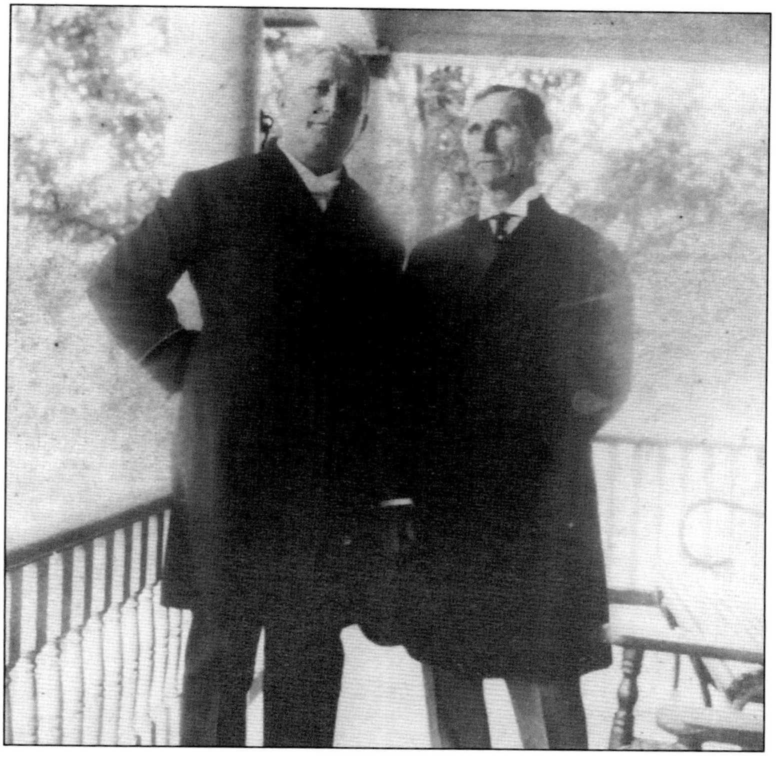

Solomon (left) Klotz and Dr. E.T. Dugas (right) formed an insurance agency in 1904 called Klotz and Dugas. A hardworking lodge member, Klotz served as supreme representative of the Grand Lodge Knights of Honor. The insurance agency continued after the deaths of the original partners by their families. (Courtesy of Catherine T. Maloney.)

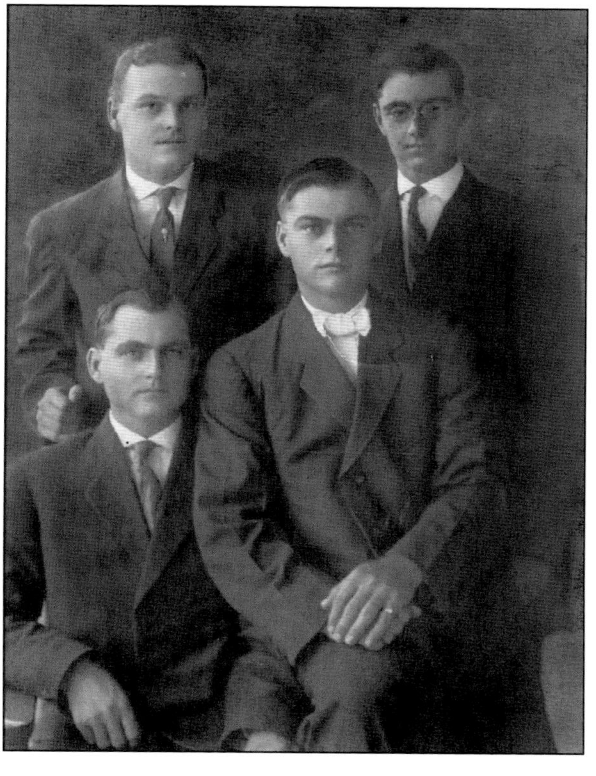

This photograph of the Talbot brothers was taken in the late 1800s. Aubert, Edward, Alwin, and Arthur Talbot were popular local athletes in youth and professionals in adulthood. Aubert became a lawyer; his son Aubert Talbot and grandson Donald Carmouche both served as district attorney. (Courtesy of Catherine T. Maloney.)

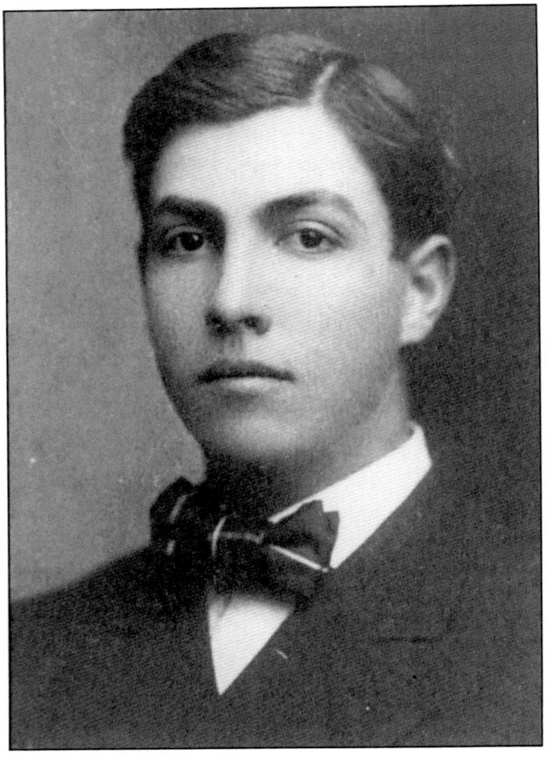

Charles L. Triche and sons Risley and Charles purchased Long Branch Plantation from Joseph U. Folse in 1917. This 1909 portrait shows Charles W. Triche, manager of a plantation in the upper part of Assumption Parish. Charles Walter Triche V, his descendant, resides in the Lafayette area today. (Courtesy of Renee Gilbert Baxter.)

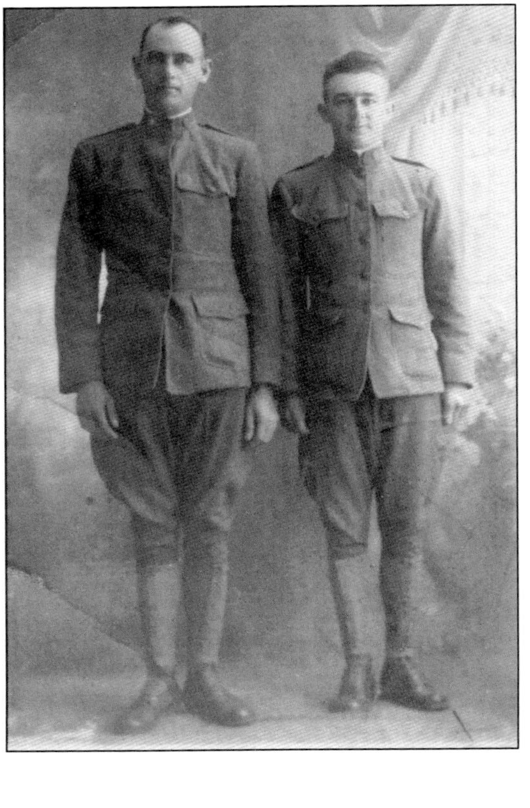

Shelby Talbot and Bronier L. Thibaut are pictured in this late-1910s photograph in World War I uniforms. Bronier purchased Madewood Plantation in 1946 from R.L. Baker. (Courtesy of the John "Sonny" and Carolyn W. "Tini" Thibaut estate.)

Napoleonville native Charles Adolph appears on horseback in this World War I–era photograph. He later became a practicing dentist in New Orleans; a nephew claims that Adolph enjoyed a lifestyle of wine, women, and song. He died a bachelor in 1927. (Courtesy of the Adolph family.)

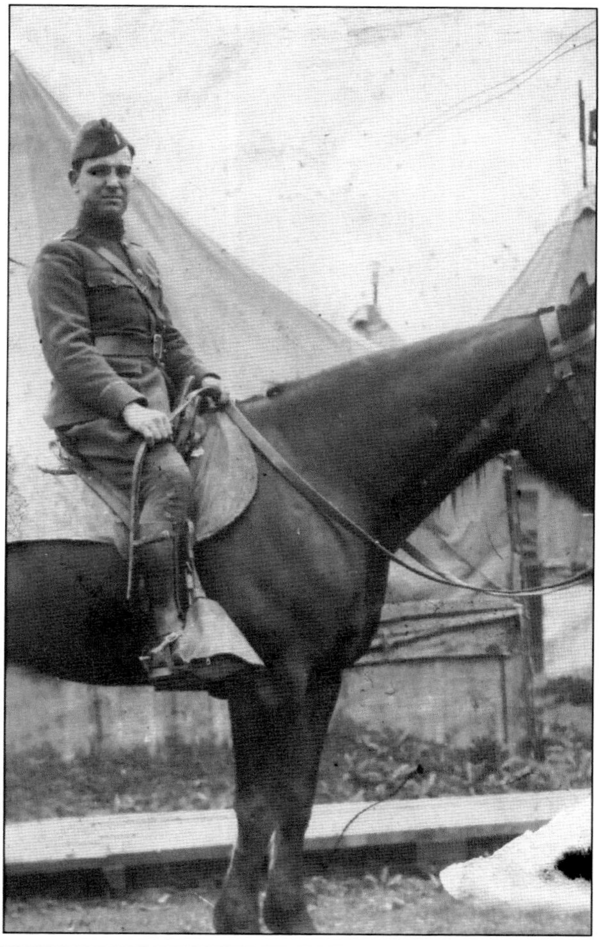

Edgar Breaux (far right) was a popular teacher and the principal at this public schoolhouse. Breaux was the son of Camille Breaux and was married to Annie Adolph, a daughter of Emile and Lelia Templet Adolph. (Courtesy of the Adolph family.)

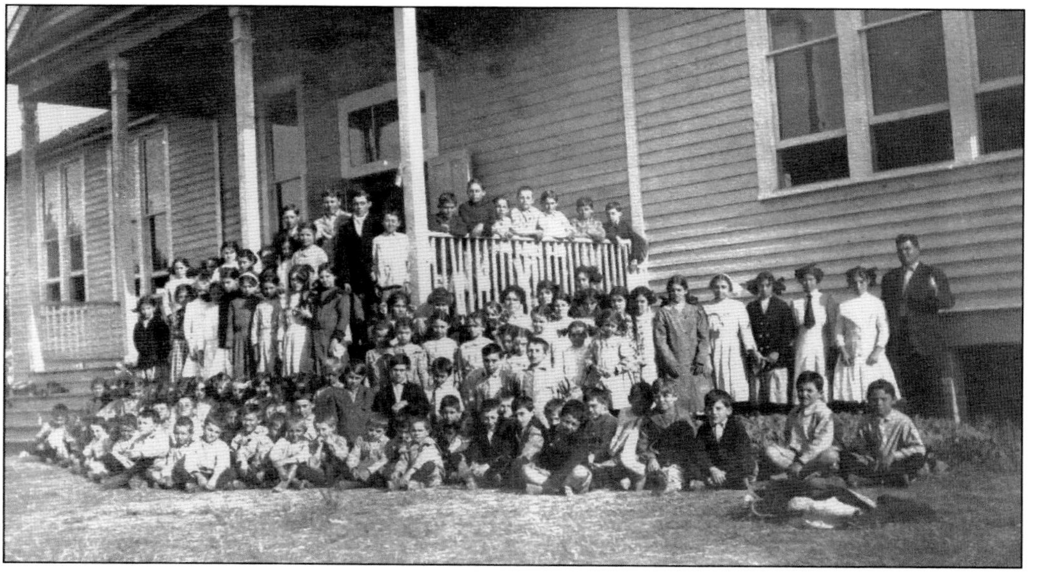

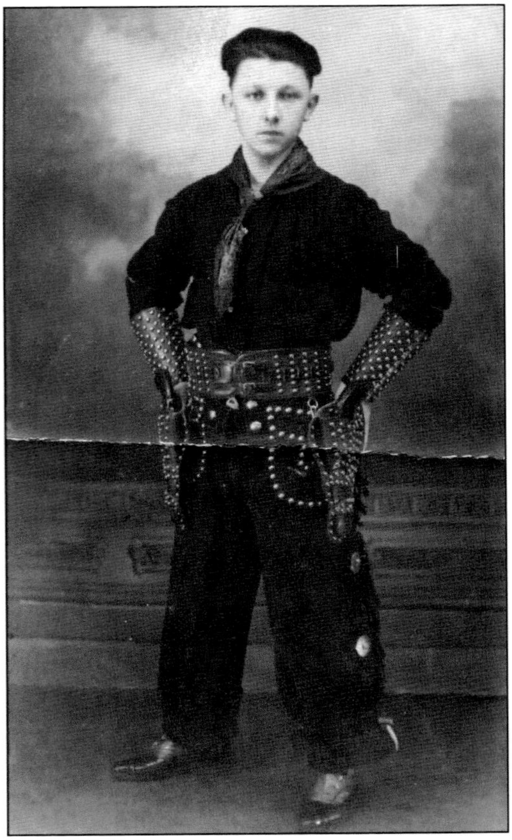

Influenced by popular dime novel stories that told of the exploits of Buffalo Bill, Wild Bill Hickock, Jessie James, and Hopalong Cassidy, this young boy has donned a cowboy costume. (Courtesy of the Adolph family.)

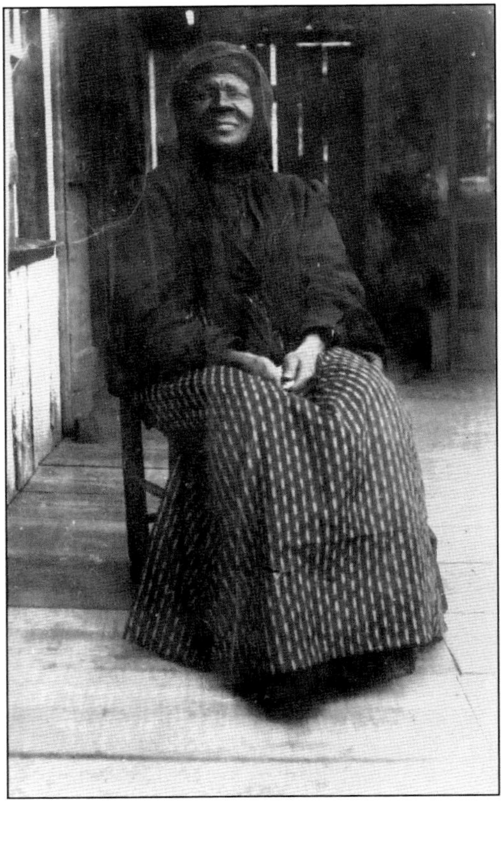

The woman in this photograph is relaxing on the family porch of Emile Adolph. Family employees were often included in household portraits. (Courtesy of the Adolph family.)

Frances Gilbert, daughter of James and Heloise Adolph Gilbert, sports an Edwardian dress in this 1910s photograph. She would later marry Joseph Clay LeBlanc and remained a parish resident throughout her life. (Courtesy of the Adolph family.)

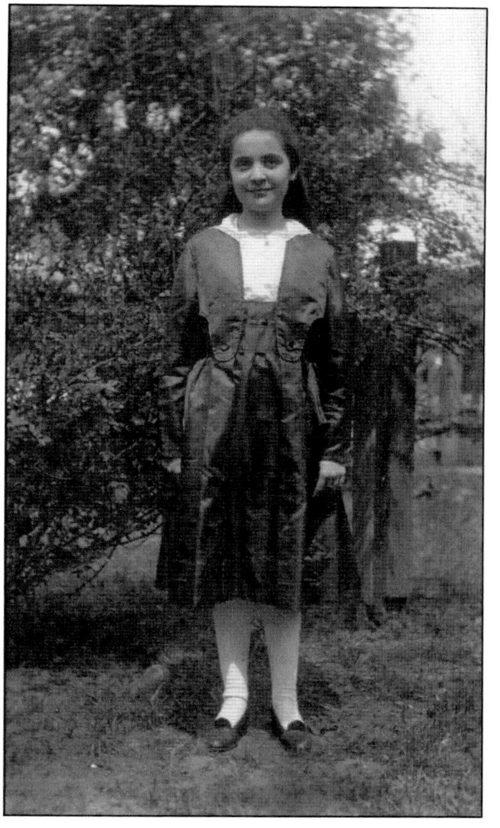

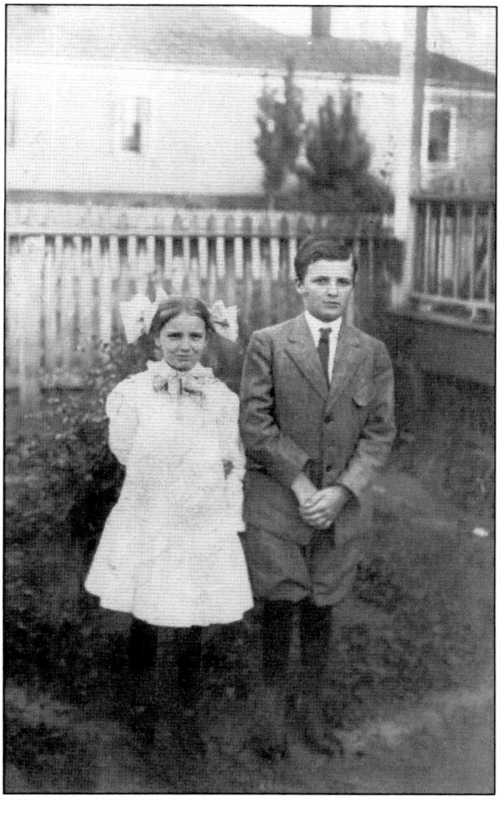

Children's costumes of the 1910s were distinguishable from other periods. Pleats, buttons, bows, and attention to other details were especially popular in children's clothing during this era. (Courtesy of the Adolph family.)

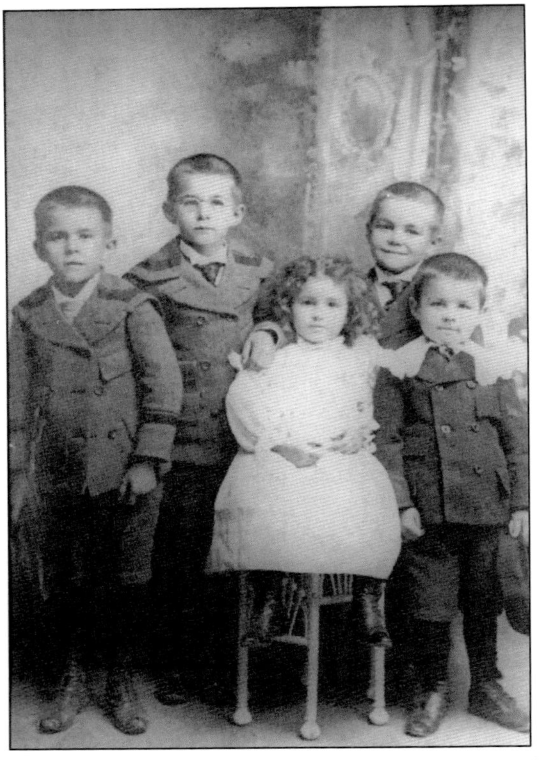

Brooks Brothers introduced the polo coat to boys clothing in the United States around 1910. These children's stylish wardrobes reflect changing fashions in a post-Victorian era. (Courtesy of the John "Sonny" and Carolyn W. "Tini" Thibaut estate.)

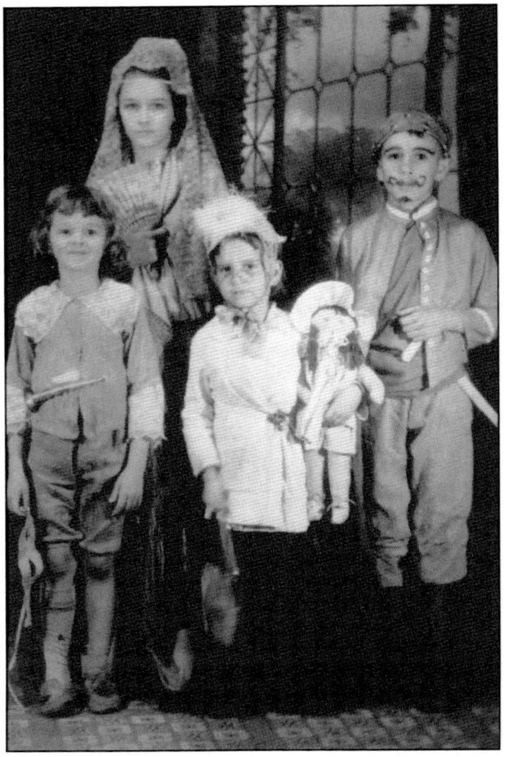

In the 1910s, Halloween was an opportunity for young people to showcase their creativity. These children in elaborate costumes may have been preparing for such a celebration. (Courtesy of the John "Sonny" and Carolyn W. "Tini" Thibaut estate.)

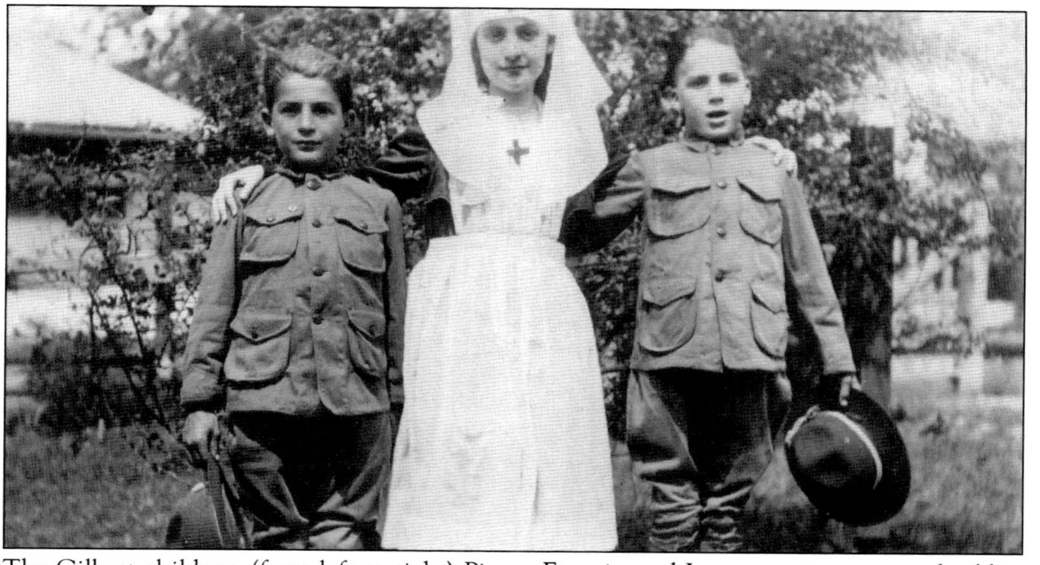

The Gilbert children, (from left to right) Pierre, Francis, and James, are in nurse and soldier costumes inspired by the day's popular heroes, the men and women who served in the armed forces. They are dressed in preparation for a homecoming parade dedicated to the servicemen of World War I. (Courtesy of the Adolph family.)

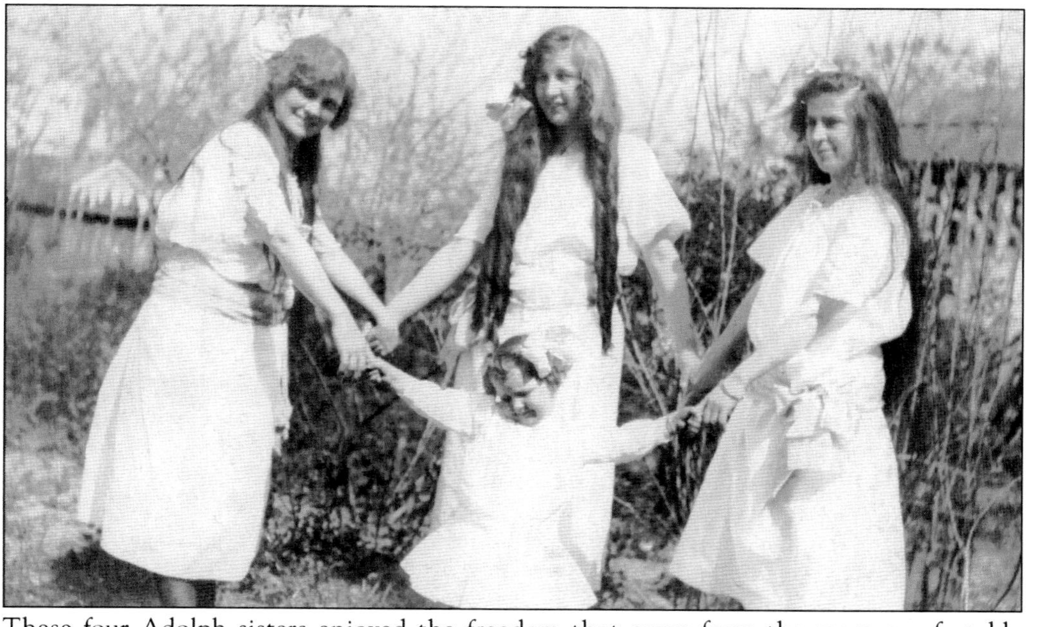

These four Adolph sisters enjoyed the freedom that came from the more comfortable Edwardian-era attire; prior to this time, women's clothing was heavily corseted. (Courtesy of the Adolph family.)

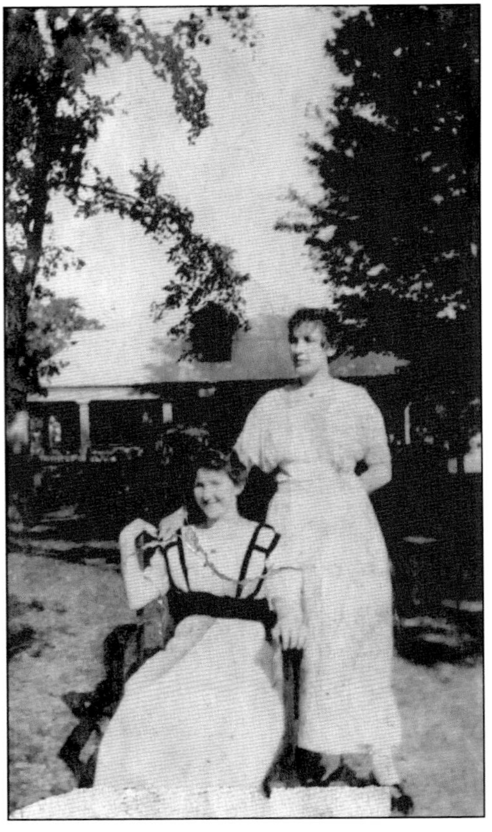

These women from Enola Plantation are wearing the skirts and blouses that became common in the early 1900s. (Courtesy of the Adolph family.)

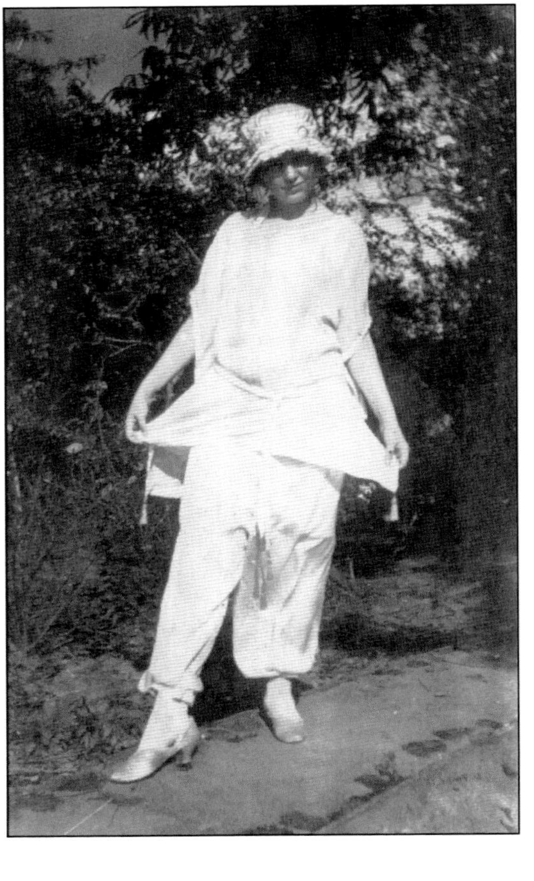

This outfit depicts the growing rage in fashion with the introduction of the "Gibson Girl," a fictitious character created in the graphic illustrations of Charles Dana Gibson. The Gibson Girl was meant to represent the sophisticated, independent woman of the turn of the century that influenced the feminine ideal for the next 20 years. (Courtesy of the Adolph family.)

The dress worn in this late-1910s photograph shows a higher hemline that left ankles exposed, a departure from Victorian modesty. (Courtesy of the Adolph family.)

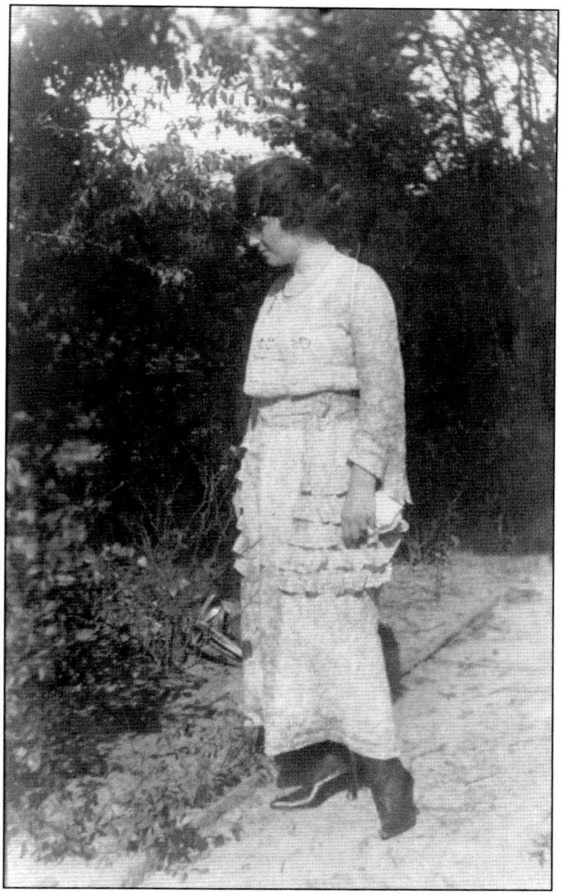

The large bow on the dress of this woman, relaxing on Adolph family porch, was a popular fashion statement of the Edwardian era. These outfits were hand sewn and were labor intensive to create. (Courtesy of the Adolph family.)

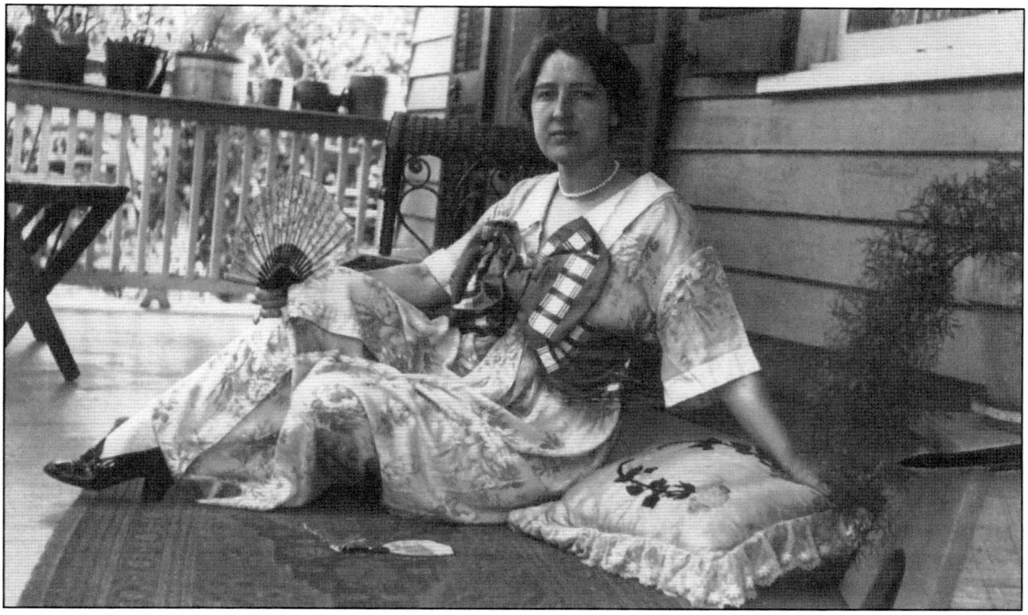

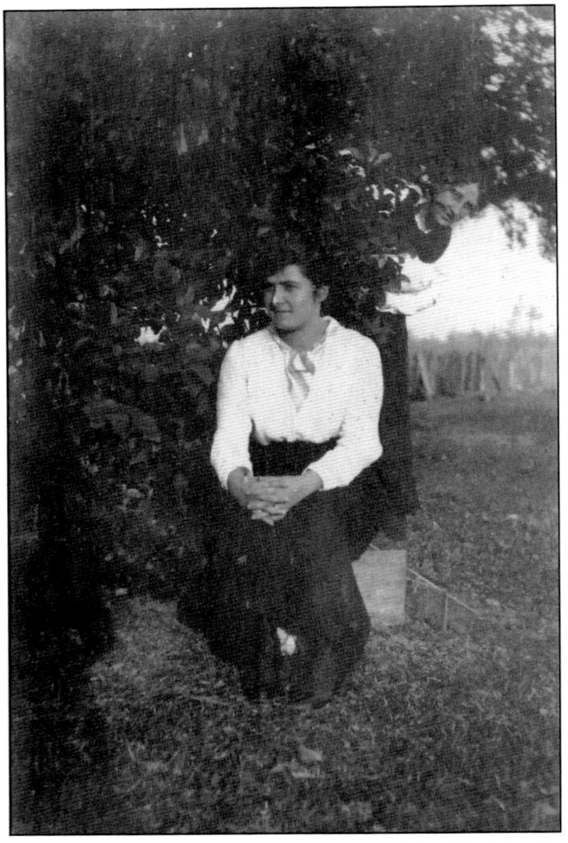

Shade was important in southern Louisiana, as air-conditioning would not be available until the mid-1920s, nearly a quarter century after this photograph. (Courtesy of the Adolph family.)

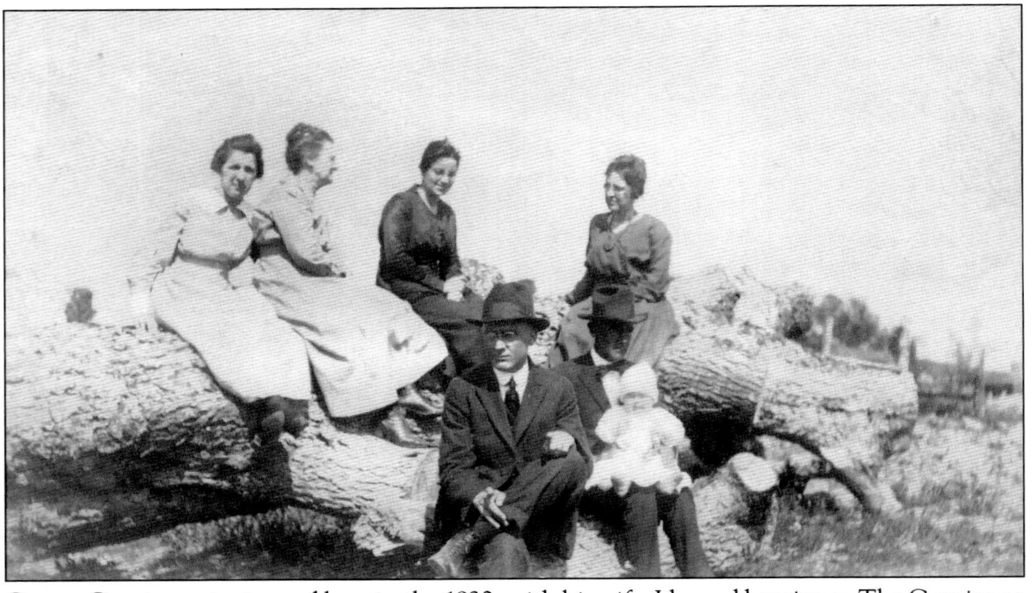

George Cancienne is pictured here in the 1920s with his wife, Ida, and her sisters. The Cancienne and Adolph families were sugar planters in Assumption. George's brother John was married to Ida's sister Rita Adolph. (Courtesy of the Adolph family.)

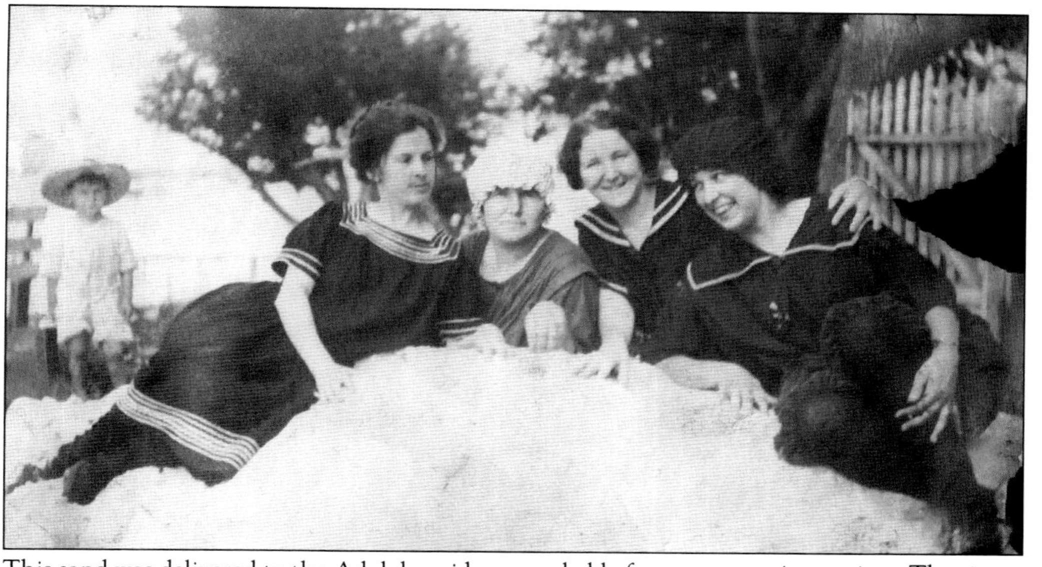

This sand was delivered to the Adolph residence probably for a construction project. The sisters are pretending they are at the beach. (Courtesy of the Adolph family.)

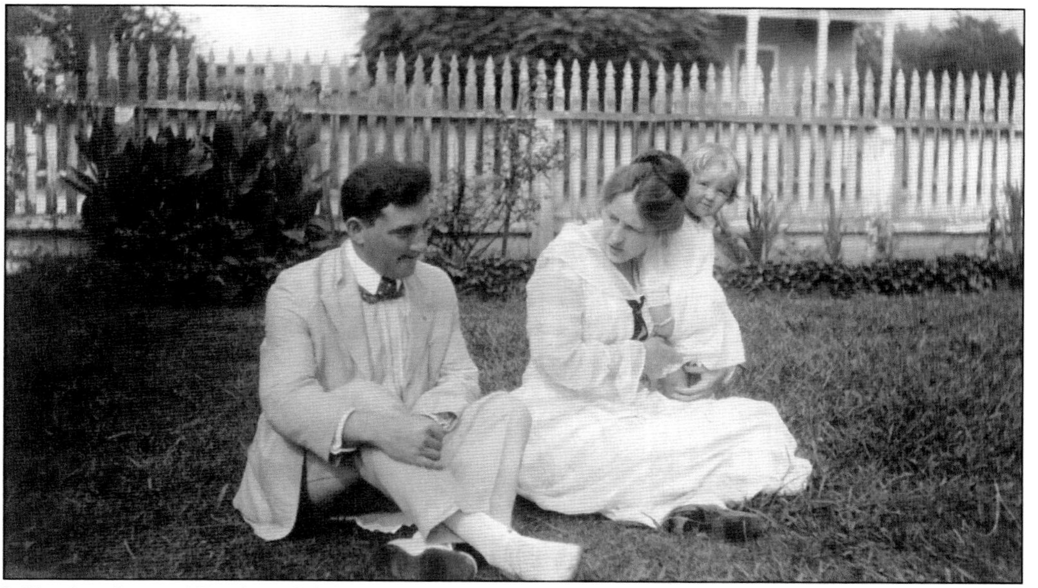

Lilly, daughter of Emile Adolph, was the second wife of Aloysios Bourgeois, a merchant from Lutcher. She married Bourgeois when he was widowed from her sister Emilie and raised her sister's children. (Courtesy of the Adolph family.)

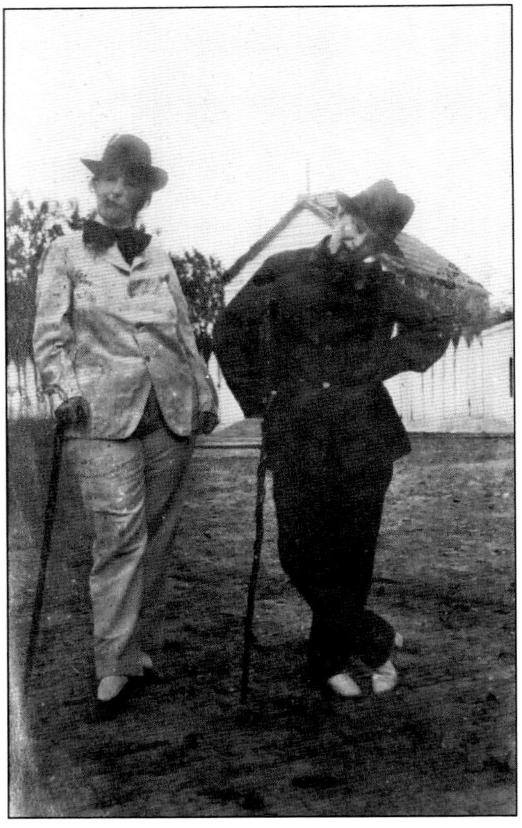

Baggy pants, derby hats, and floppy shoes were typical of these Vaudeville-inspired costumes, worn in jest by two pranksters. (Courtesy of the Adolph family.)

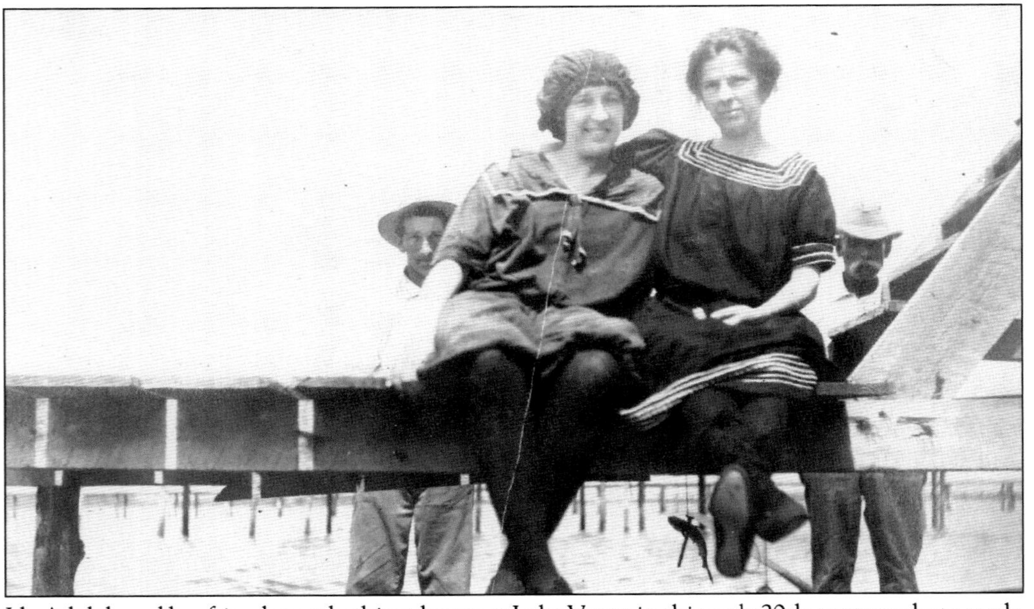

Ida Adolph and her friend sport bathing dresses at Lake Verret in this early-20th-century photograph. They were typically navy trimmed in nautical details and consisted of a blouse and bloomer combination. (Courtesy of the Adolph family.)

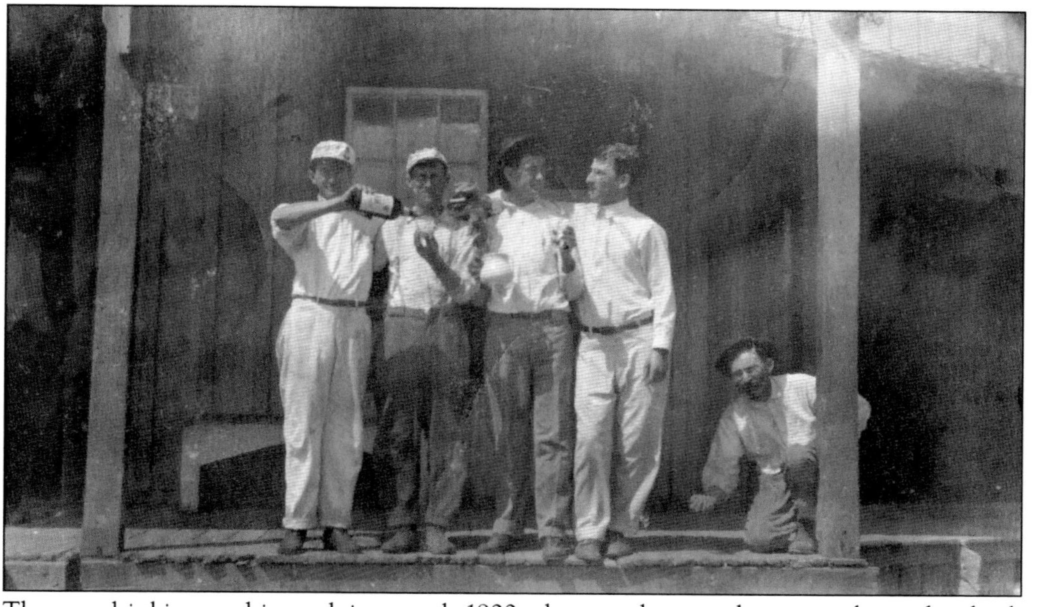

The men drinking on this porch in an early-1900s photograph appear happy to relax with a drink after a hard day's work. (Courtesy of the Adolph family.)

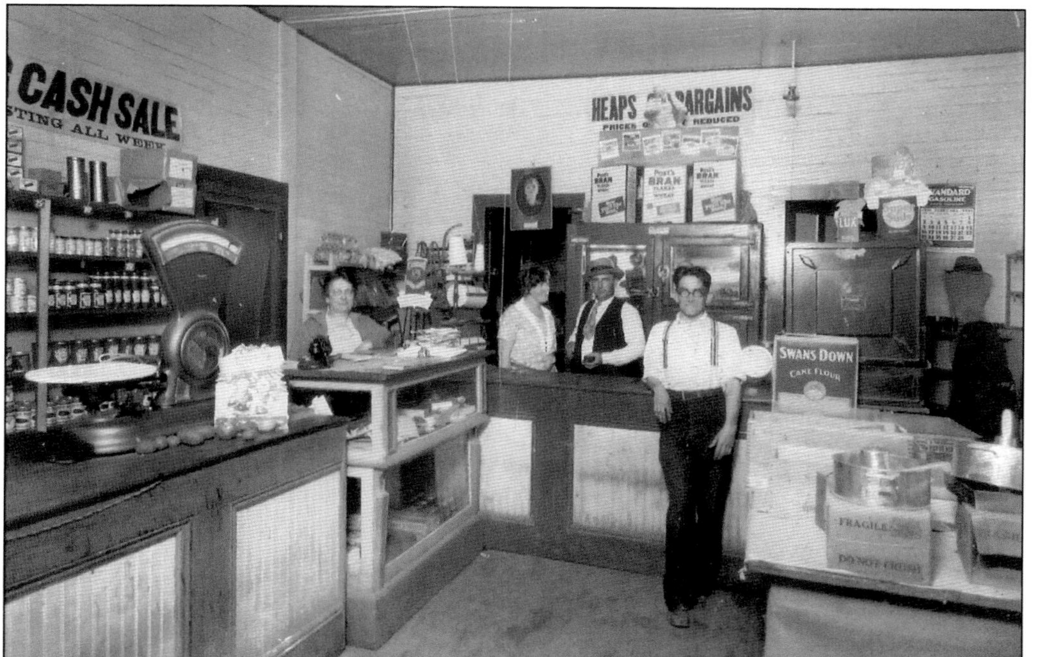

James Gilbert's Cosmopolitan grocery store on Franklin Street in Napoleonville provided fancy and staple groceries, country produce, crockery, glassware, and general supplies. Emile Gilbert is posing in the foreground in this 1920s photograph. (Courtesy of Nick and Loretta Carrier.)

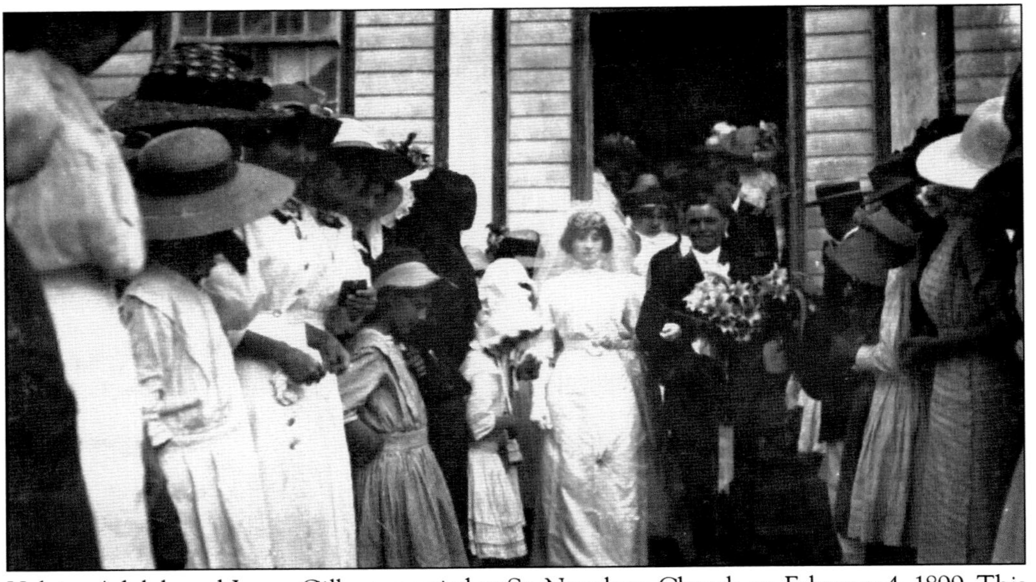

Heloise Adolph and James Gilbert married at St. Napoleon Church on February 4, 1899. This photograph was a contribution from the bride's descendents. (Courtesy of the Adolph family.)

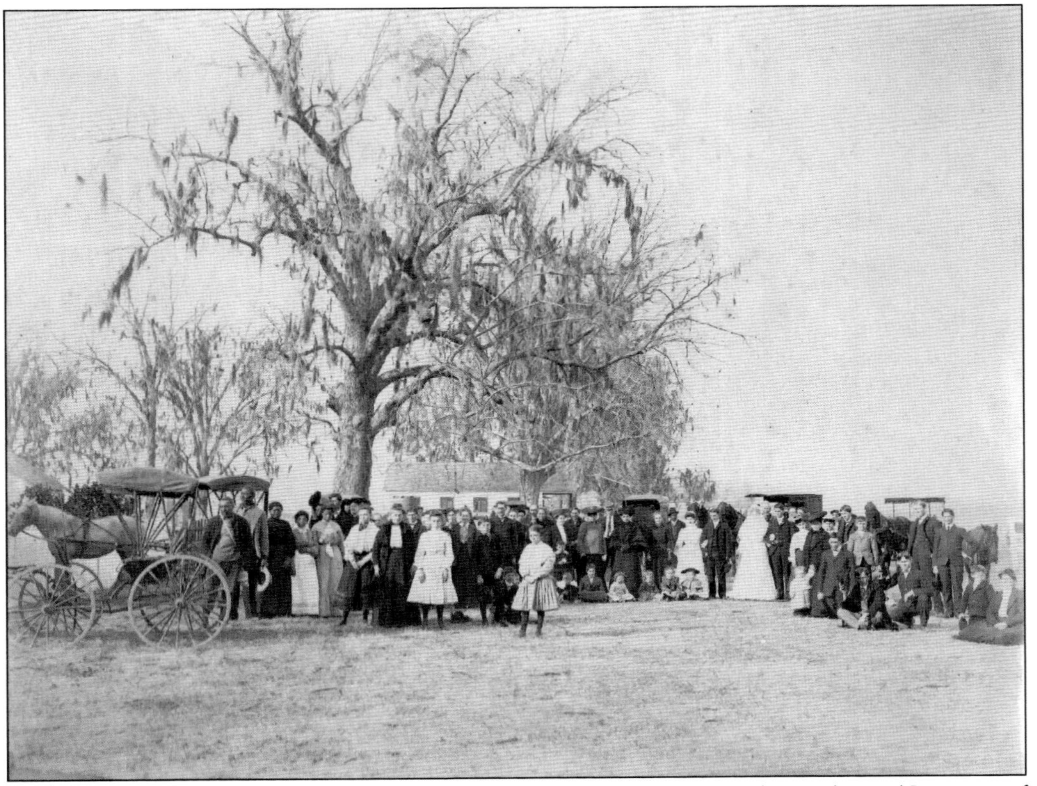

Here is a photograph of the wedding party contributed by the groom's descendents. (Courtesy of Nick and Loretta Carrier.)

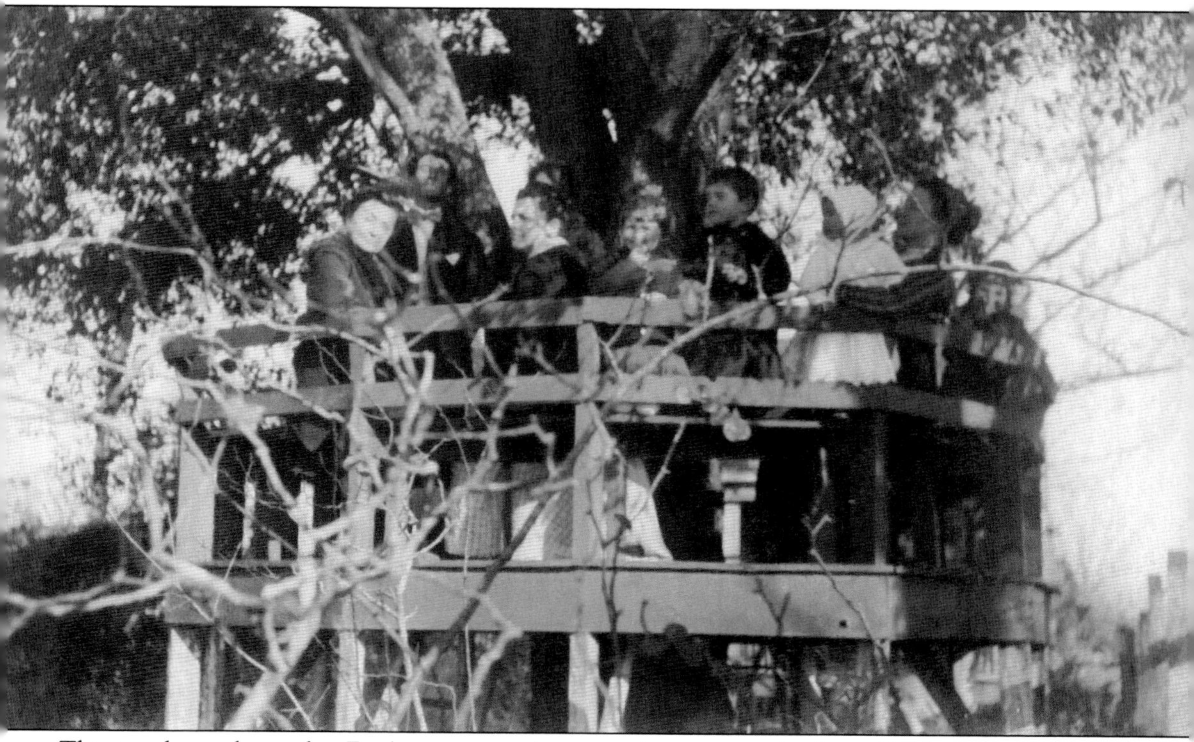

This tree house located at Enola was a popular recreation spot on the farm. Unlike today's tree houses, this sanctuary was equally prepared to be a respite for adults as for children. (Courtesy of the Adolph family.)

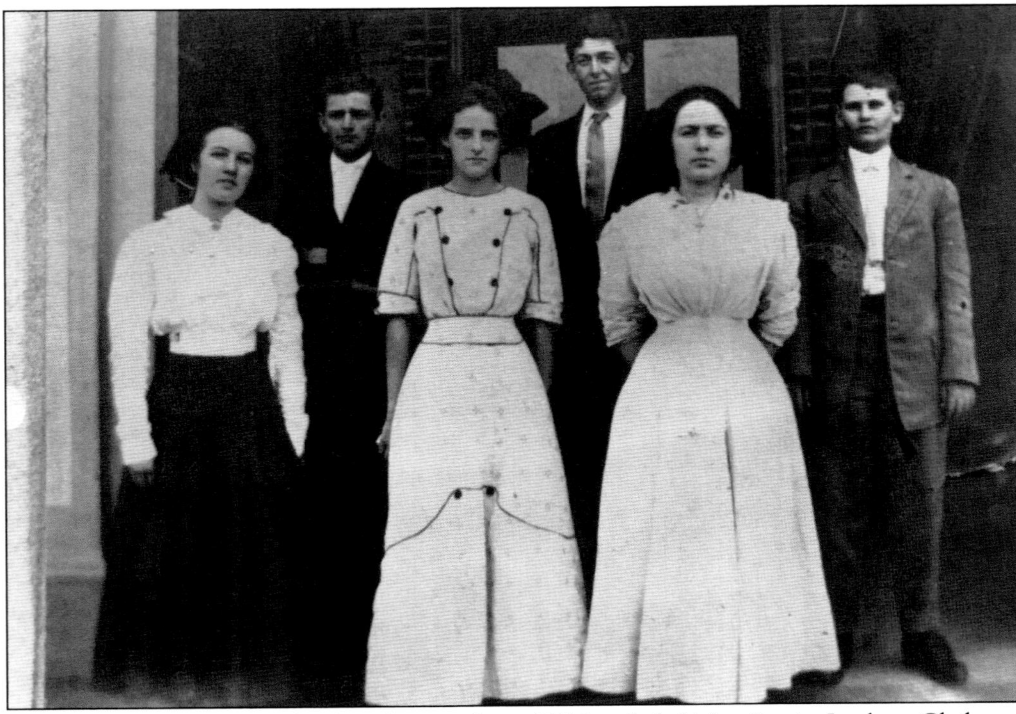

The Napoleonville High School graduating class of 1911 included Mary Louise Lockett, Claiborne Talbot, Josie Pugh, E. Monnot Lanier, Clara Guillot, and W.L. "Litt" Martin. (Courtesy of William Littlejohn Martin Collection, Archives and Special Collections, Nicholls State University, Thibodaux, Louisiana.)

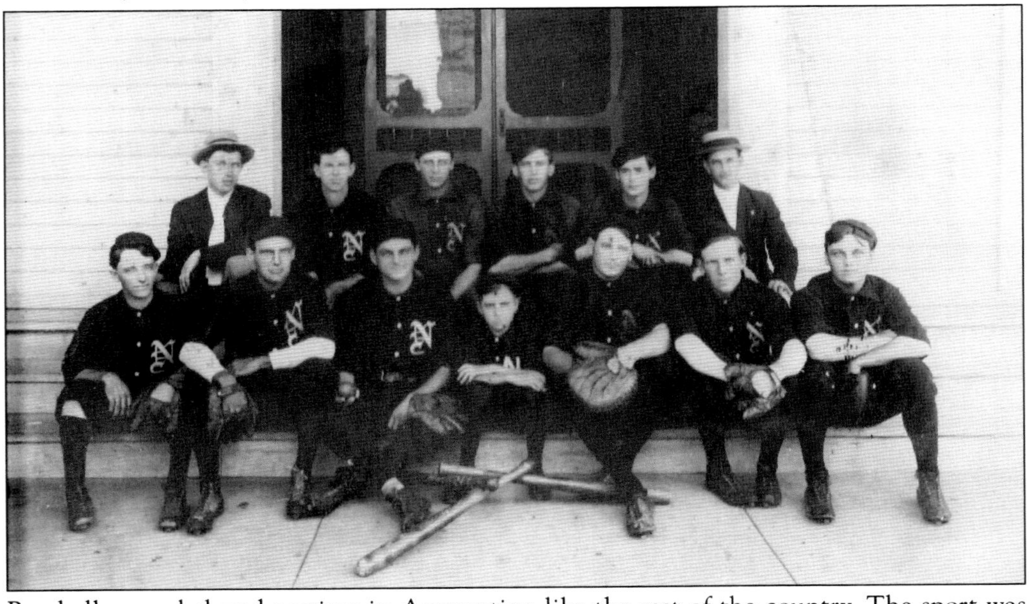

Baseball was a beloved pastime in Assumption like the rest of the country. The sport was already 40 years old when this Napoleonville baseball team posed in 1907. (Courtesy of Nick and Loretta Carrier.)

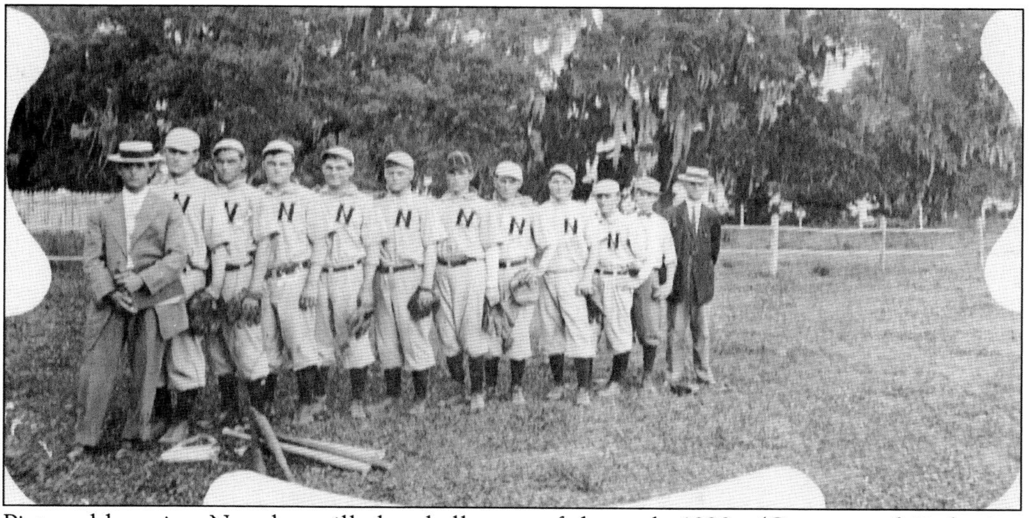

Pictured here is a Napoleonville baseball team of the early 1920s. (Courtesy of Catherine T. Maloney.)

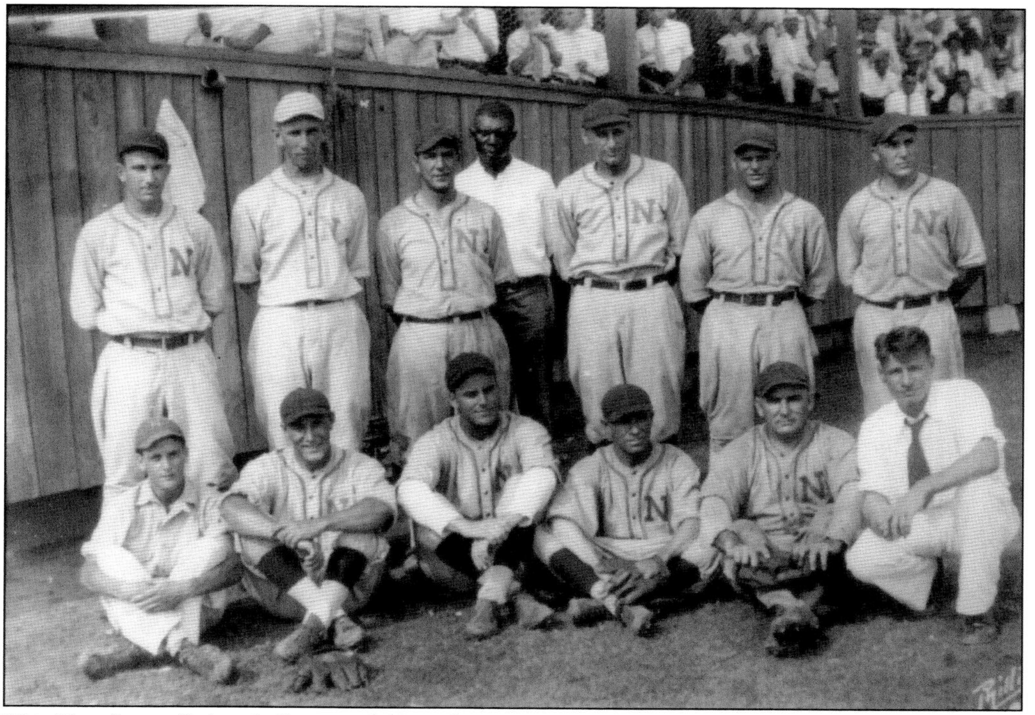

This Napoleonville baseball team of the early 1930s enjoyed the luxury of playing in a newly created ballpark. Contrast the uniforms in the two previous photographs; eras were easily discernable by the style of uniform worn by the players. Pictured here are, from left to right, (sitting) Henry Gilbert, Leroy Gilbert (shortstop), Louis "Nootsey" Landry (first base), Brian Gilbert (second base), Louis "Tooke" Dugas (left field), and George "Cabbage" Rodrigue (scorekeeper); (standing) Bill Lietz (pitcher), Harvey "Cotton" Blanchard (catcher), Philip "Pete" Gilber (third base), ? Parker (groundskeeper), Rev. Fr. Jules Toups, Francis "Mack" Rodrigue (center field), and James W. Gilbert (right field). (Courtesy of Donald and Billie Eris Blanchard.)

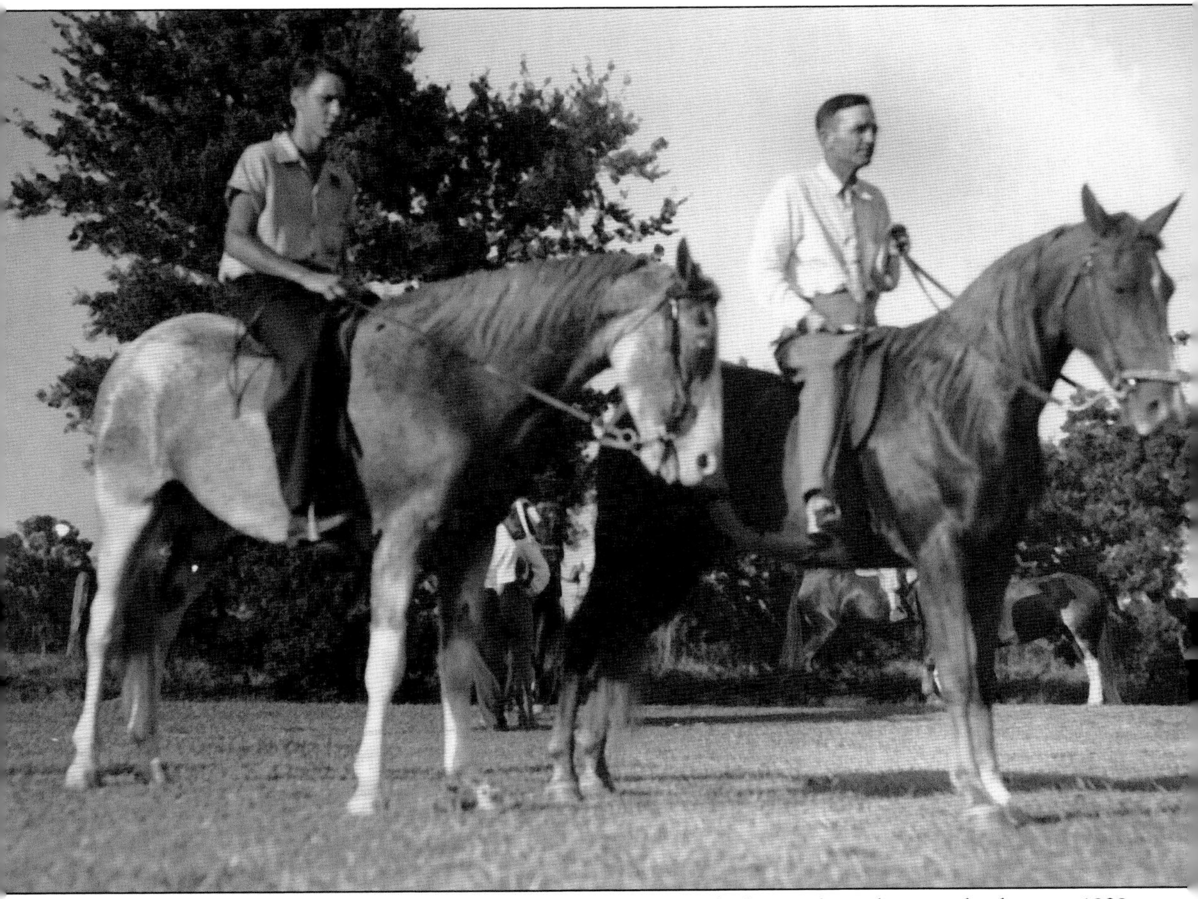

John "Sonny" (left) and Bronier Thibaut are getting ready for a ride with several others in 1939. Bronier was a banker, sugarcane farmer, and auto dealer, with farming interests throughout the parish. Sonny served as president of the American Sugar Cane League of the USA, an organization devoted to agricultural research; the Assumption Bank and Trust; former Glenwood Inc; and was founding president of the Louisiana Crawfish Association, the non-profit trade association representing nearly 1,500 crawfish farm operations across the state. (Courtesy of the John "Sonny" and Carolyn W. "Tini" Thibaut estate.)

Two

SUGAR AND NATURAL PARADISE

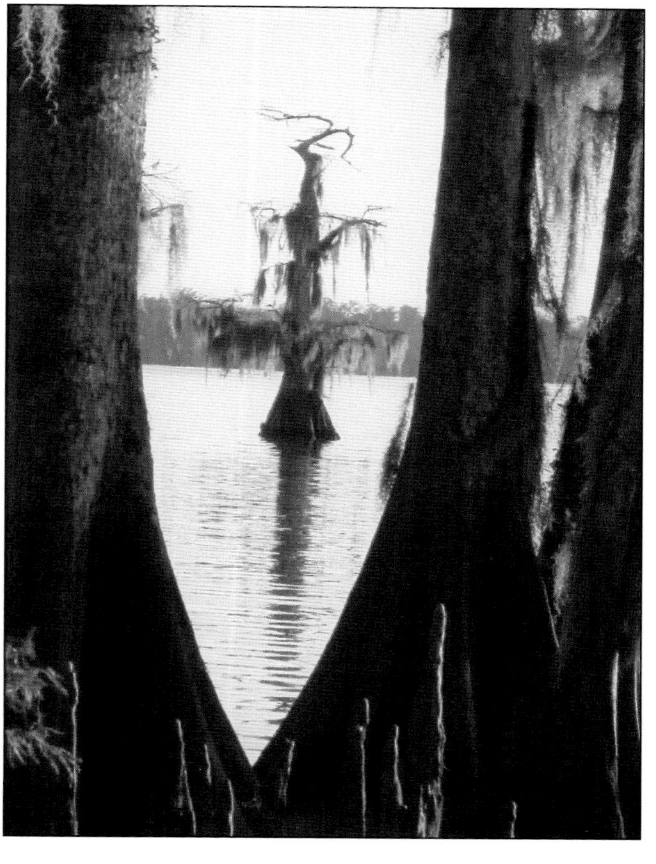

A popular fishing and duck-hunting destination, Lake Verret covers 23 square miles and is peppered with public boat-launching ramps, many private camps, and lake houses. Some local historians believe that the lake got its name from Nichols Verret, one of the earliest parish officials. (Courtesy of Renee B. Richard.)

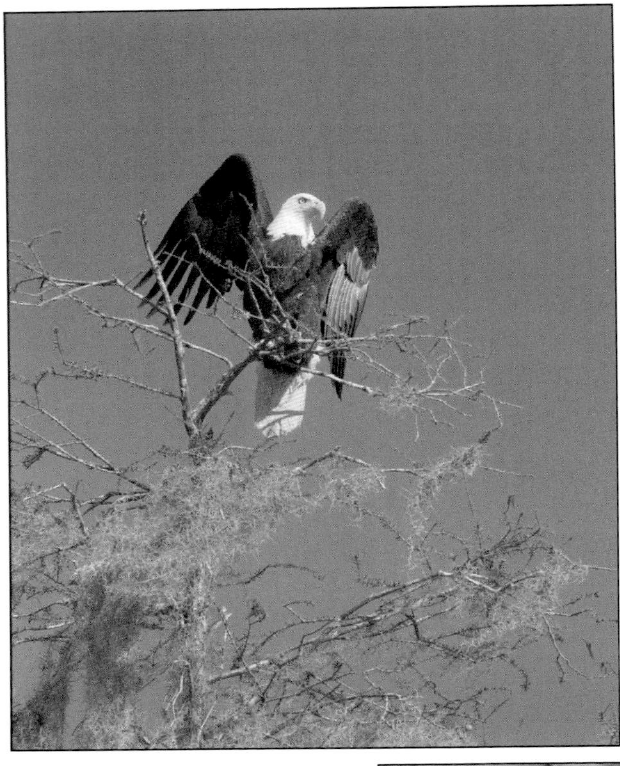

A significant population of bald eagles makes its home on Lake Verret. Eagles nest in the tall cypress trees that line the lake. (Courtesy of Kim Blanchard Comeaux.)

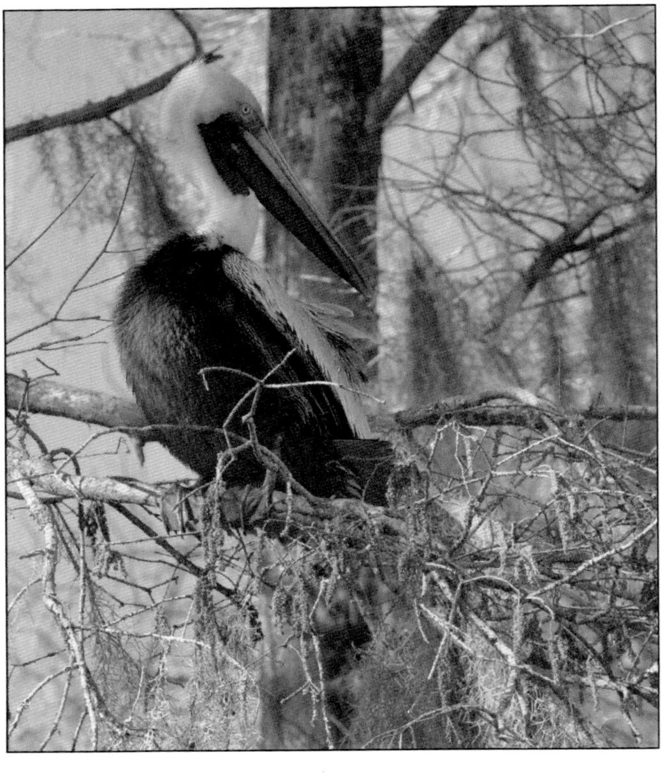

Although not designated the state bird of Louisiana until 1966, early European settlers of the area were impressed with the pelican's generous and nurturing attitude towards its young; it has been a symbol ever since. Declared an endangered species in 1970, the bird has been declared recovered. Over 40,000 brown pelicans are estimated in the state. (Courtesy of Kim Blanchard Comeaux.)

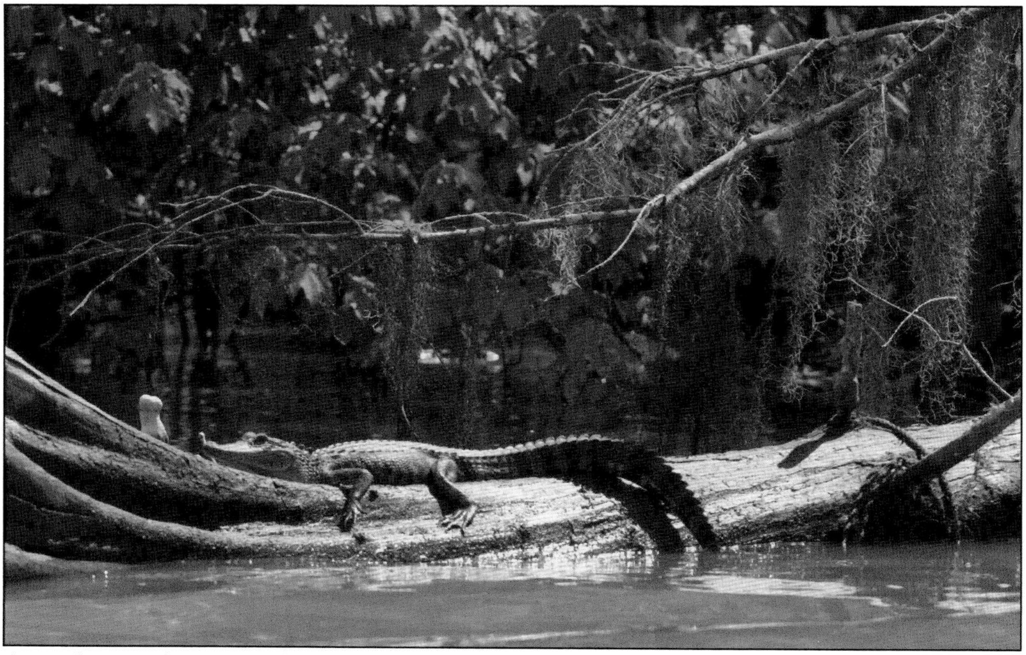

According to the 2005 *Scholastic Book of World Records*, Louisiana is the state with the largest alligator population, numbering over a million. During cold weather, alligators enter semi-hibernation, called brumation, where they do not eat and seldom move. (Courtesy of Kim Blanchard Comeaux.)

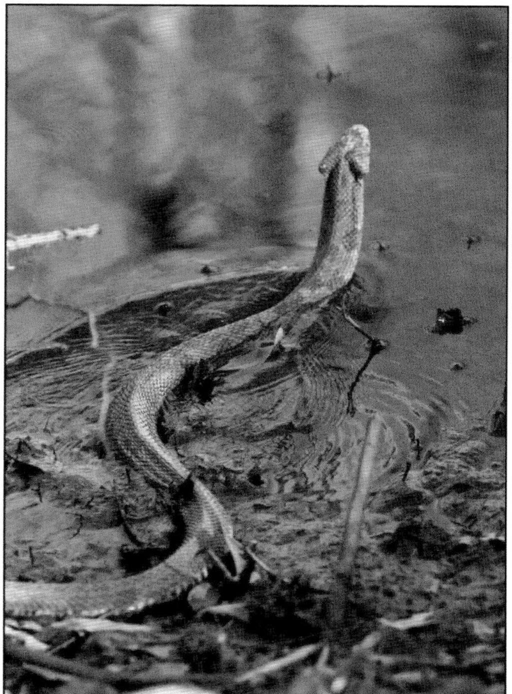

Alternatively known as a cottonmouth or gapper, the water moccasin is the world's only semiaquatic snake. Its reputation as aggressive and highly poisonous makes it a feared striker; it can even bite under water. (Courtesy of Kim Blanchard Comeaux.)

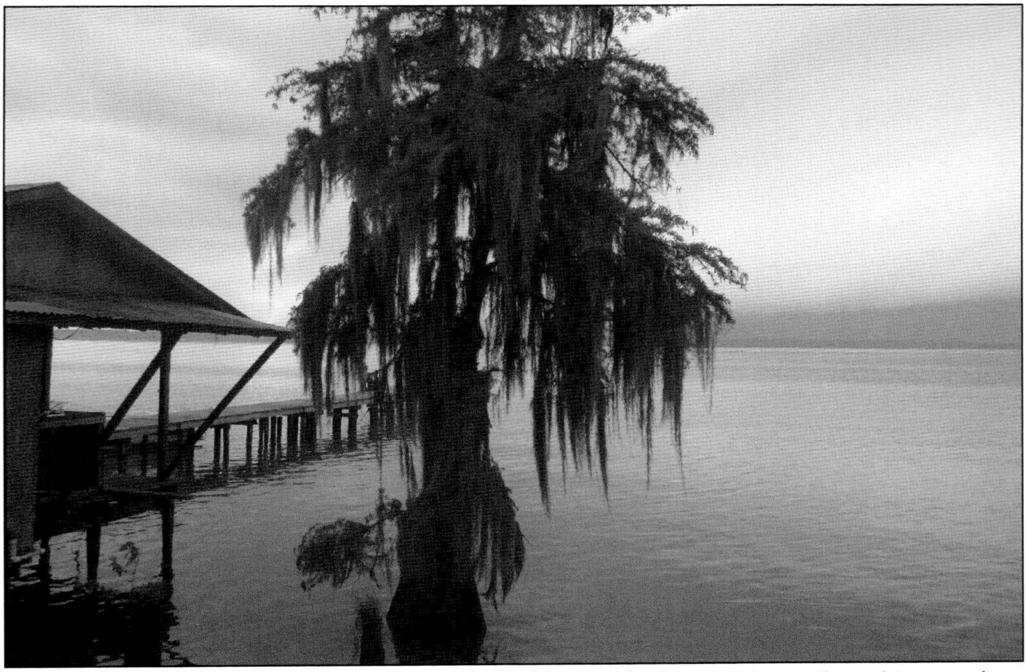

Moss-covered cypress trees are common to Lake Verret. Used in soft home furnishings such as mattresses and upholstery prior to the manufacturing of synthetic fabrics, moss was also employed extensively for binding mud or clay in plastering houses. Known for its durability, Spanish moss is in the plaster binder of New Orleans' famous Absinthe House. (Courtesy of Renee B. Richard.)

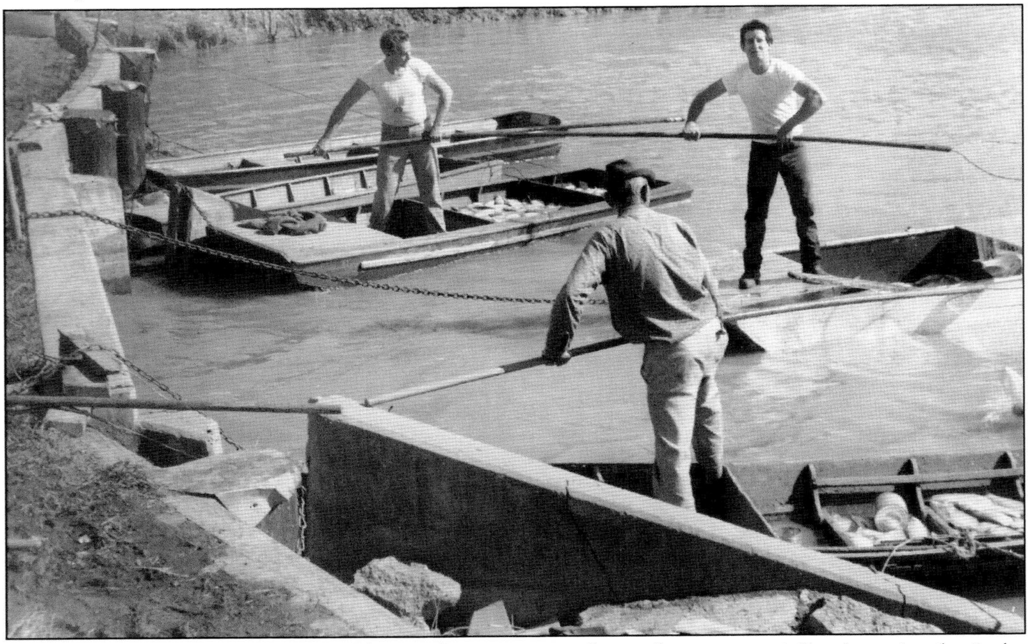

Fishing has provided a means of living for many parish residents, especially those in the Lake Verret and Pierre Part area. Here, fishermen enjoy a bounty of a good day's catch while net fishing in the 1960s. (Courtesy of the Gerald and Olivia Chenevert family.)

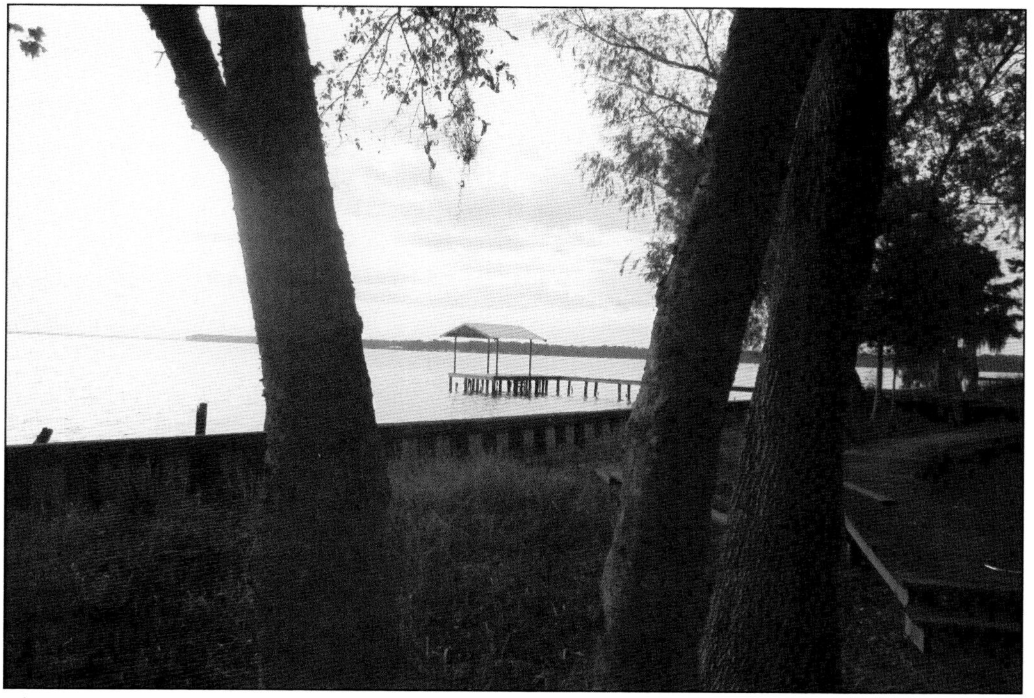

There are few better spots to watch a sunset than a dock on Lake Verret. Many recreation camps line the shore and can only be reached by boat. (Courtesy of the Renee B. Richard.)

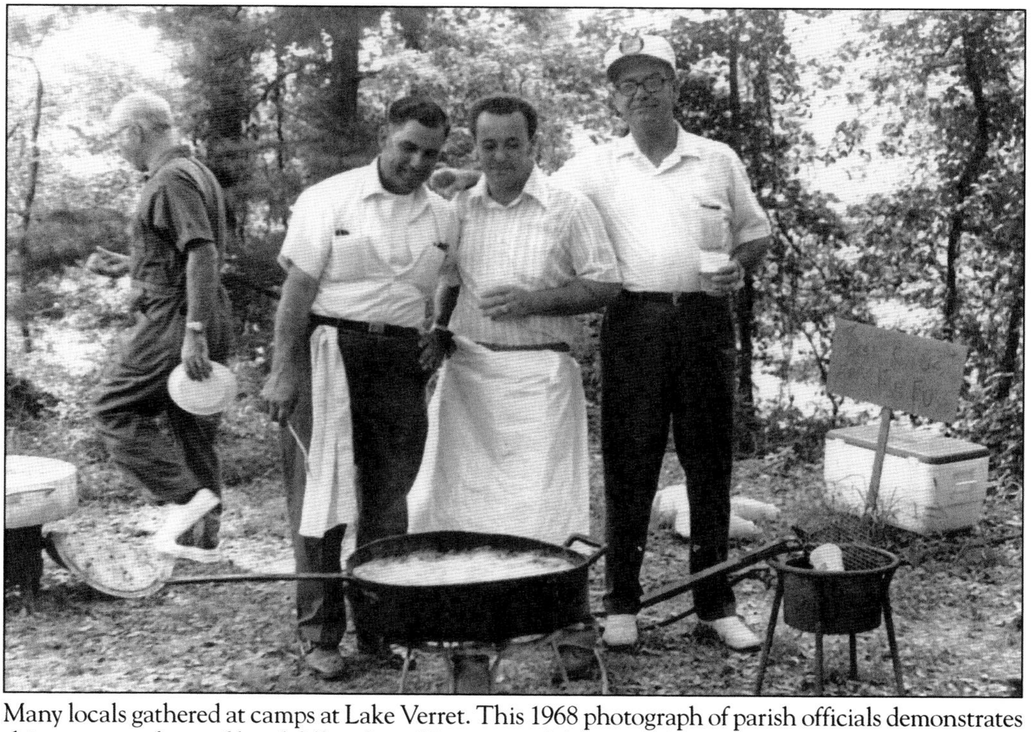

Many locals gathered at camps at Lake Verret. This 1968 photograph of parish officials demonstrates this common form of local fellowship. (Courtesy of the Gerald and Olivia Chenevert family.)

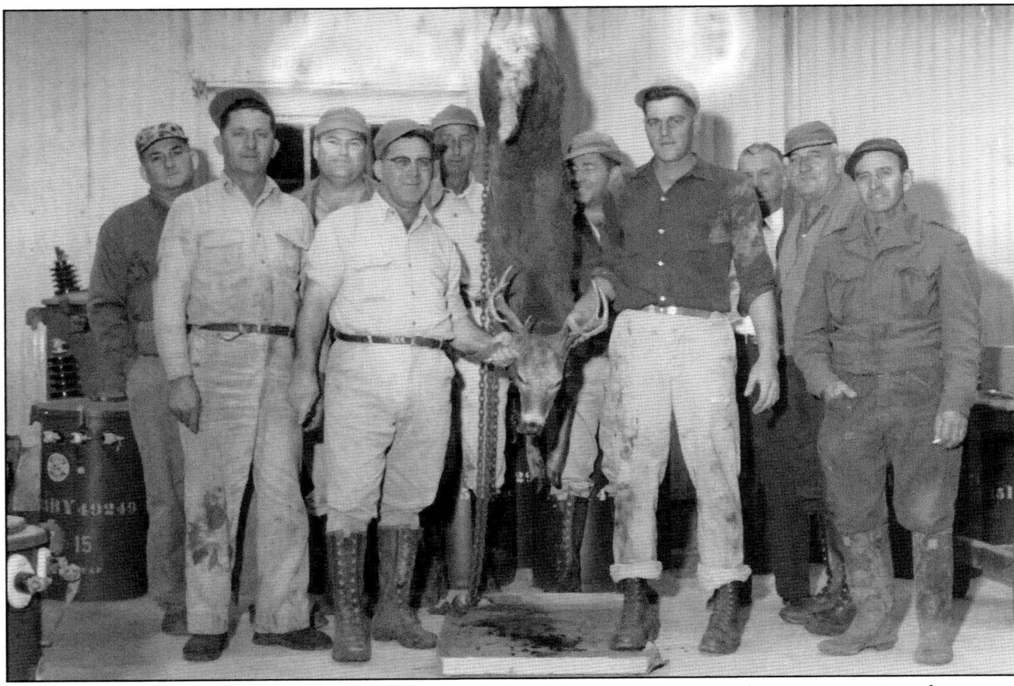

Hunters dress this recently shot deer in the mid-1950s. Hunting has always been an activity of necessity and sport in Assumption Parish. (Courtesy of the Gerald and Olivia Chenevert family.)

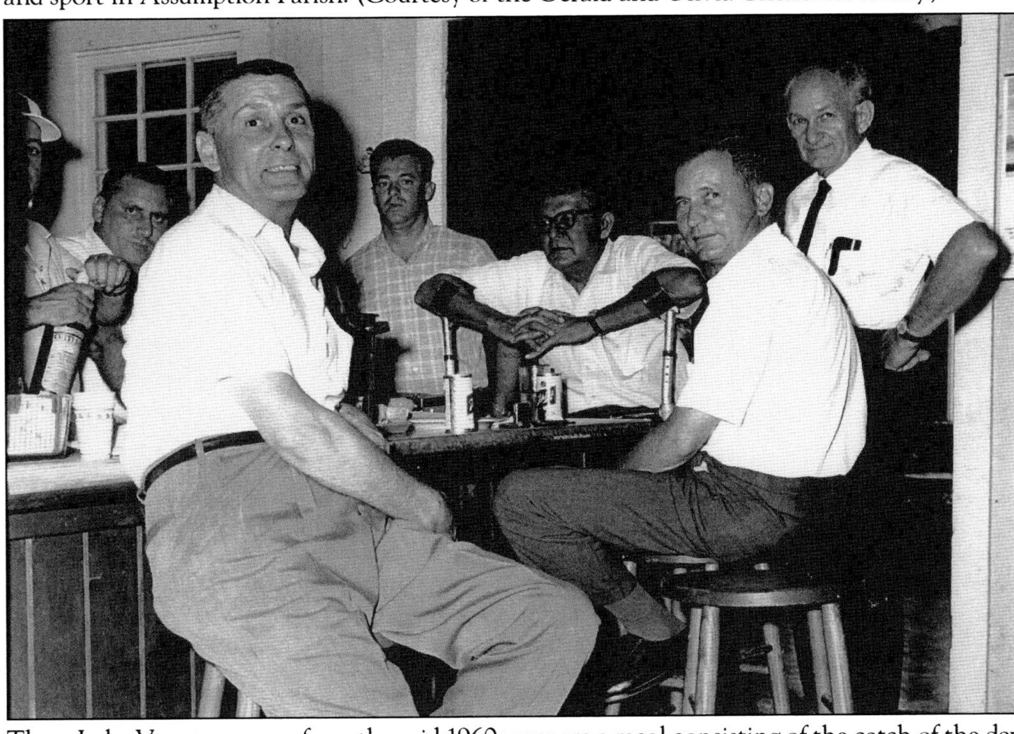

These Lake Verret campers from the mid-1960s prepare a meal consisting of the catch of the day. (Courtesy of the Gerald and Olivia Chenevert family.)

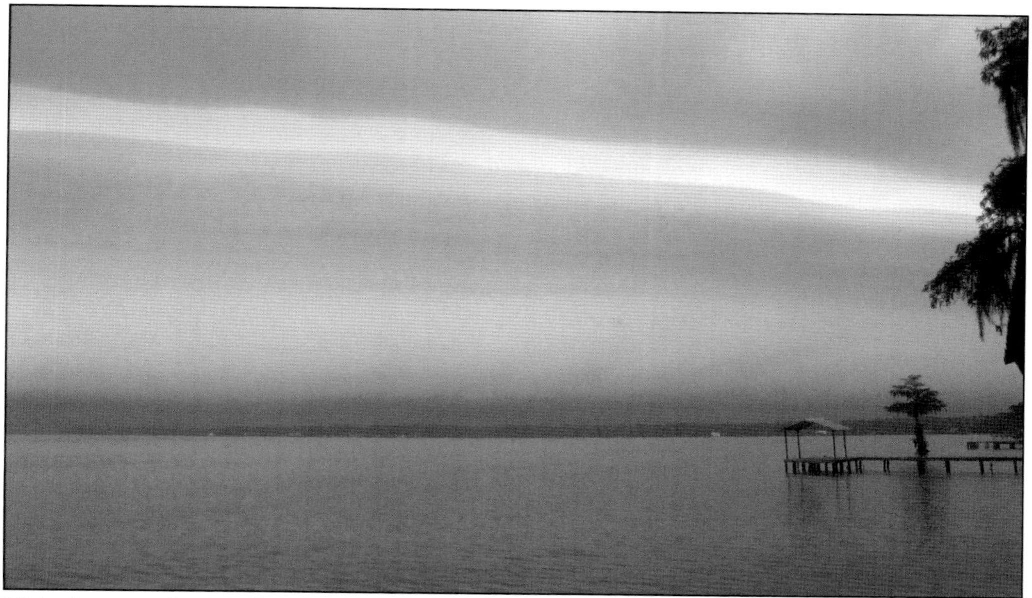

This photograph was taken just as bands from tropical storm Lee appeared over Lake Verret. By the time these bands were overhead, it was too late for the campers to cross the water to get to dry land; they rode the storm out unharmed. (Courtesy of Renee B. Richard.)

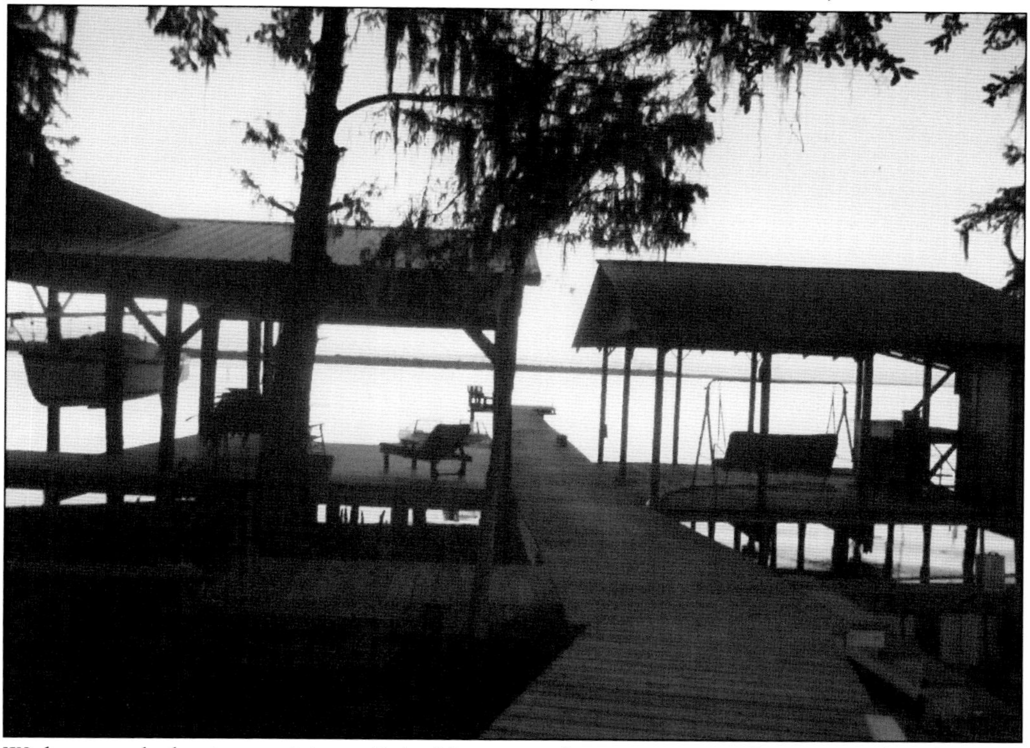

With as much daytime activity as Lake Verret gets from sportsmen, the quiet night takes over with the sun setting over the water. The bench on the dock is the perfect spot to enjoy the end of a day. (Courtesy of Renee B. Richard.)

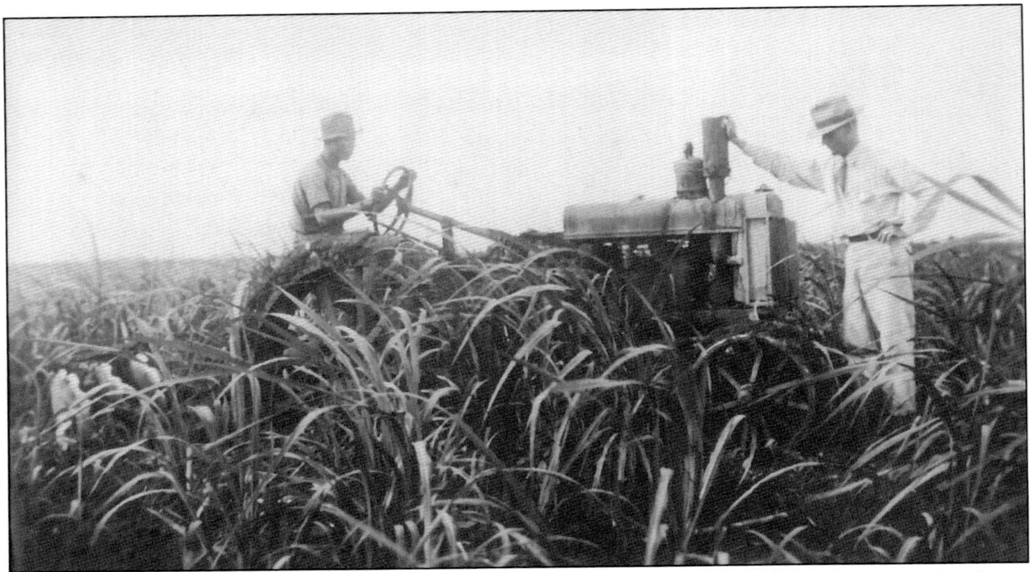

This early tractor at Wildwood Plantation was among the first ever brought onto the farm. Sam Bergeron inspects the day's progress made by this Aliss-Chalmer. (Courtesy of Don and Diane Bergeron.)

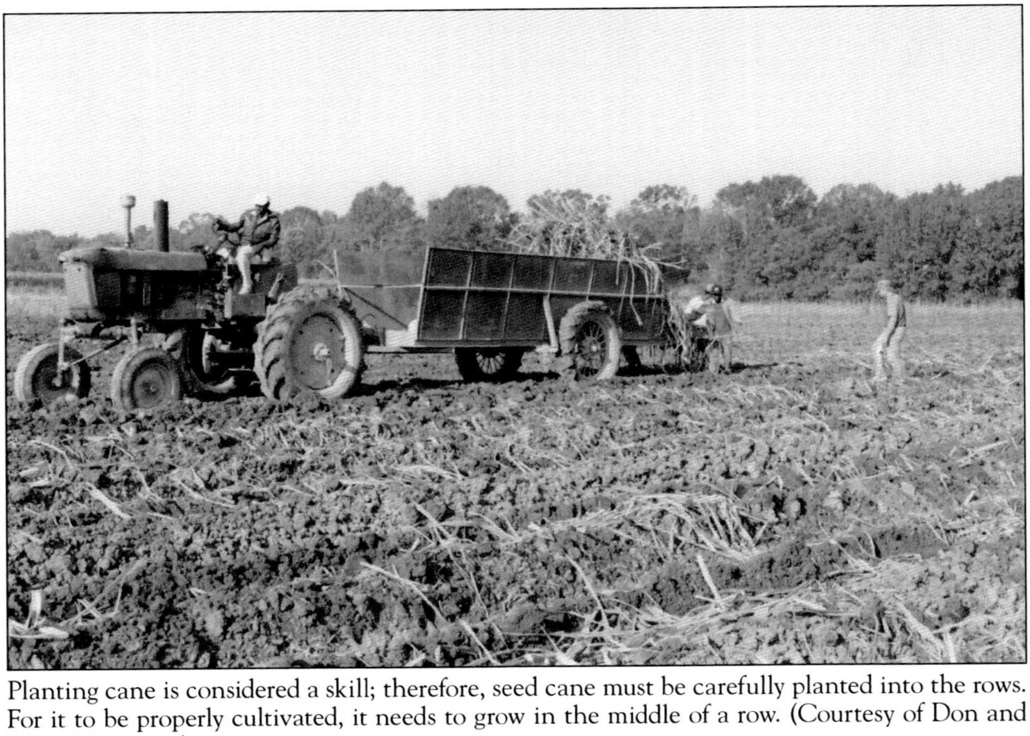

Planting cane is considered a skill; therefore, seed cane must be carefully planted into the rows. For it to be properly cultivated, it needs to grow in the middle of a row. (Courtesy of Don and Diane Bergeron.)

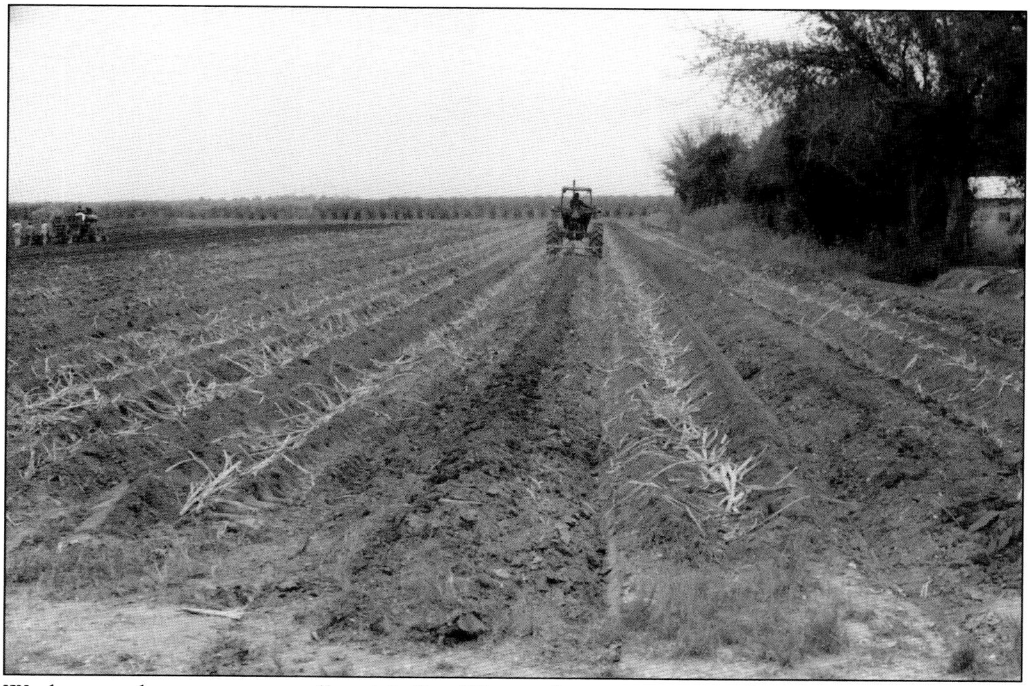

Workers use hoes to cover stalks with dirt. The seed cane, a section of a mature cane stalk with one or more buds or bud eyes, is covered with two to four inches of dirt. (Courtesy of Don and Diane Bergeron.)

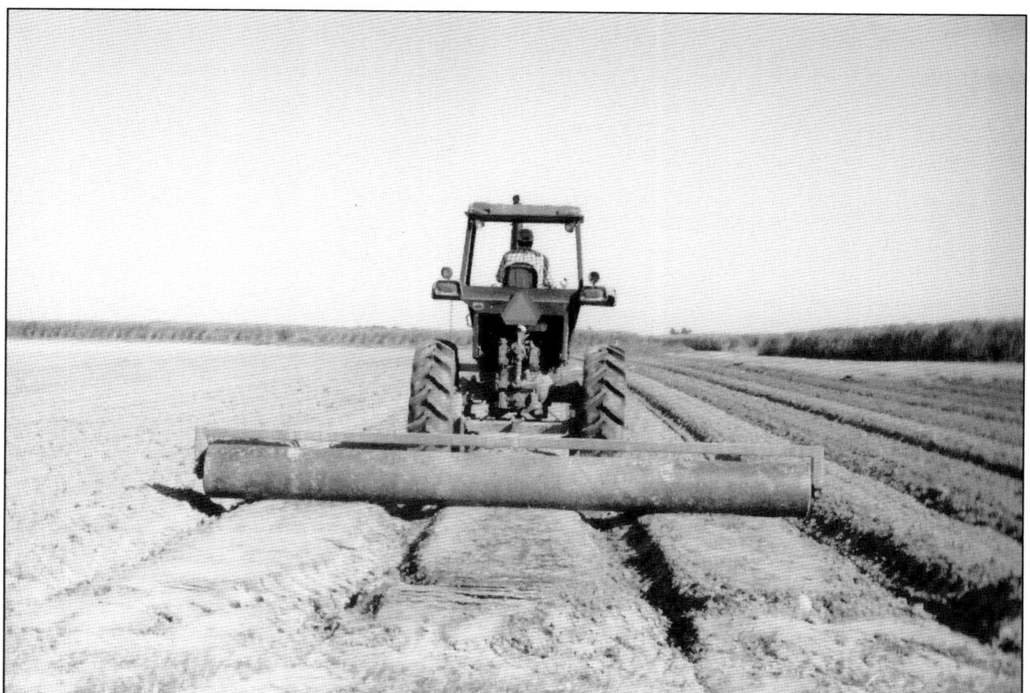

Dirt is then packed down by rolling over the rows. (Courtesy of Don and Diane Bergeron.)

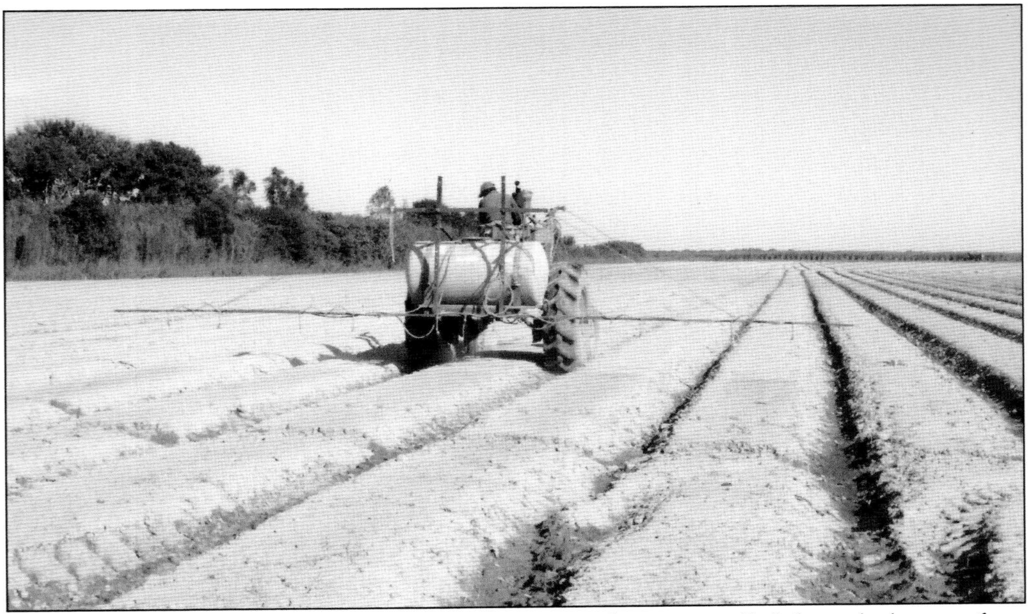

Weeds are controlled through the use of chemicals. Insects can also cause extensive damage to commercial sugar crops. (Courtesy of Don and Diane Bergeron.)

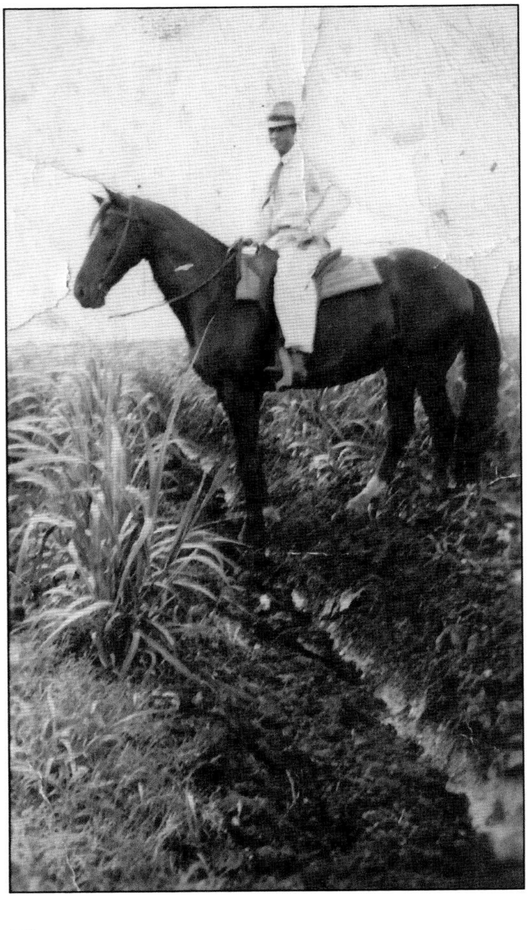

Planters were dependent on their horses to move around the farms quickly. Sam Bergeron is pictured on horseback in 1936. Today, four-wheelers and trucks are a much more common sight in the fields. (Courtesy of Don and Diane Bergeron.)

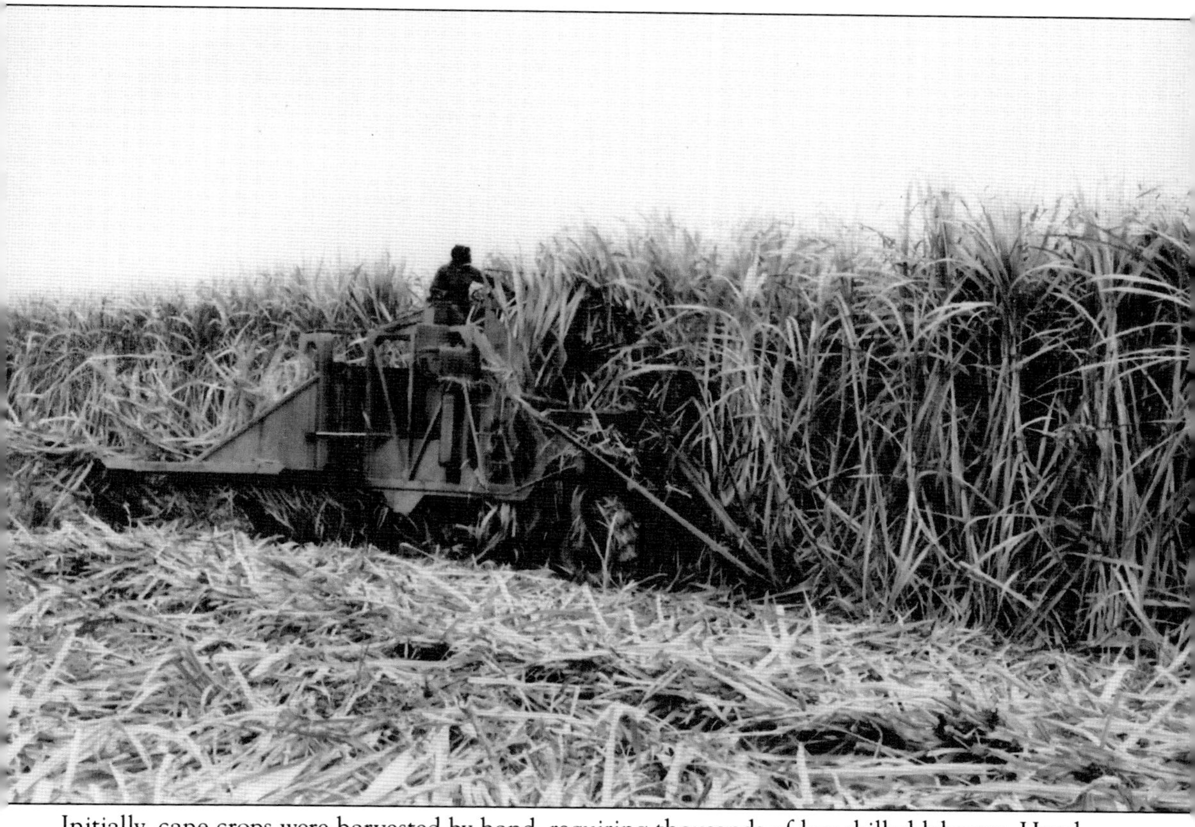

Initially, cane crops were harvested by hand, requiring thousands of low-skilled laborers. Hand chopping used heavy knives to slice at the base of stalks left standing in the field. The one-row harvester became affordable for most farmers by the 1950s. This breakthrough in sugarcane harvesting did the work of 75 men. Technological breakthroughs have only been one element necessary to the survival of the industry. Administrative organization, reorganizations, and cooperatives have kept farmers on the cutting edge of best industry practices. Most recently, Louisiana Refining has been formed as the largest single investment in the sugar industry in more than 40 years. The refinery is capable of refining two billion pounds of white sugar annually. (Courtesy of Don and Diane Bergeron.)

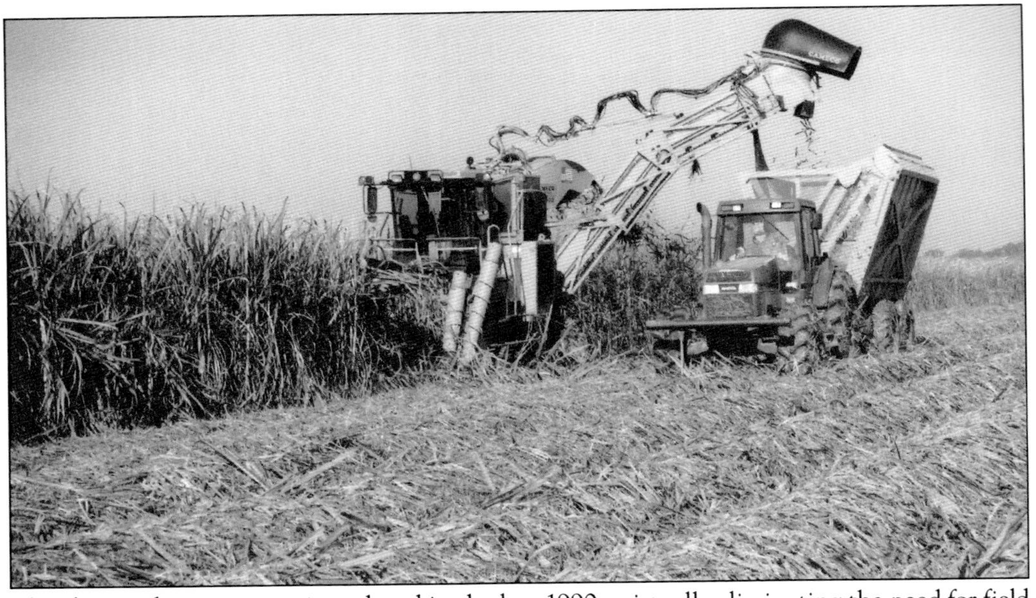

The chopper harvester was introduced in the late 1990s, virtually eliminating the need for field scrappers. It cuts the cane at the top and bottom and then chops it into smaller pieces. Large fans blow green leaves away as the conveyer belt propels stalks into collection wagons. (Courtesy of Don and Diane Bergeron.)

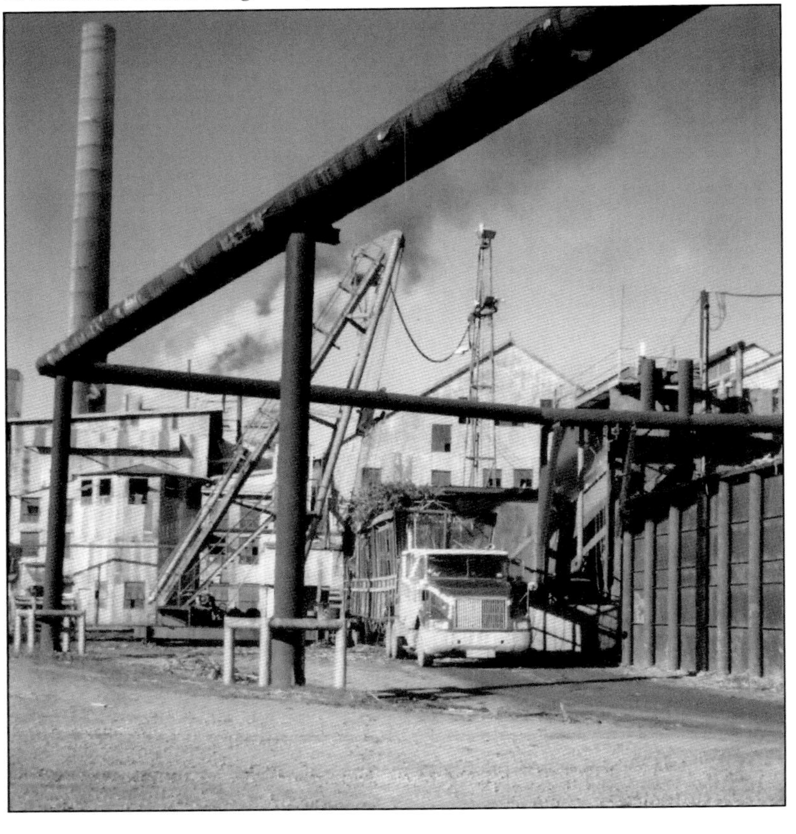

From the collection wagon, the cane is loaded into large trucks and sent to the mill. Here is an example of cane being delivered to the Glenwood mill. (Courtesy of Don and Diane Bergeron.)

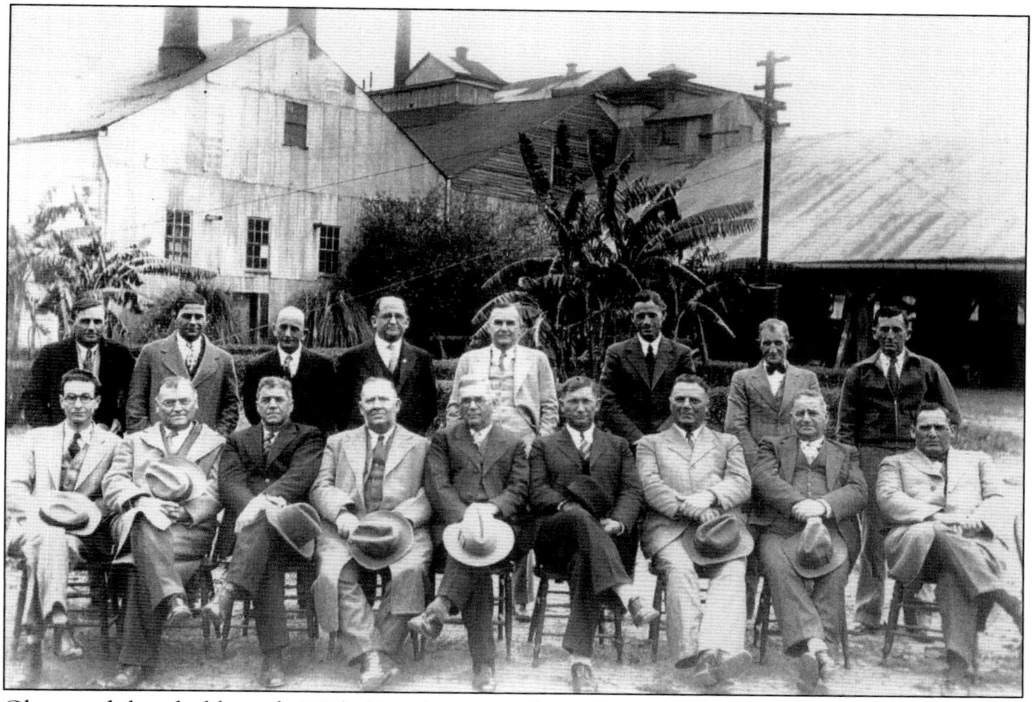

Glenwood shareholders of 1933 held stakes not only in Glenwood but were also concerned about the well-being of the entire sugar industry of the region. The sugar industry's survival came from the continual investment of farmers, who searched for continual improvement in technologies and administration and put in seriously hard work. Pictured here are, from left to right, (sitting) Lawrence Toups, Aubert Talbot, Henry Landry, F.U. Landry, Alphonse Blanchard, Richard Melancon, Numa Caballero, Gustave Landry, and Charles Thiac; (standing) Bronier Thibaut, Angelo Simoneaux, Ben Simoneaux, Walter Lemann, Jean Templet, Dubourg Thibaut, Emile Thibodeaux, and Ardonne Simoneaux. (Courtesy of Don and Diane Bergeron.)

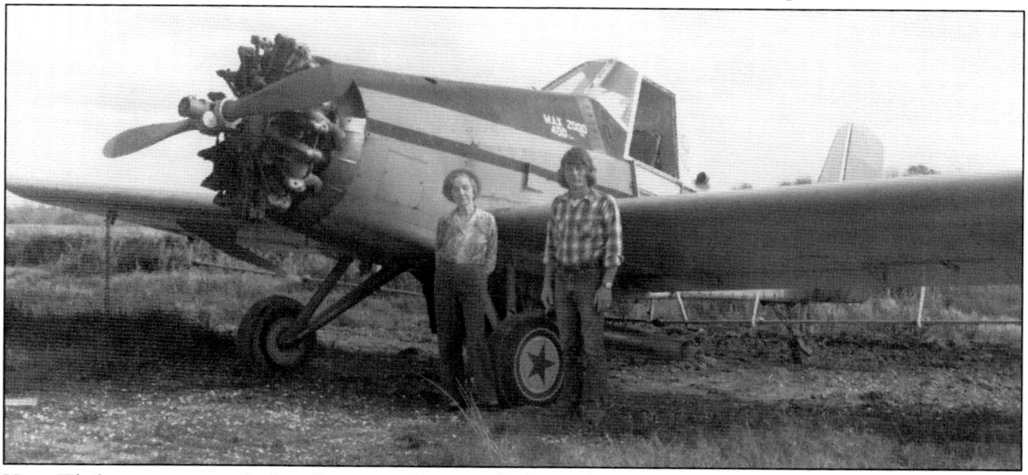

Kate Thibaut prepares for her first crop-dusting flight with Tommy Watson. He will drop chemicals on the fields below to combat the sugarcane borer. This pest, a non-native species of moth introduced to Louisiana around 1855, was responsible for 20 percent of insect damage to Louisiana cane. (Courtesy of the Gerald and Olivia Chenevert family.)

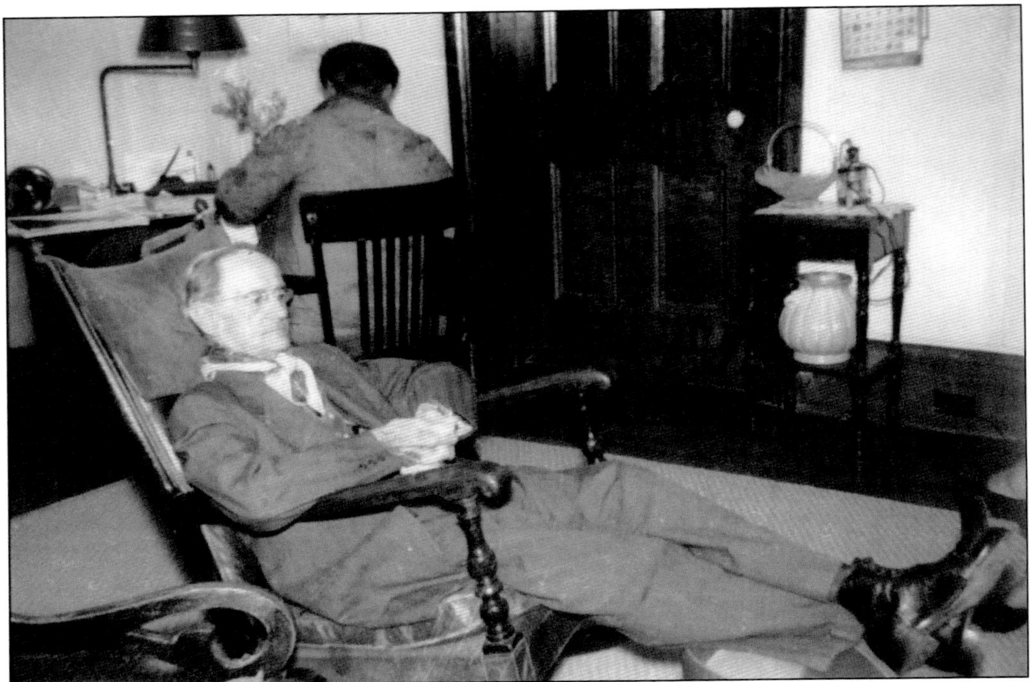

For over 100 years, Bergeron family members have owned, operated, and lived on Wildwood Plantation. In this late-1930s photograph, a retired Willie Noah relaxes as his son Sam Bergeron works on the books in the Wildwood office. (Courtesy of Don and Diane Bergeron.)

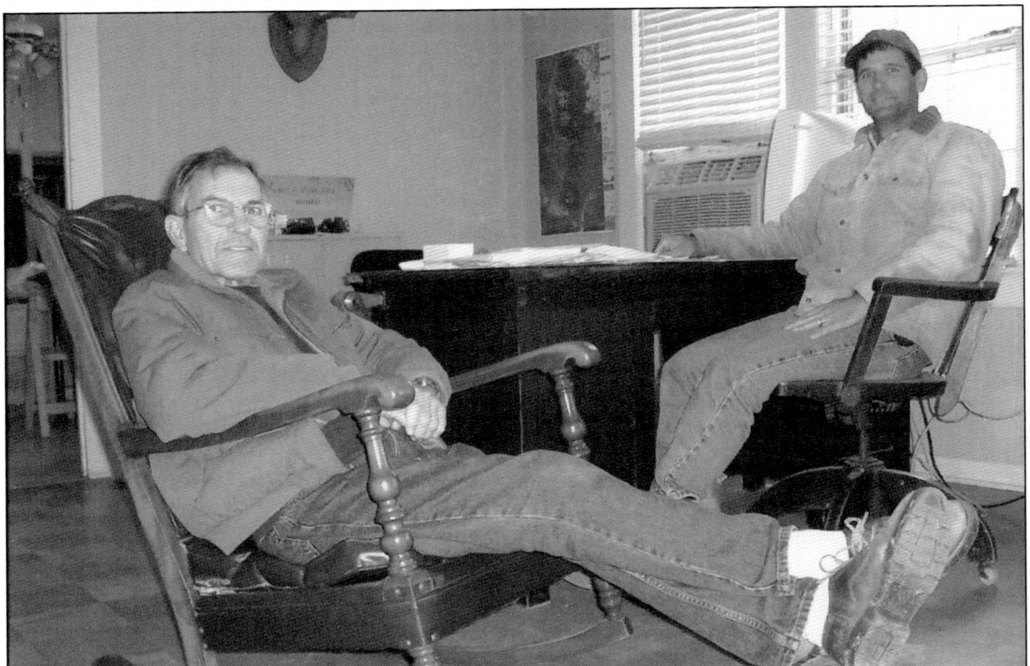

Two generations later, Sam Bergeron's son Don and grandson Mark continue work in the same office occupied for four generations. (Courtesy of Don and Diane Bergeron.)

Three

ARCHITECTURE

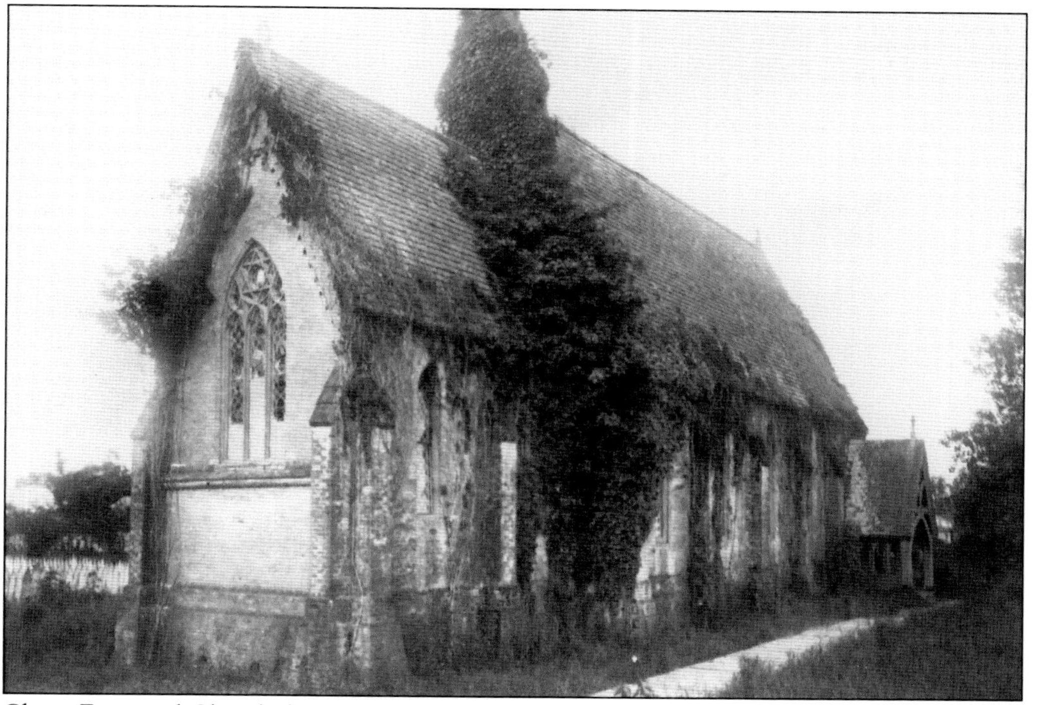

Christ Episcopal Church, built in 1853 and consecrated by the Right Reverend Leonidas Polk in 1854, served as a place of worship for English Protestants of Napoleonville. It was designed by Frank Wills, who also designed the Gothic Revival–style building of the New York Ecclesiological Society. Christ Episcopal Church was added to the National Register of Historic Places in 1977. (Courtesy of William Littlejohn Martin Collection, Archives and Special Collections, Nicholls State University, Thibodaux, Louisiana.)

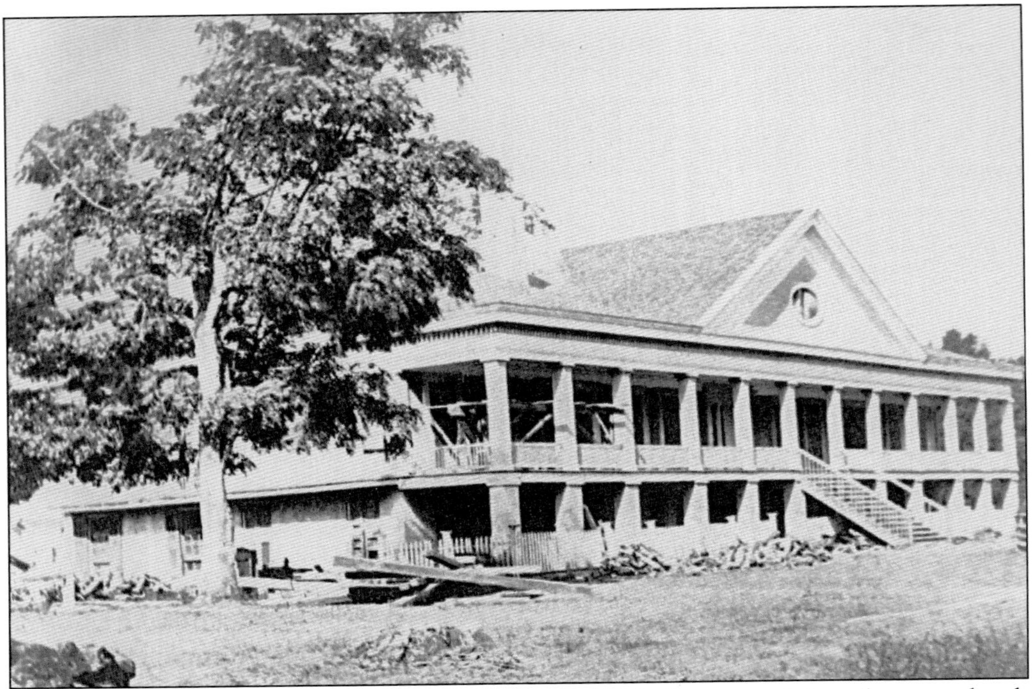

Prior to the Civil War, sugar planters lived in luxury. With the war and the subsequent harsh Reconstruction wreaking havoc on the fortunes of these sugar barons, few original owners retained their lifestyles. E.E. Kittredge died in 1867 at his Tennessee summer residence. He built this home on Elm Hall Plantation but did not live to share in the devastating experience of the Civil War. (Courtesy of LARBC Heritage '76 Collection, Archives and Special Collections, Nicholls State University, Thibodaux, Louisiana.)

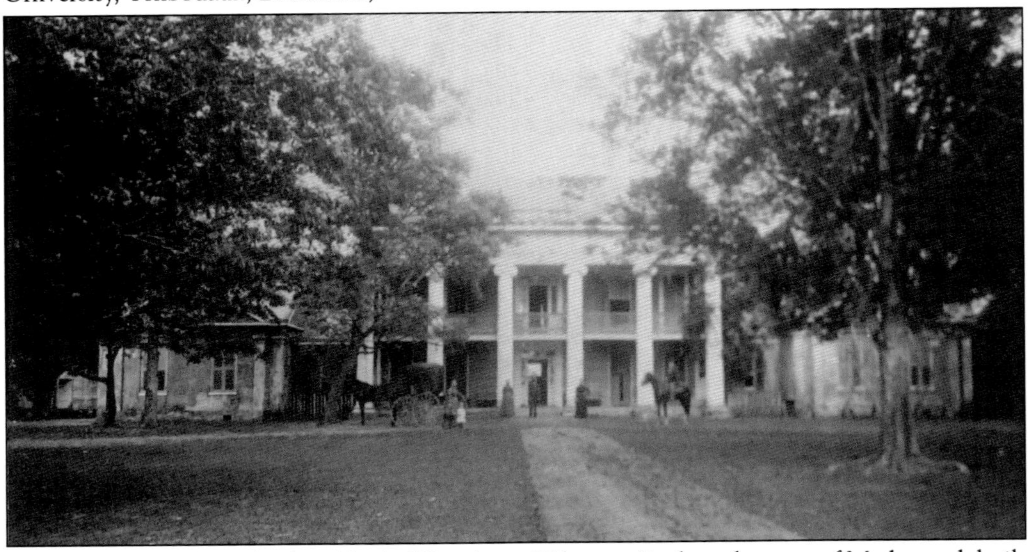

William Whitmell Pugh, the older half-brother of Thomas Pugh and owner of Madewood, built Woodlawn in 1840. Wings were added to this formidable Greek Revival–style home in 1850. It was demolished in the 1940s. (Courtesy of William Littlejohn Martin Collection, Archives and Special Collections, Nicholls State University, Thibodaux, Louisiana.)

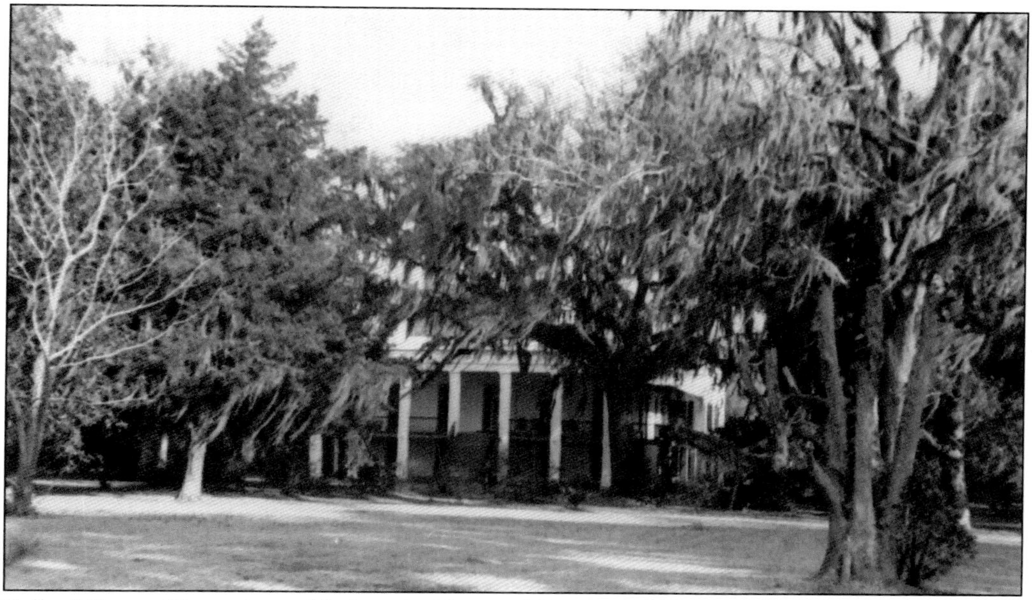

Belle Alliance Plantation, added to the National Register of Historic Places in 1998, is located on the east bank of Bayou Lafourche, about two miles north of Belle Rose on Highway 308, in an area originally settled as Valenzuela. Don Juan Vives, a physician and Spanish military officer, was granted a 7,000-acre plot. Vives participated in the 1779 expedition against the British in Baton Rouge, led by Spanish governor Don Bernardo Galvez. Vives received the Bayou Lafourche land grant Valenzuela during the Spanish occupation of Louisiana. Spanish military settlers from the Canary Islands came to the area to secure Spanish interests. Much of the success of this Spanish military outpost was due to financial support from the Spanish government for several years until the area became self-sufficient. Familiar family names remain as direct descendants of the original settlers from this community. (Both, courtesy of William Littlejohn Martin Collection, Archives and Special Collections, Nicholls State University, Thibodaux, Louisiana.)

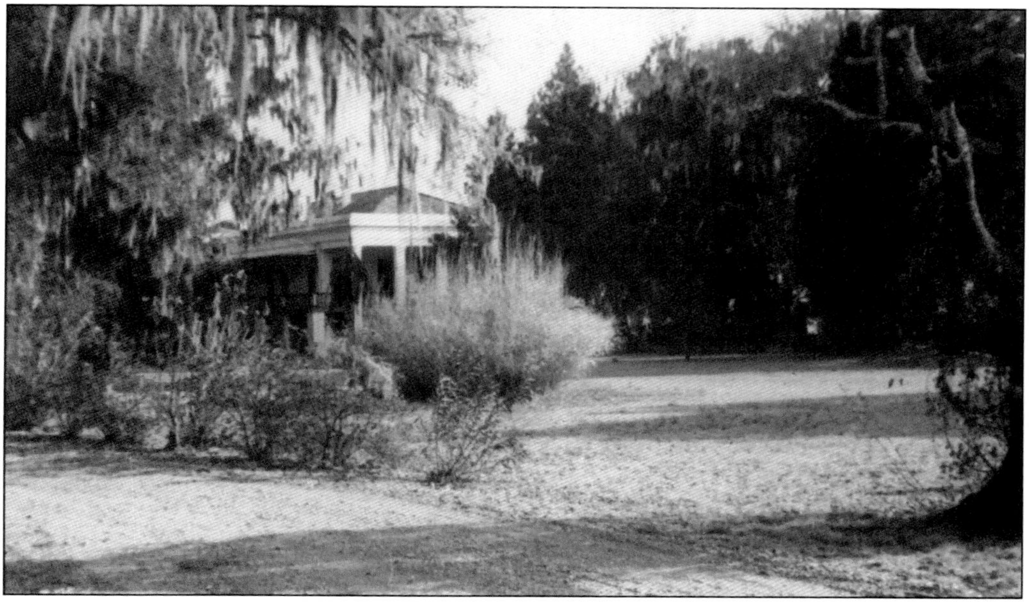

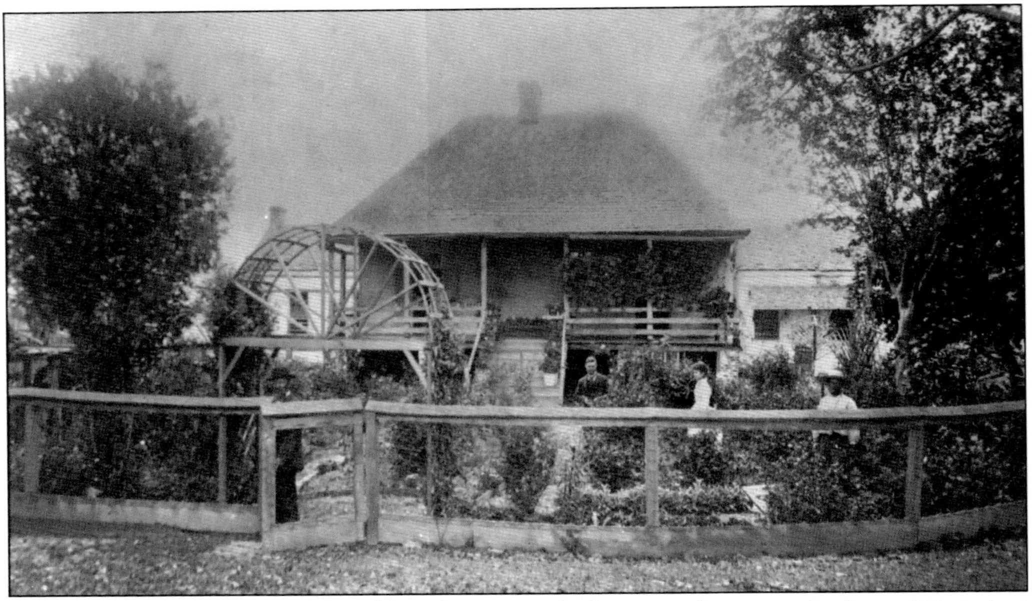

Albemarle, built in 1787, is the oldest documented plantation home in the lower Mississippi Valley. Acquired by Robert Campbell Martin Sr. in 1940, it is run by descendents as the longest continually owned and operated plantation in Assumption Parish. It is named for the Albemarle Sound, the tidewater area near Bertie County, North Carolina, where Martin's father was born. (Courtesy of William Littlejohn Martin Collection, Archives and Special Collections, Nicholls State University, Thibodaux, Louisiana.)

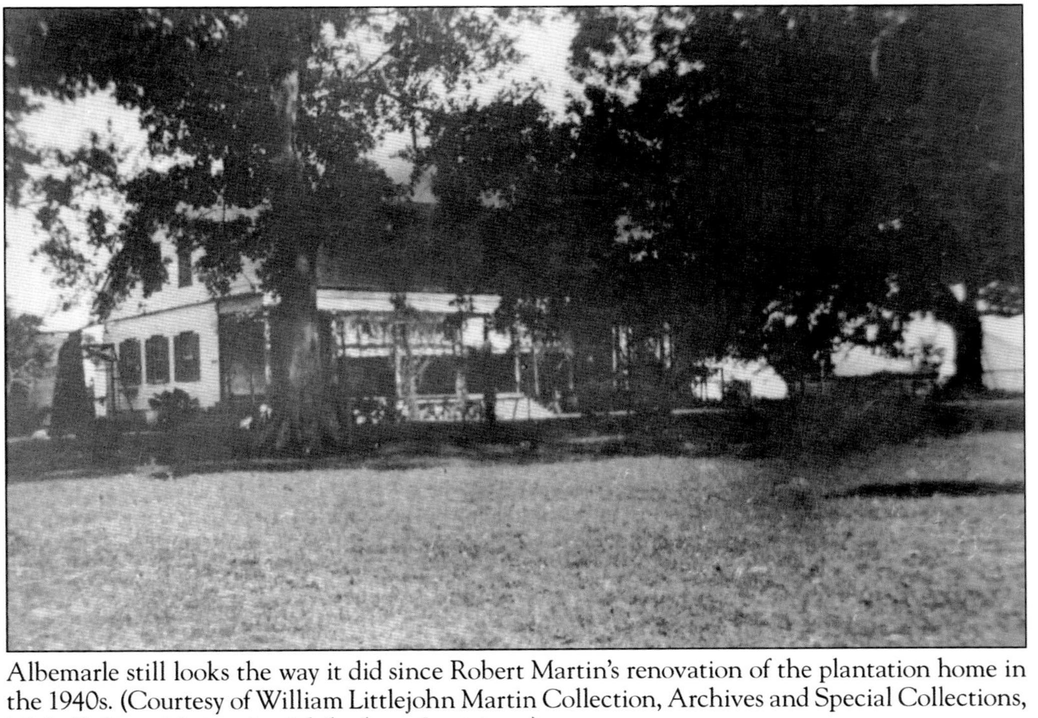

Albemarle still looks the way it did since Robert Martin's renovation of the plantation home in the 1940s. (Courtesy of William Littlejohn Martin Collection, Archives and Special Collections, Nicholls State University, Thibodaux, Louisiana.)

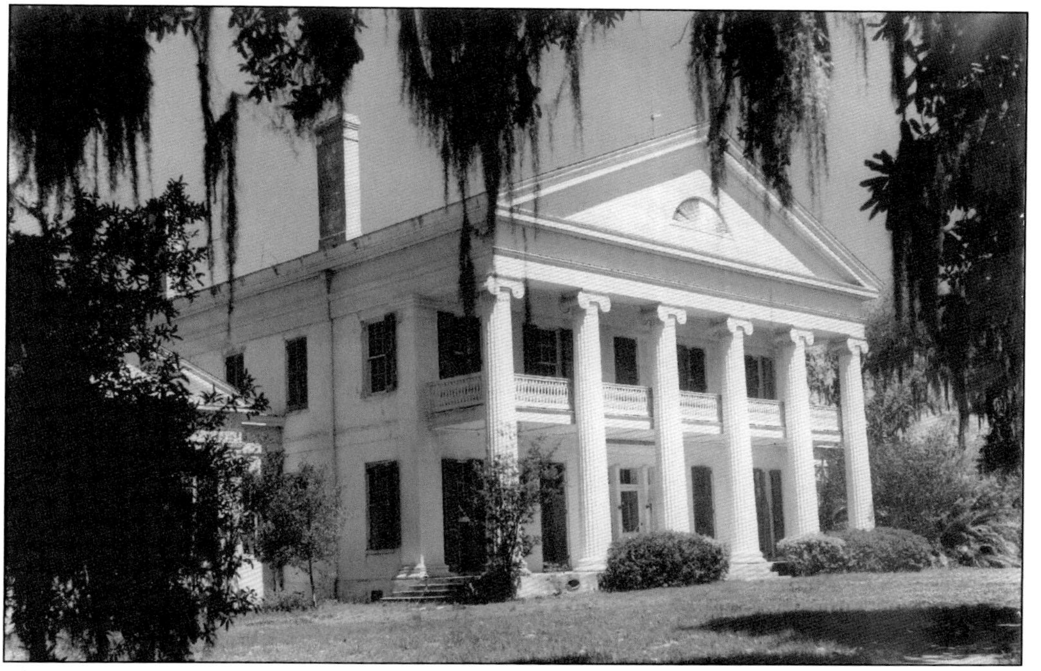

The Greek Revival–style Madewood Plantation home was built between 1840 and 1848 by Eliza Foley Pugh and her husband, Col. Thomas Pugh. It was owned by the Thibaut family when this 1955 photograph was taken. It is currently owned by the Marshall family. (Courtesy of the Gerald and Olivia Chenevert family.)

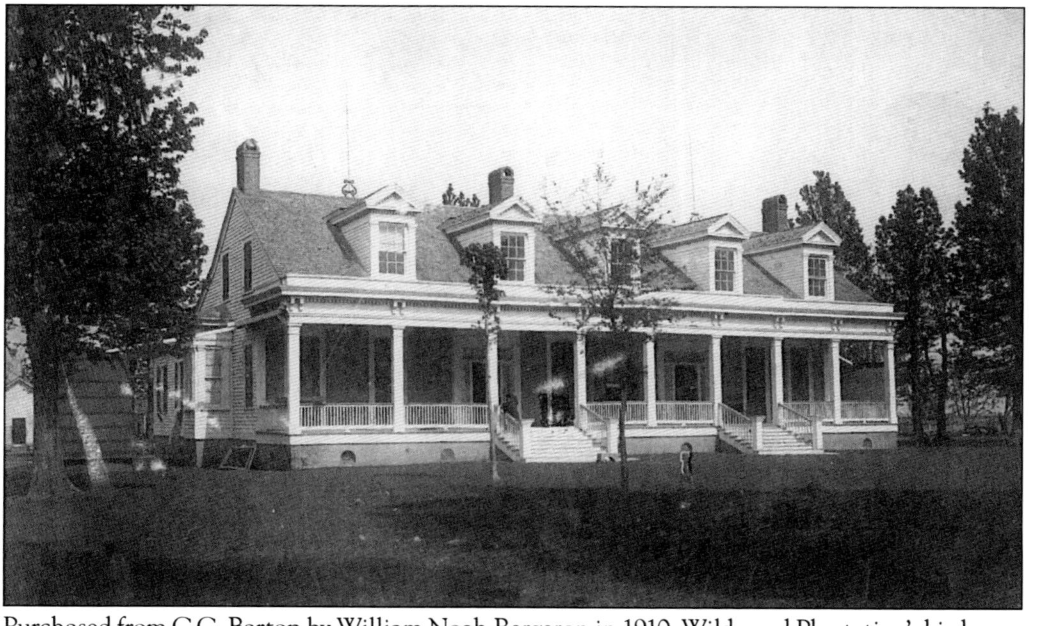

Purchased from C.C. Barton by William Noah Bergeron in 1910, Wildwood Plantation's big house was originally built in the 1830s by Gabriel Beasley. Since acquiring the plantation, the Bergeron family has worked and lived on the plantation continuously for over 100 years. (Courtesy of the Yvette B. Winston.)

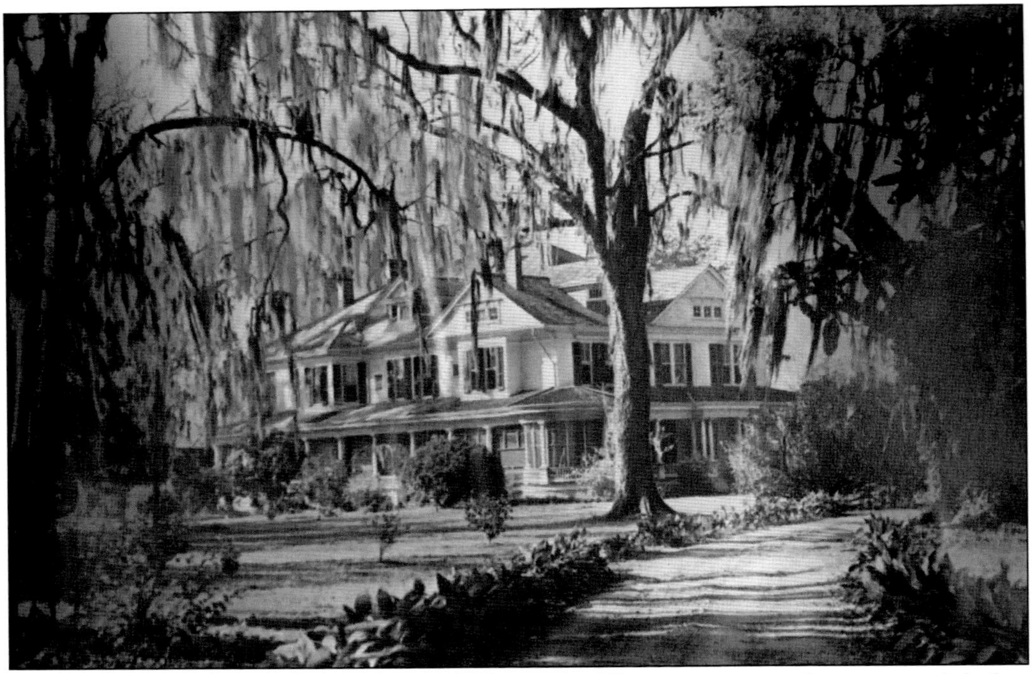

The Munson family owned the Glenwood Plantation. This picture was taken one week before the home burned in 1955. (Courtesy of the Gerald and Olivia Chenevert family.)

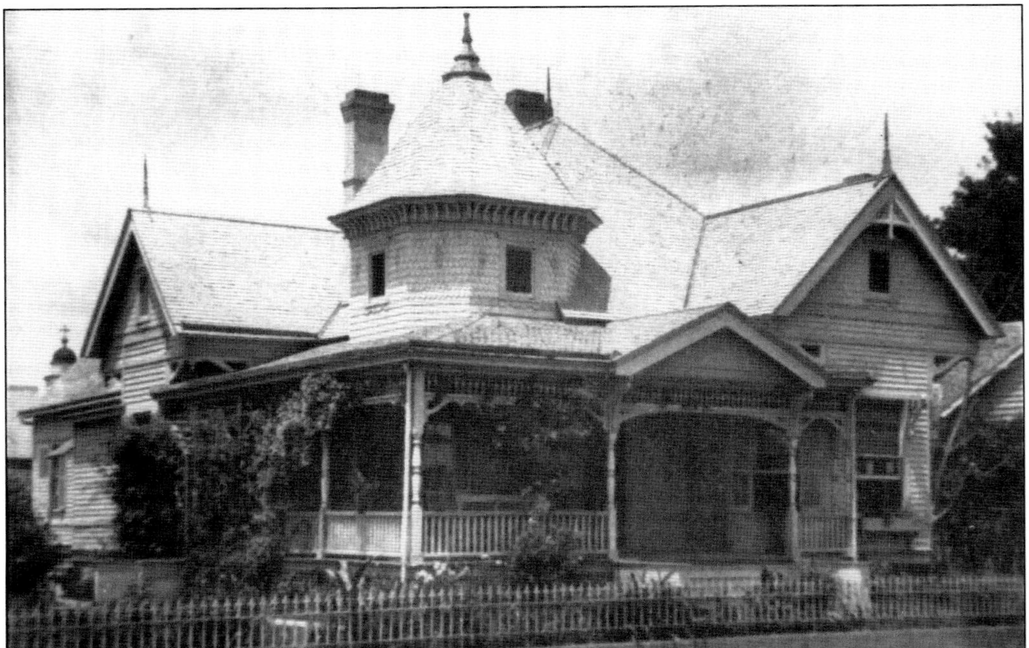

This is the home of Judge Whitmell P. Martin, the second son of Albemarle owner Robert C. Martin. He was the only Louisiana congressional representative to serve as a member of Teddy Roosevelt's Bull Moose Party. (Courtesy of William Littlejohn Martin Collection, Archives and Special Collections, Nicholls State University, Thibodaux, Louisiana.)

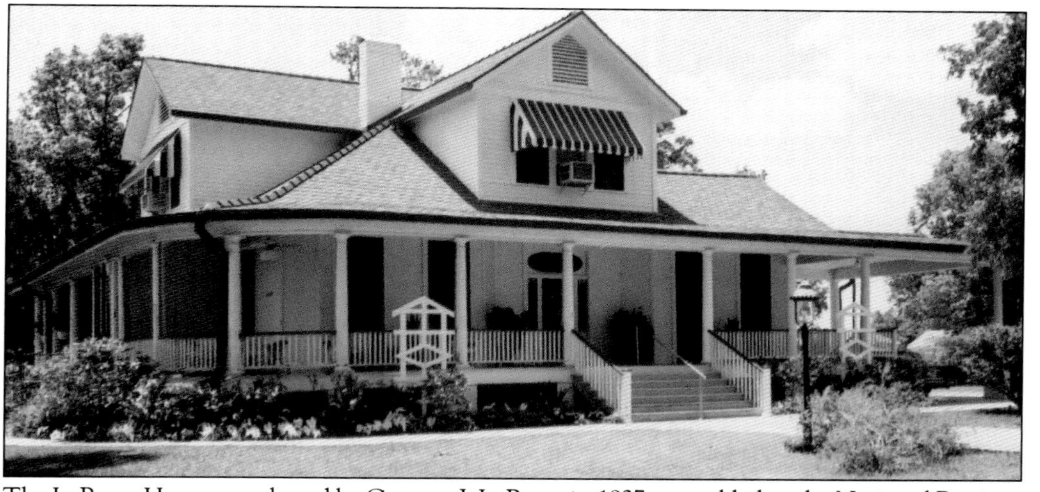

The LaBarre House, purchased by Gustave J. LaBarre in 1937, was added to the National Register of Historic Places in 2008. Built by Napoleonville attorney George Seth Guion in 1909, it is owned by LaBarre's daughter Marlene and her husband, Dr. Raymond Folse. (Courtesy of Dr. Raymond and Marlene LaBarre Folse.)

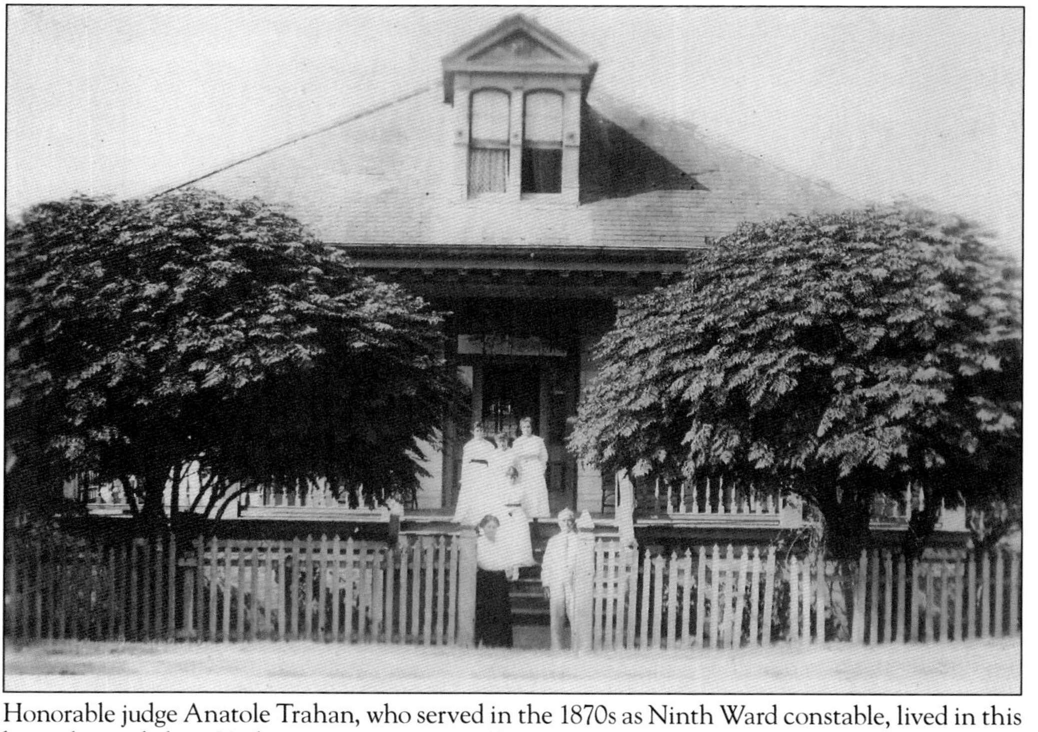

Honorable judge Anatole Trahan, who served in the 1870s as Ninth Ward constable, lived in this house located along Highway 1 in Paincourtville. This 1910s photograph was taken near the time Judge Trahan's daughter Louise married Frank Newchurch, son of Henry and Eldah Newchurch. Henry served the Confederacy in the Civil War until the day General Lee surrendered to General Grant at Appomattox in 1865. (Courtesy of Martha Newchurch.)

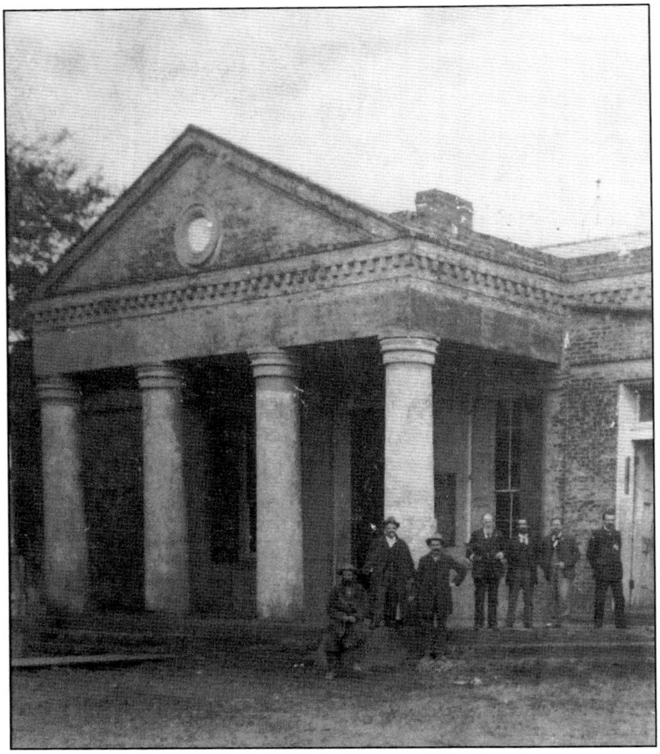

This Greek Revival–style municipal building, constructed after 1818, served as the Assumption Parish Courthouse until it was replaced in 1896. It is speculated that mantels found in the new courthouse may have been salvaged from this building because of their similarity to Federal-style mantels popular earlier in the 1800s. (Courtesy of Donald and Billie Eris Blanchard)

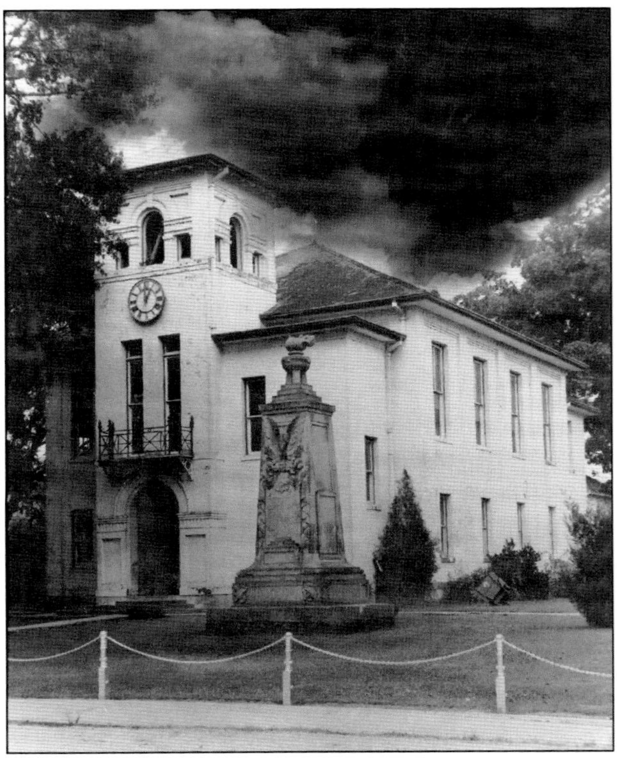

Built in 1896, the Assumption Parish Courthouse and Jail was added to the National Register of Historic Places in 1997 as an example of Italian Villa–style architecture. (Courtesy of Cecile M. LeBlanc.)

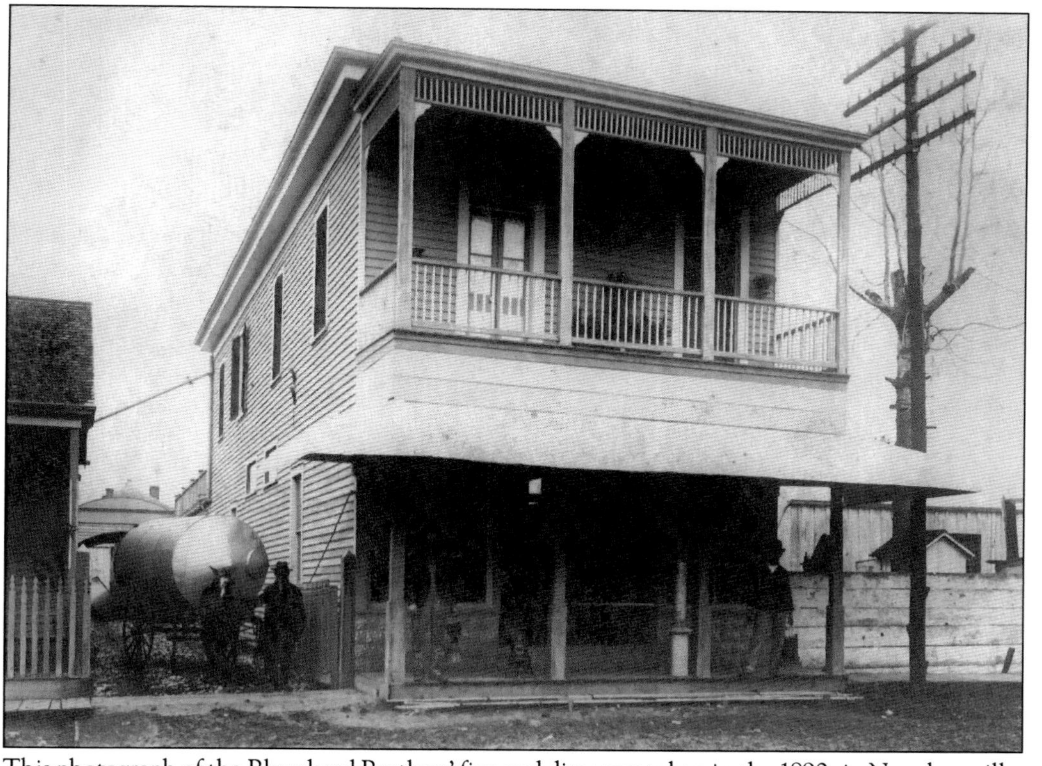

This photograph of the Blanchard Brothers' five and dime was taken in the 1890s in Napoleonville. The store, which no longer exists, was a popular market in town. (Courtesy of Donald and Billie Eris Blanchard.)

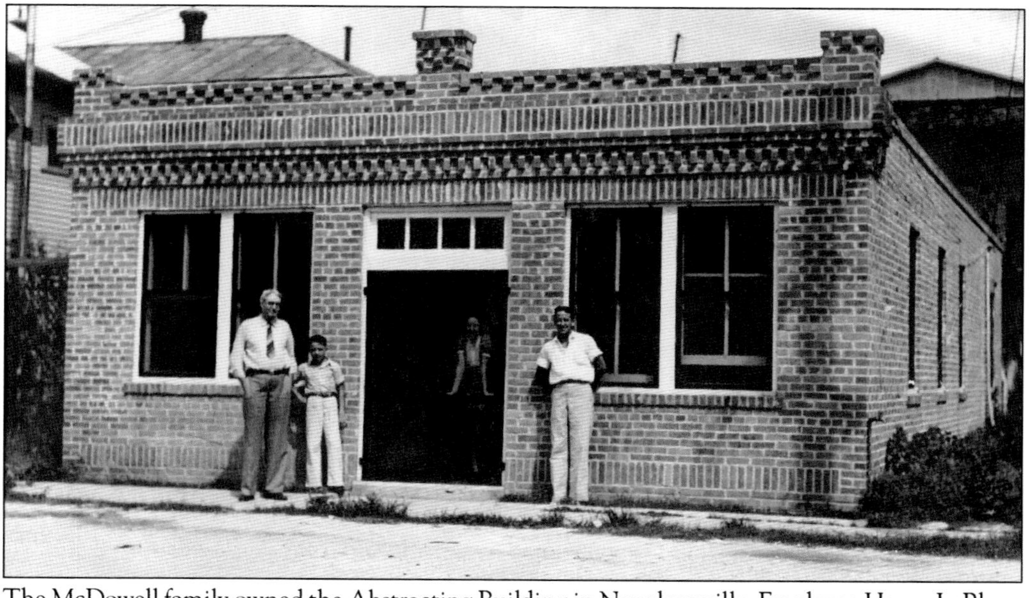

The McDowell family owned the Abstracting Building in Napoleonville. Employee Henry LeBlanc is pictured (far right) with the owner and staff. The building was located on Washington Street in Napoleonville. (Courtesy of Cecile M. LeBlanc.)

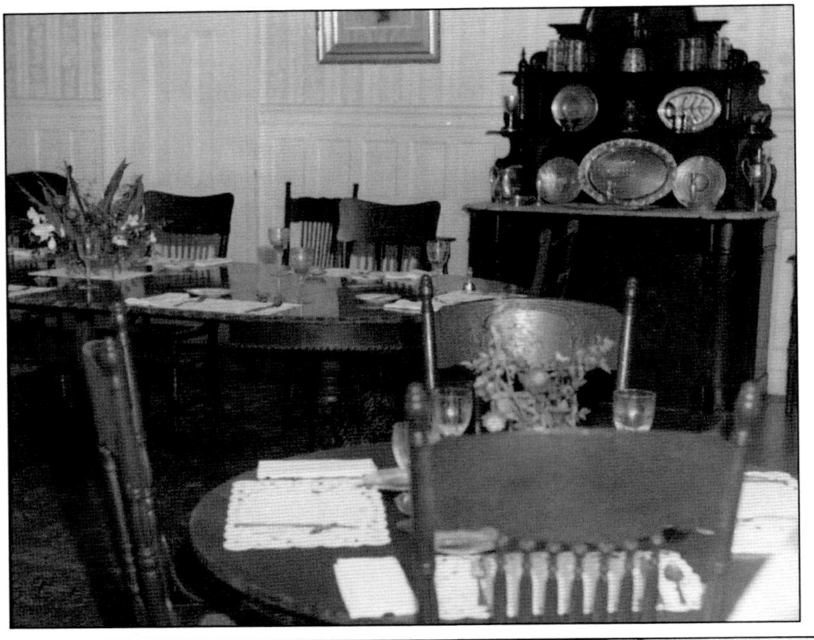

This photograph of the Glenwood dining room was taken by Gerald Chenevert for a travel piece on Assumption Parish in *New Orleans Magazine* in 1955. It was taken only a week before the mansion burned. (Courtesy of the Gerald and Olivia Chenevert family.)

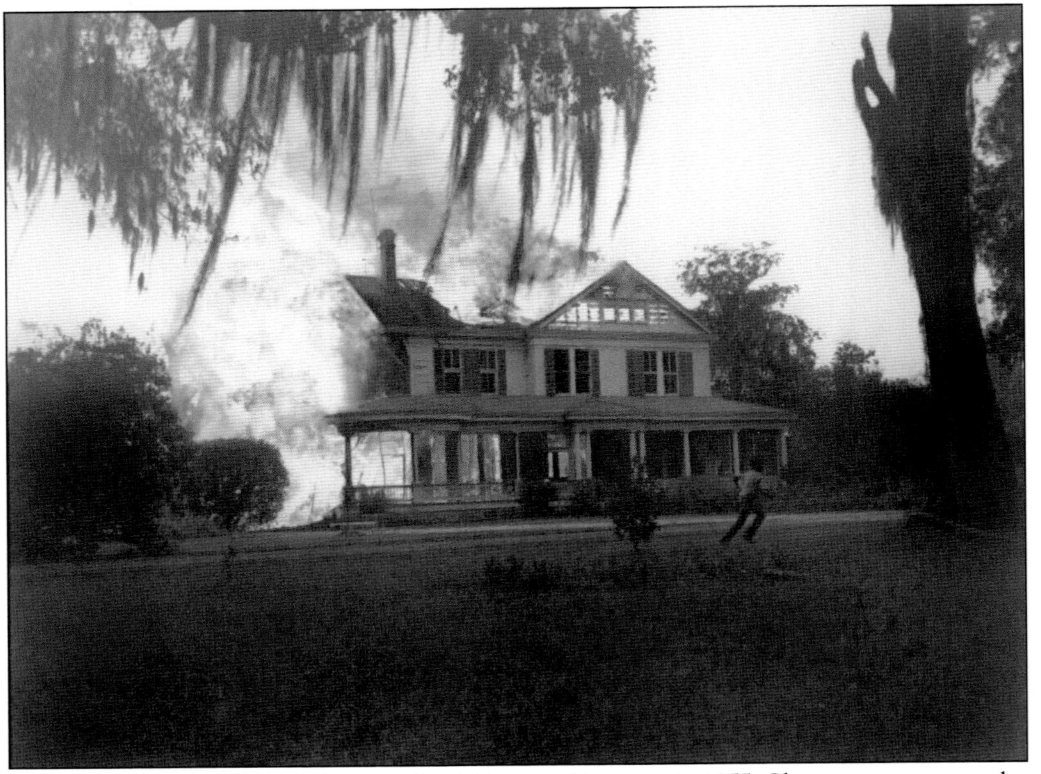

Gerald Chenevert took this photograph of Glenwood burning in 1955. Chenevert was a popular photographer (as well as volunteer fireman) in the parish and happened to have his fully loaded camera in his vehicle when the volunteer firemen responded to the blaze. (Courtesy of the Gerald and Olivia Chenevert family.)

The African Americans plea to the diocese, "Give us a priest, and we will build the church," was heeded in the late 1800s. From this request, St. Benedict the Moor Church in Bertrandville and its mission church in Klotzville, St. Augustine, were born. Fr. Benoit Favard of the Society of St. Joseph became the first pastor of St. Benedict, pictured here in 1922. (Courtesy of St. Benedict the Moor Catholic Church.)

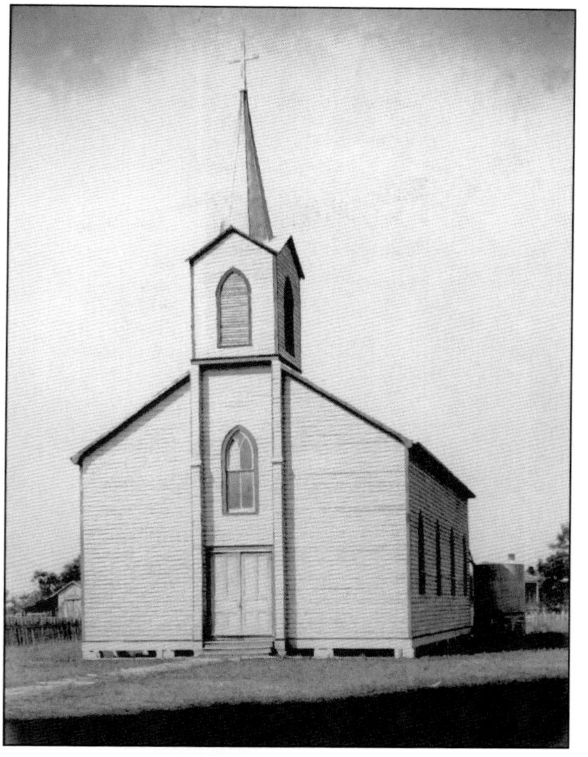

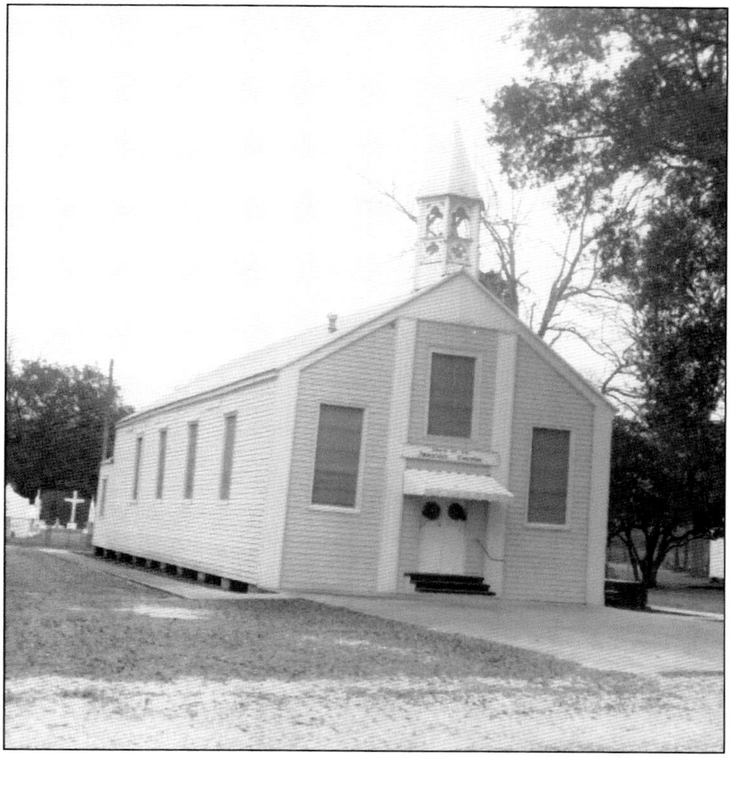

The Church of the Immaculate Conception, established in 1857 and located on Highway 401 south of Napoleonville, is a chapel church of St. Anne. The church is still there and appears unchanged from the time this photograph was taken. (Courtesy of the Gerald and Olivia Chenevert family.)

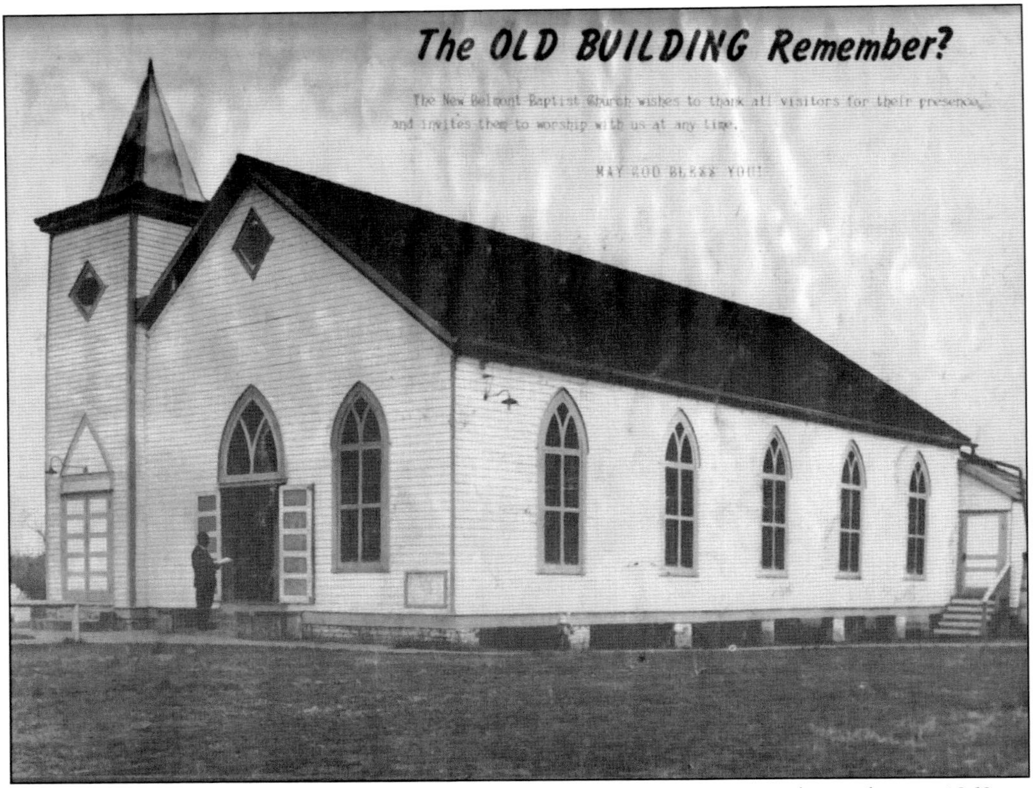

The New Belmont Baptist Church was established when a group joined together in 1869 on Melrose Plantation to dedicate their new congregation to the service of God. Under the leadership of Rev. Washington Brown, the New Belmont Church bought land from plantation owner Simon Abraham in 1891. (Courtesy of Mildred Sylvester.)

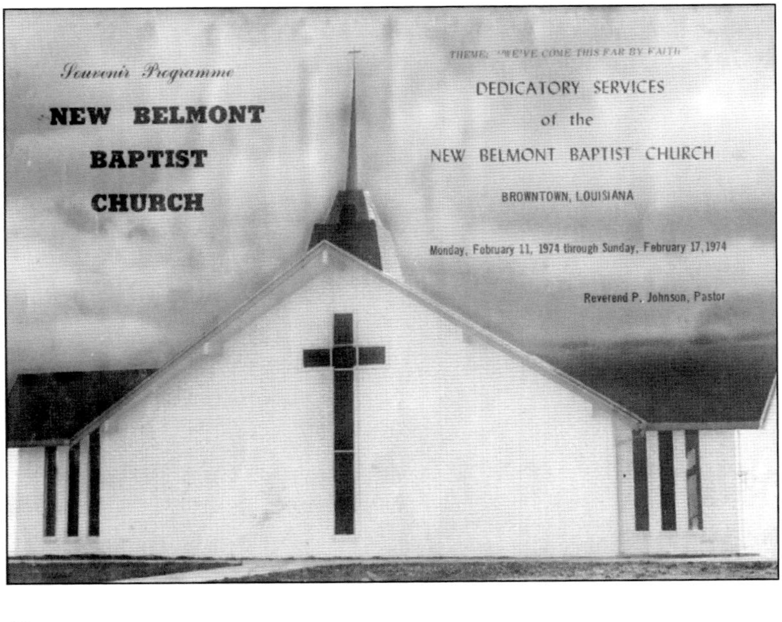

The New Belmont Baptist Church congregation took occupancy of their new building in 1974. The current pastor, Rev. Johnny E. Johnson Jr., leads the congregation at the same site where the steamship *HB Dickey*, depicted on page 14, was sucked into Jones Crevasse in 1883. (Courtesy of Mildred Sylvester.)

This photograph was taken of the pastor in front of the new First Baptist Church in Napoleonville in the 1970s. The mission of the church, as quoted from its website, states, "To live godly lives and share in the gospel of salvation in Jesus Christ that others may come to know Jesus Christ as Lord and Savior." (Courtesy of the Gerald and Olivia Chenevert family.)

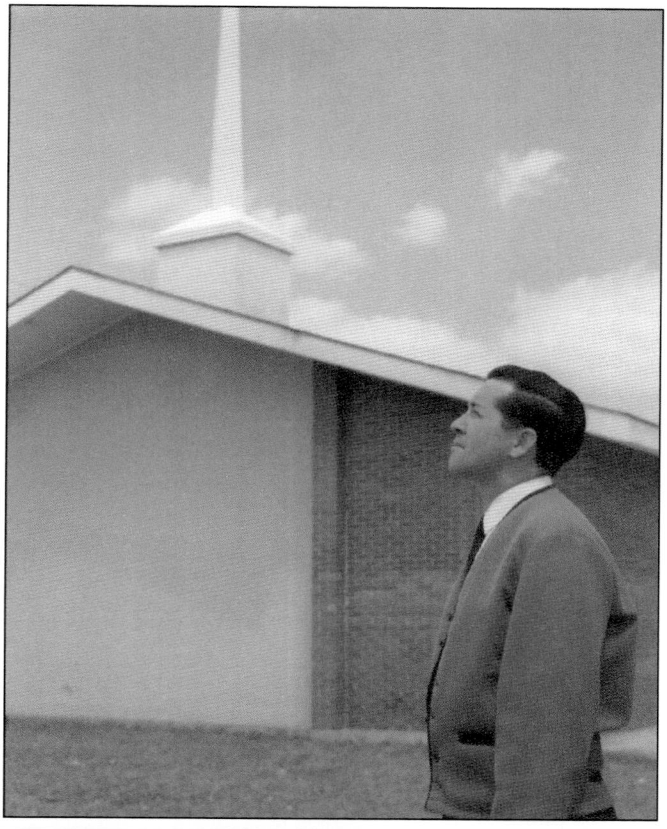

St. Anne Catholic Church was completed in Napoleonville to accommodate the growing needs of the bayou community. The stained-glass windows depict most of the mysteries of the rosary. It replaced the previously established church, St. Napoleon, that had served the area. (Courtesy of the Gerald and Olivia Chenevert family.)

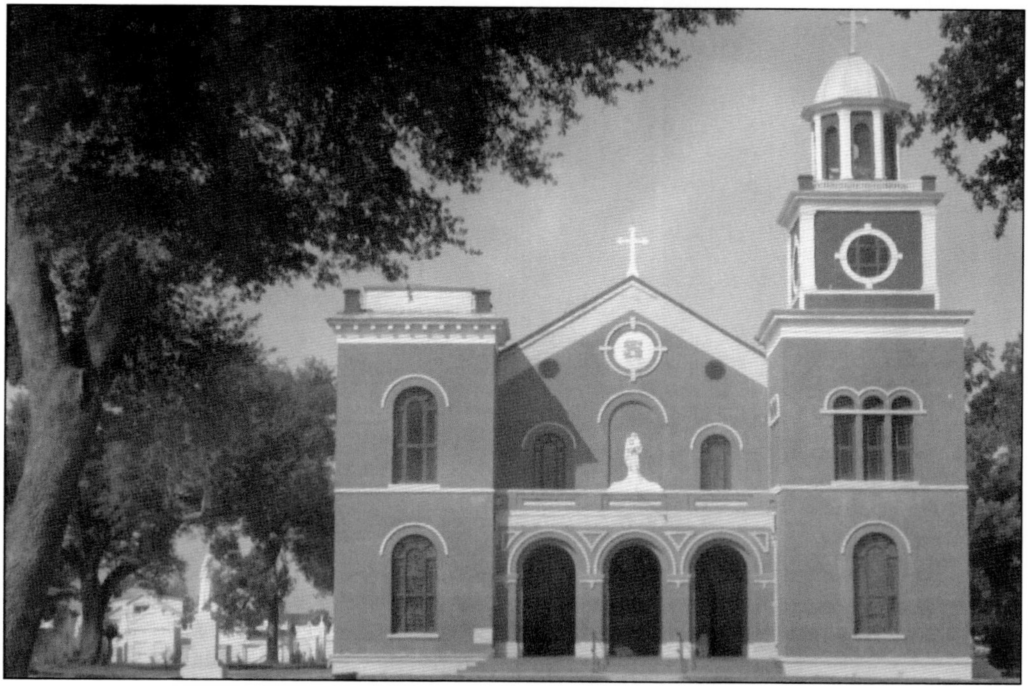

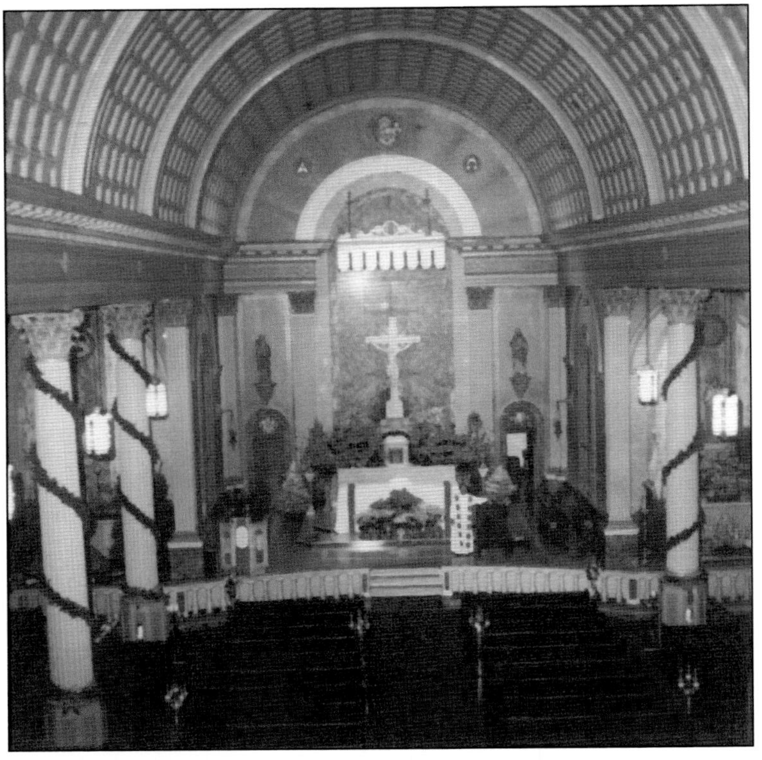

St Anne's altar is pictured here. The church was entered into the National Register of Historic Places in 2001 as an example of Romanesque architecture and boasts an exquisite imported Italian marble altar. (Courtesy of the Gerald and Olivia Chenevert family.)

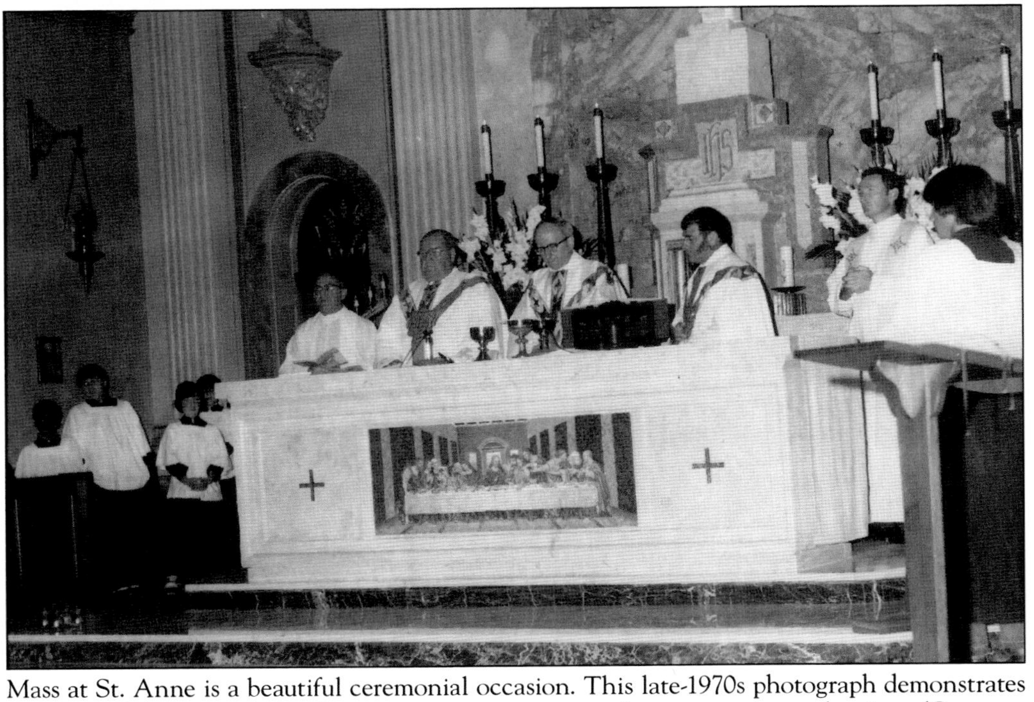

Mass at St. Anne is a beautiful ceremonial occasion. This late-1970s photograph demonstrates multiple celebrants and altar boys common in service to the community at the time. (Courtesy of the Gerald and Olivia Chenevert family.)

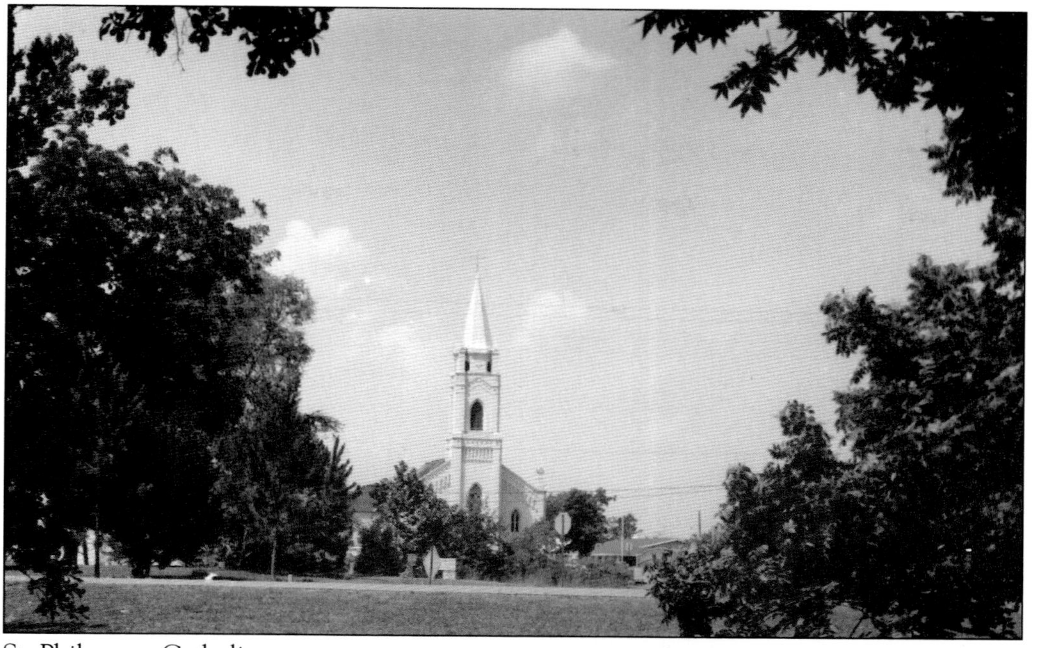

St. Philomena Catholic Church and Rectory was added to the National Register of Historic Places in 1983. Fr. Cyprian Vennisat became the first pastor of St. Philomena after its establishment in 1855. Construction on the present-day church began around 1888. (Courtesy of the Gerald and Olivia Chenevert family.)

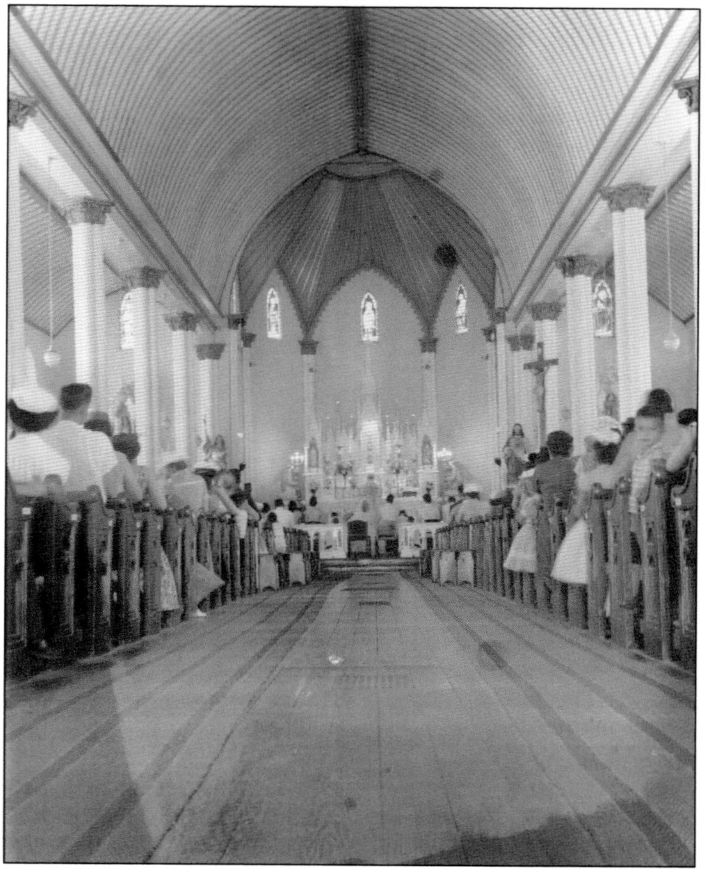

The elaborate altar woodwork of St. Philomena was a feature that figured in the approval of the church's entry in the historic register. (Courtesy of the Gerald and Olivia Chenevert family.)

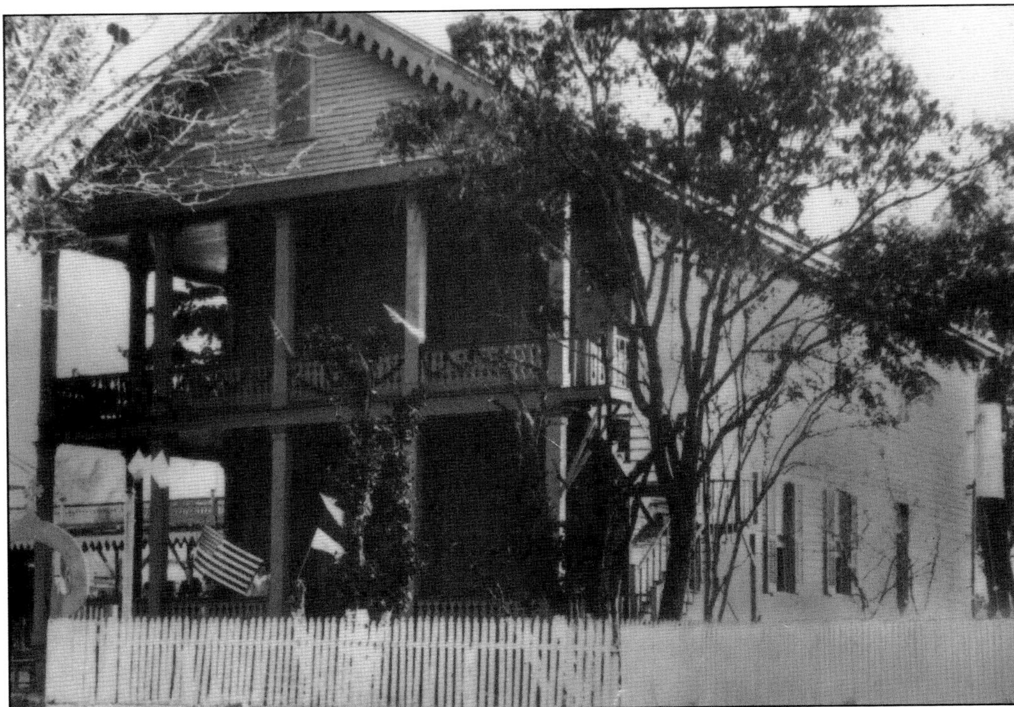

Mount Carmel School, pictured here in the 1890s, was the predecessor of St. Elizabeth School, the church school associated with Paincourtville's St. Elizabeth Catholic Church. (Courtesy of Diane LeBlanc.)

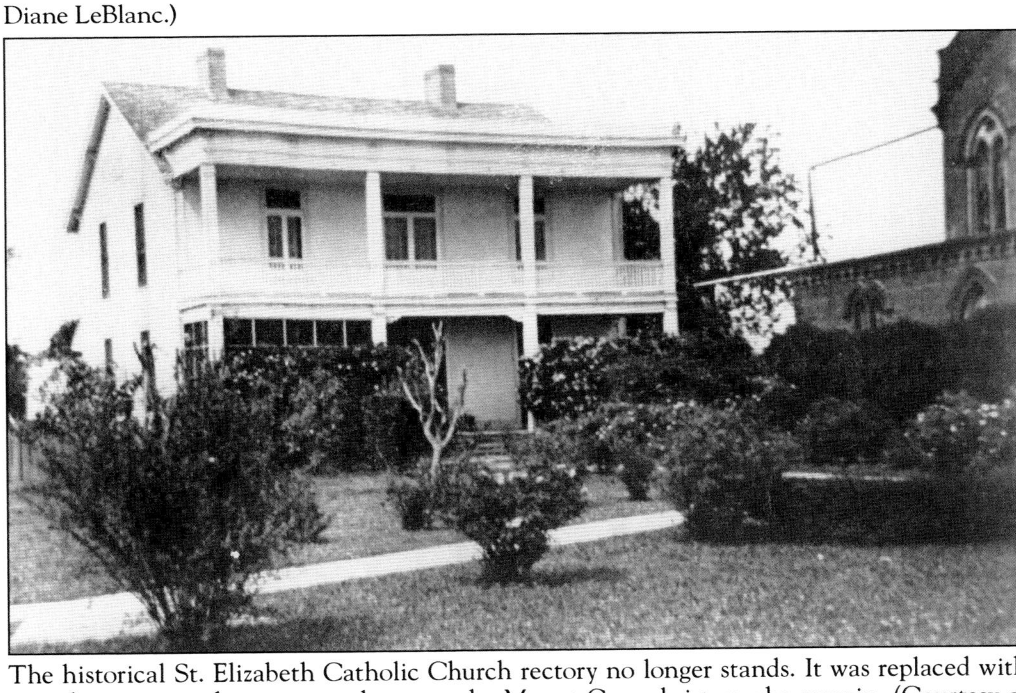

The historical St. Elizabeth Catholic Church rectory no longer stands. It was replaced with a modern rectory that serves as home to the Mount Carmel sisters who remain. (Courtesy of Diane LeBlanc.)

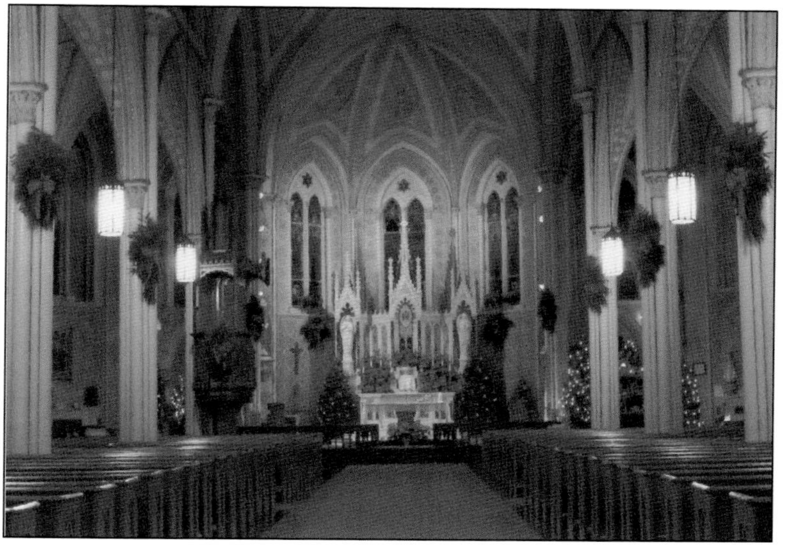

F.B. Dicharry designed St. Elizabeth Church in the early 1900s. The altar and interior of the church demonstrate Gothic architecture. The church was entered into the National Register of Historic Places in 1983. (Courtesy of Diane LeBlanc.)

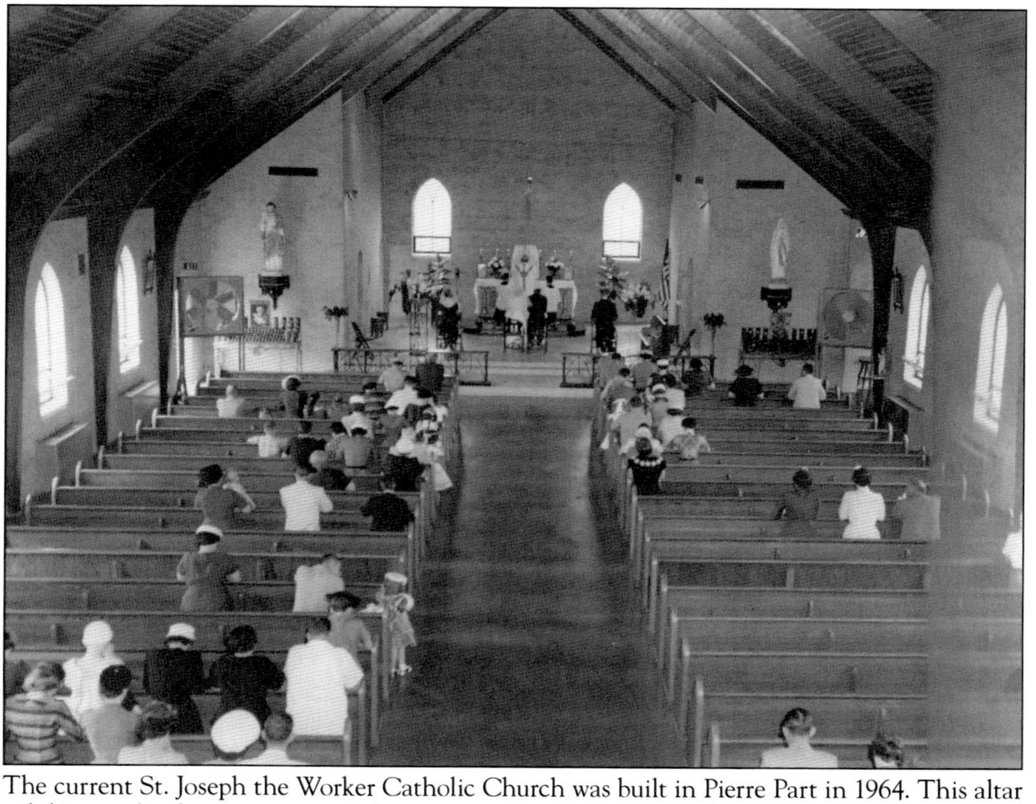

The current St. Joseph the Worker Catholic Church was built in Pierre Part in 1964. This altar exhibits a stylized, contemporary feel common in late-20th-century church construction. (Courtesy of the Gerald and Olivia Chenevert family.)

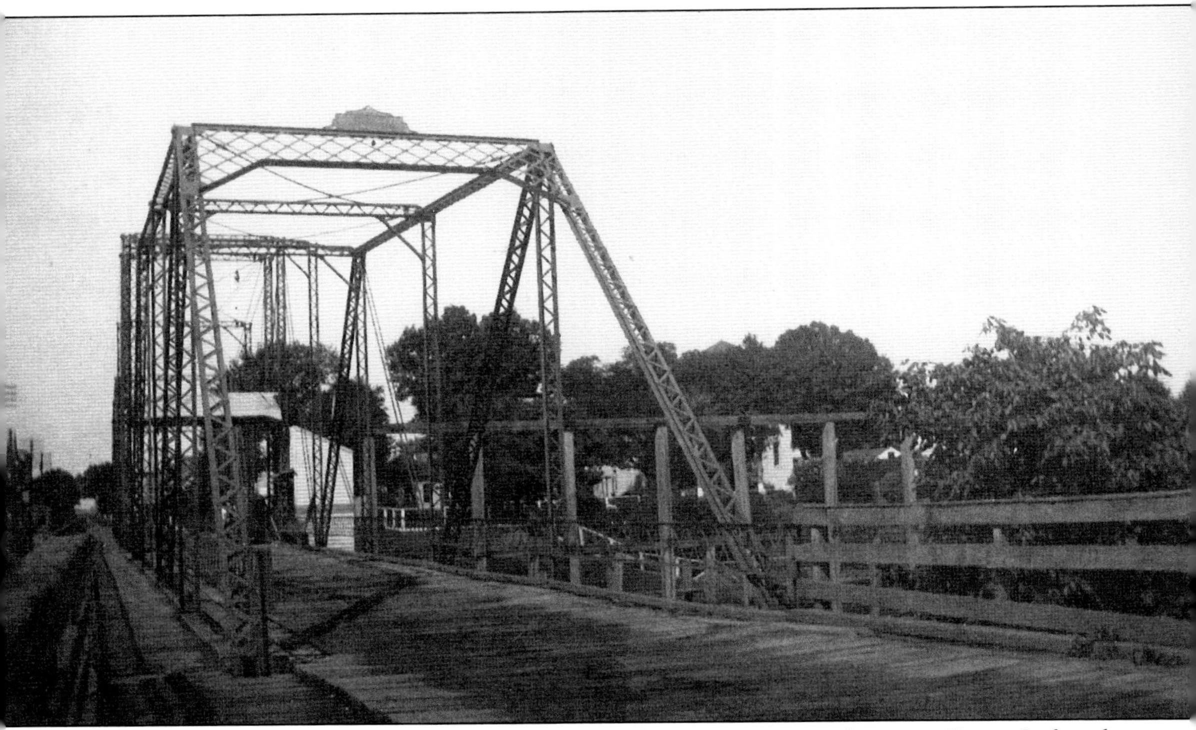

The first Napoleonville bridge was constructed after 1904. Prior to this time, Bayou Lafourche levees were too unstable and engineering did not favor construction. Ferries were commonly used before bridges were built. (Courtesy of Don and Billie Eris Blanchard.)

Four

Communities and Notables

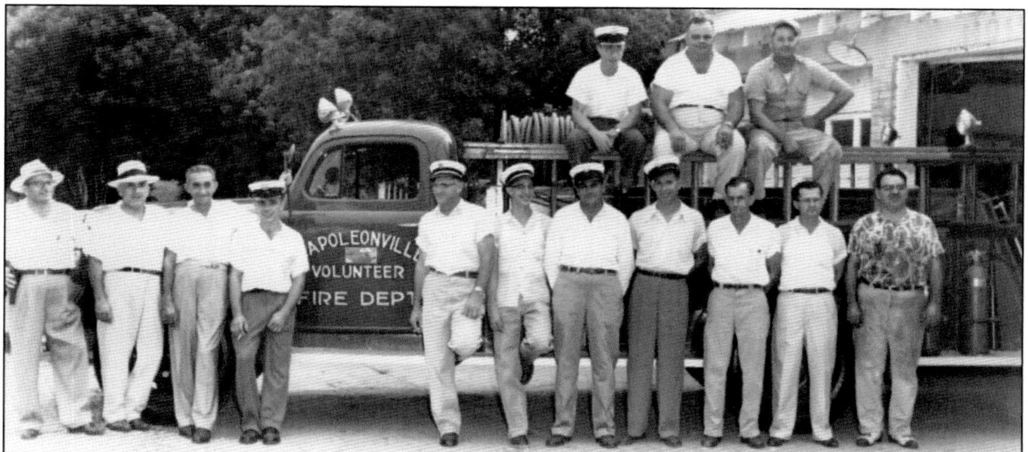

This 1950s photograph shows Napoleonville Fire Department volunteers. The fire department was established in 1878 and began with an all-volunteer force. Don Blanchard Jr. is today's chief; currently, there are 28 volunteers and 52 paid members on the force. (Courtesy of the Gerald and Olivia Chenevert family.)

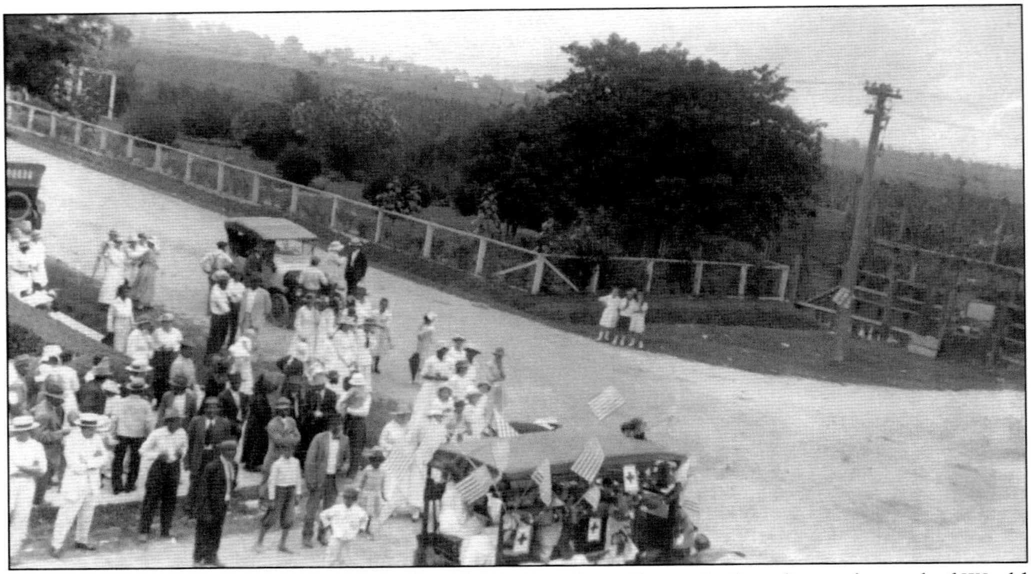

This 1919 photograph shows the parish celebration along Bayou Lafourche at the end of World War I. (Courtesy of the Adolph family.)

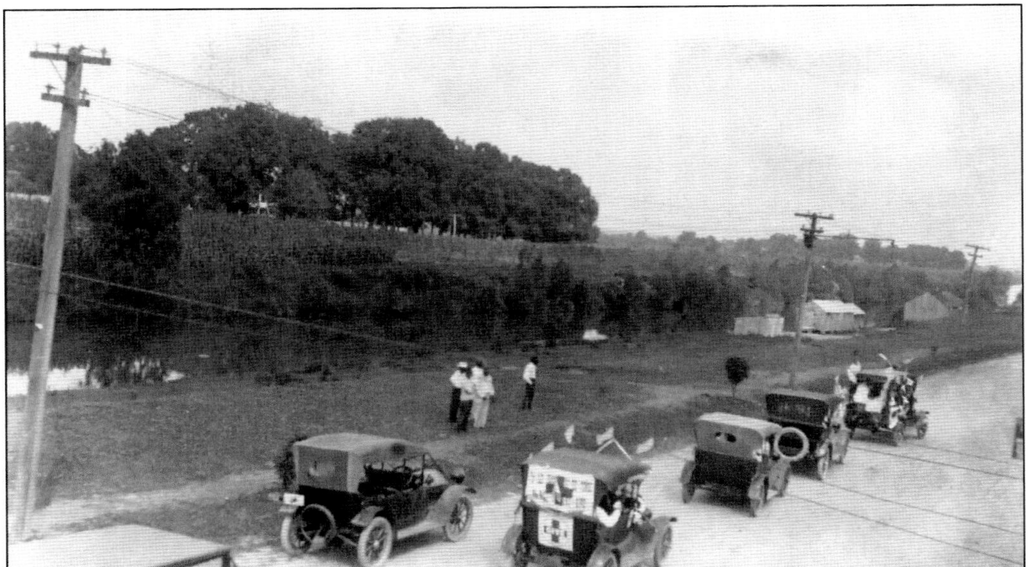

This photograph of the same World War I parade shows Bayou Lafourche at the time. (Courtesy of the Adolph family.)

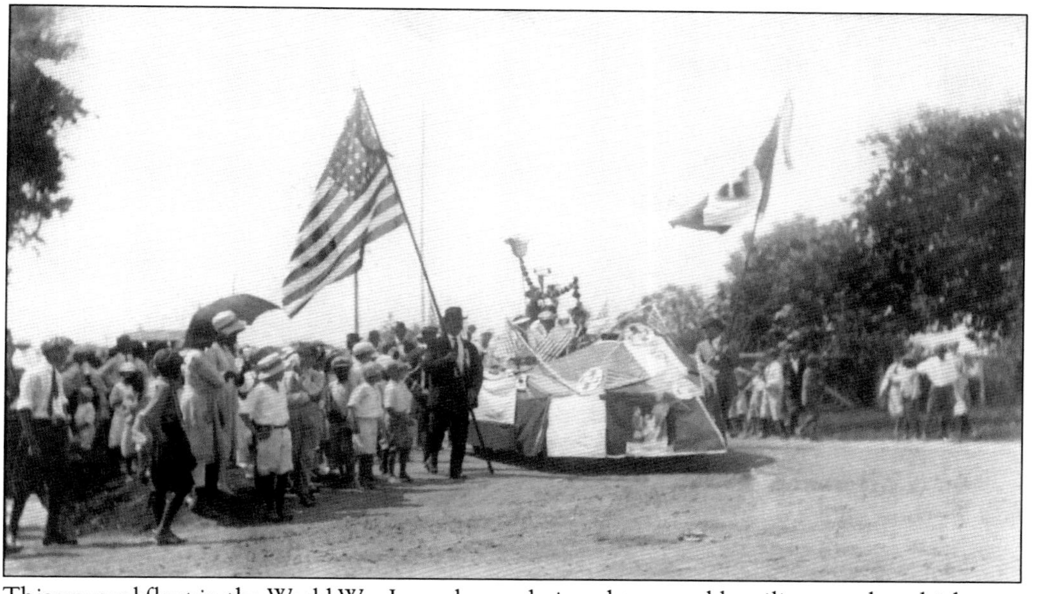

This unusual float in the World War I parade was designed to resemble military tanks, which were employed widely for the first time during that conflict. (Courtesy of the Adolph family.)

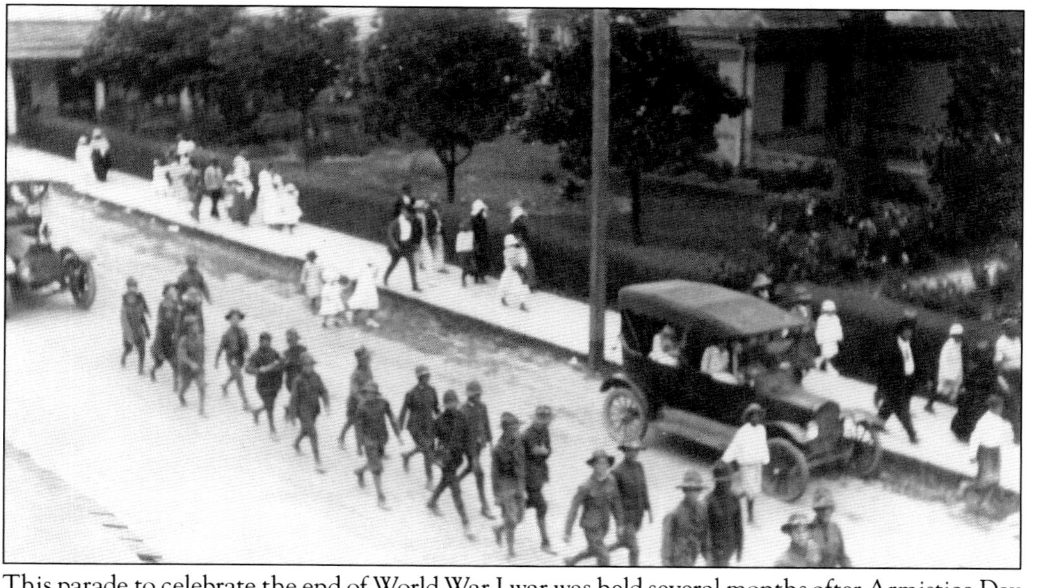

This parade to celebrate the end of World War I war was held several months after Armistice Day in 1918 and included a Red Cross canteen booth. Beginning in 1917, the Red Cross provided a canteen service, distributing food and leisure articles to troops in transit at railroad stations and embarkation and debarkation ports. (Courtesy of the Adolph family.)

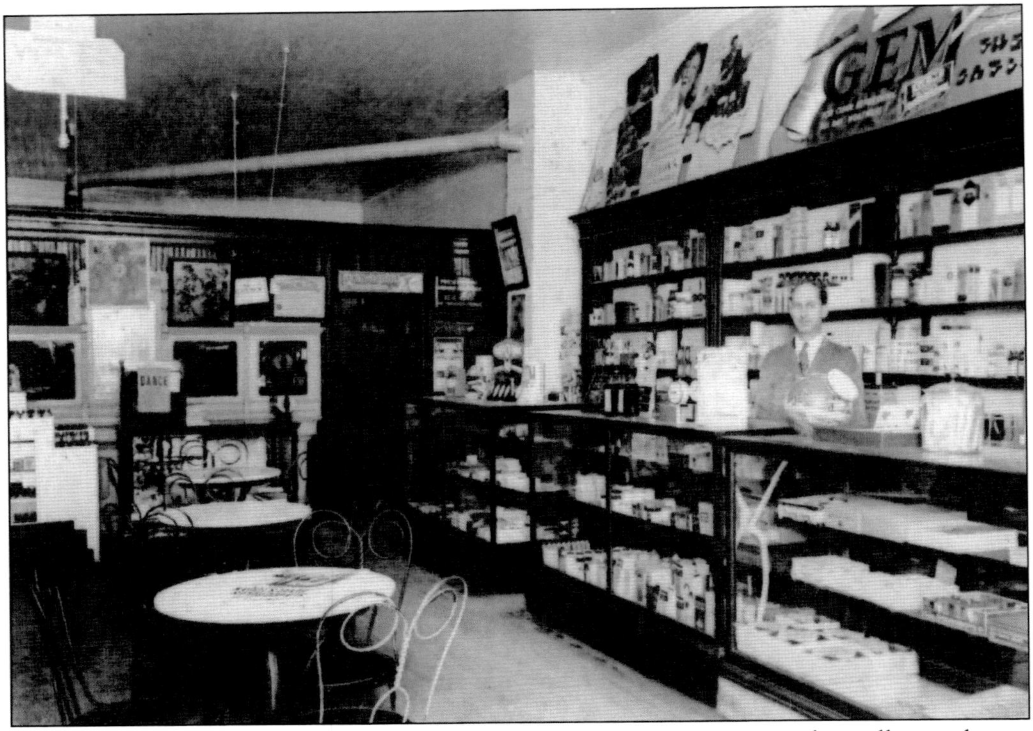

The Doc Heberts pharmacy building located on Washington Street in Napoleonville is no longer open; however, the building still stands. It was popular as a pharmacy and gathering place for locals. (Courtesy of Donald and Billie Eris Blanchard.)

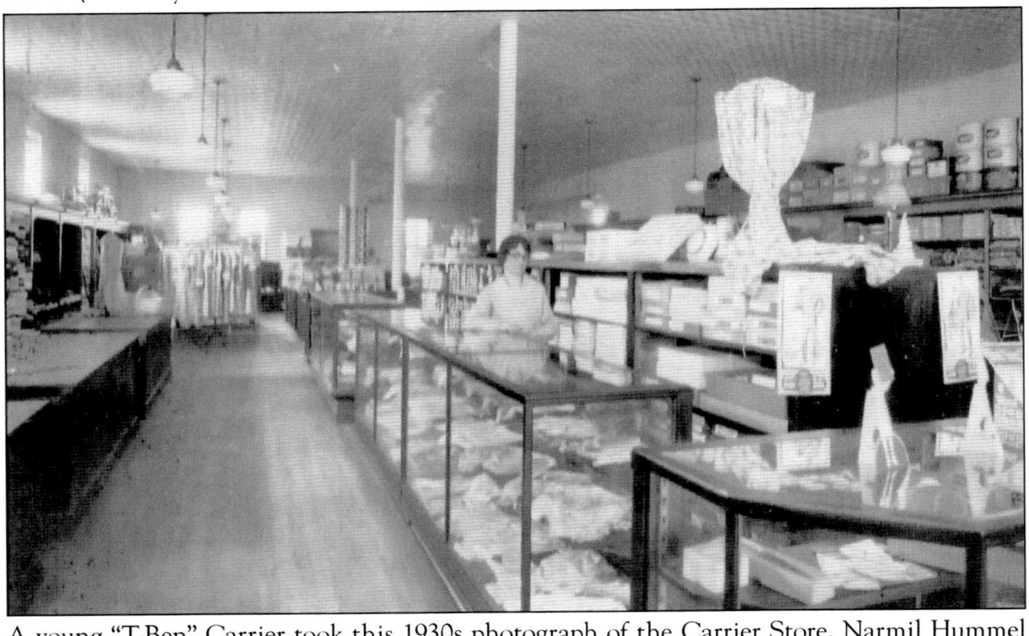

A young "T-Ben" Carrier took this 1930s photograph of the Carrier Store. Narmil Hummel Sternfels (pictured) worked at the store as a clerk for the Carrier family. (Courtesy of Nick and Loretta Carrier.)

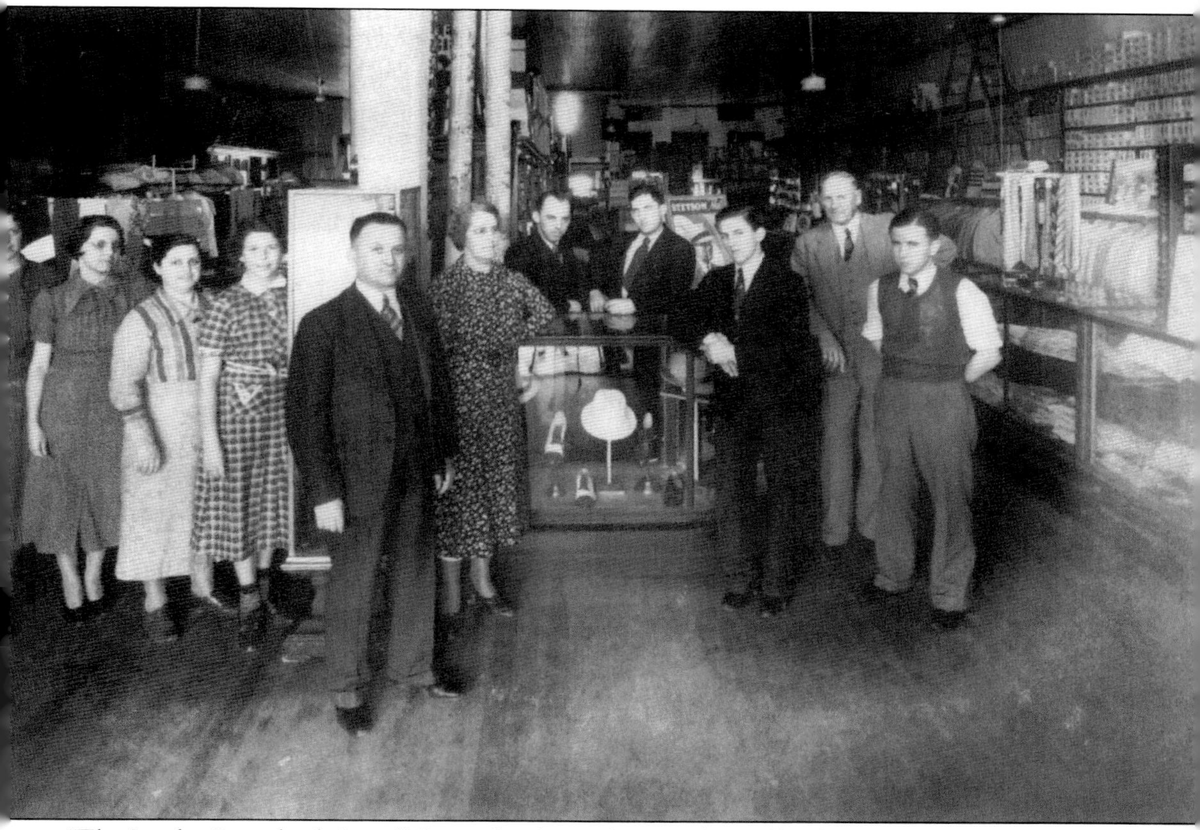

"The Leader Store leads 'em all!" was the slogan for Napoleonville's largest department store. This 1937 photograph shows the merchandise offered at the store. (Courtesy of Donald and Billie Eris Blanchard.)

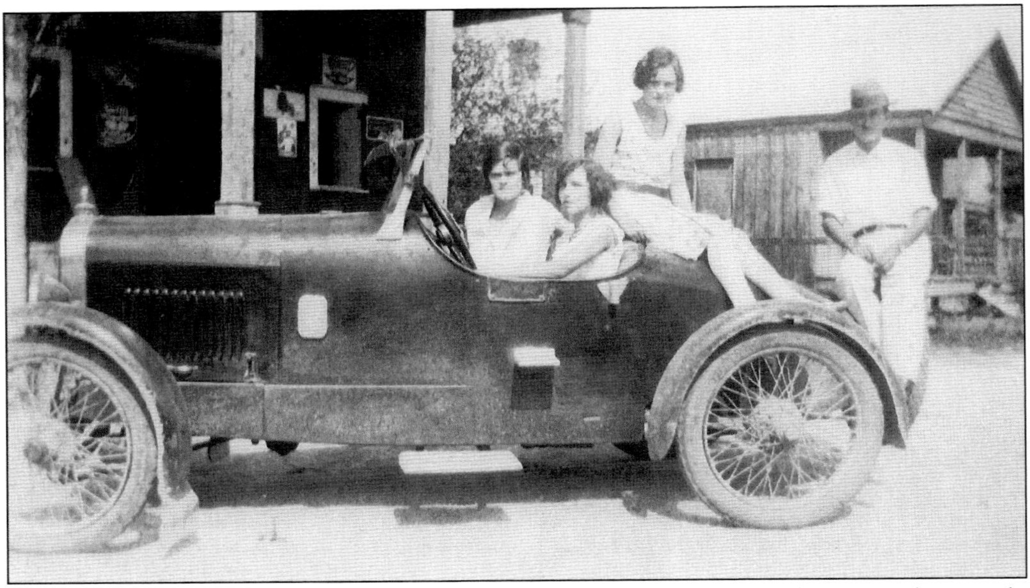

Percy Carrier shows off his Ford Racer to his future wife, Hazel Himel, in this mid-1930s photograph. They are in front of Himel's Grocery Store in Labadieville with Hazel's sisters Inez (behind the wheel) and Eva (on the passenger side). (Courtesy of Donald and Billie Eris Blanchard.)

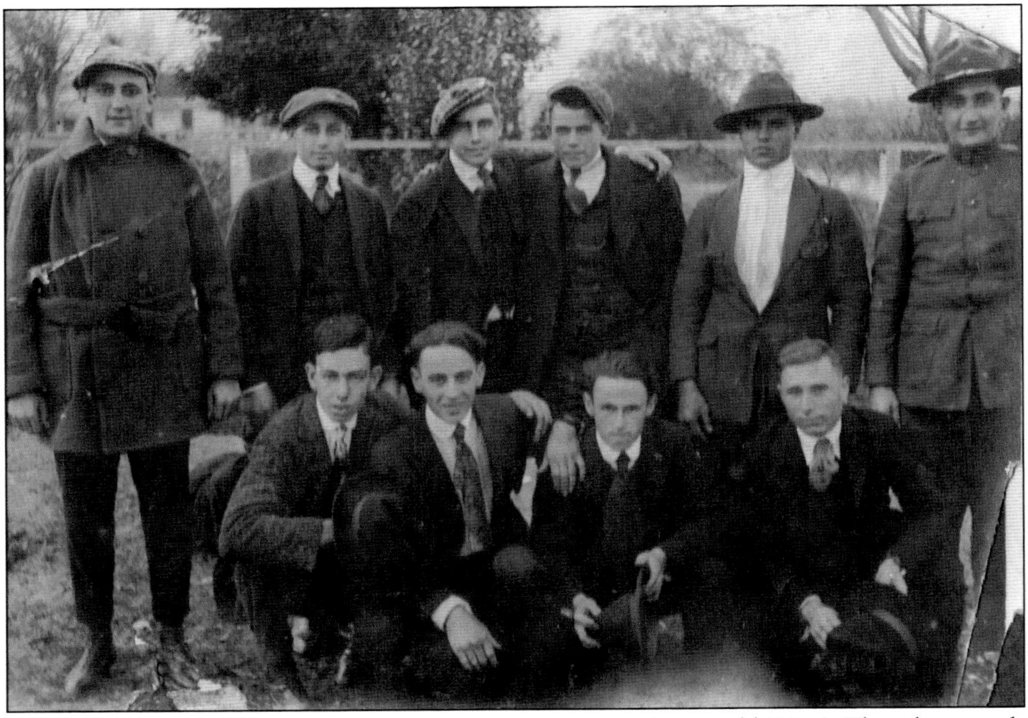

Friends gather to welcome the safe return of a native son after World War I. This photograph was most likely taken on the same day as the previous parade photographs. (Courtesy of Donald and Billie Eris Blanchard.)

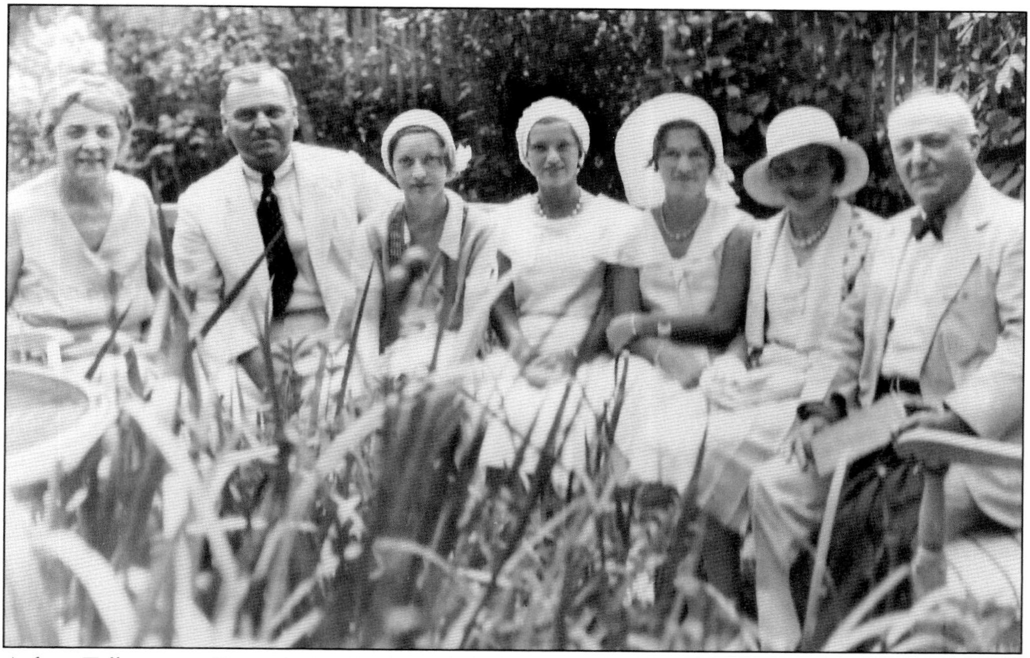

Aubert Talbot visits Dr. and Mrs. Stephens in Lafayette at the University of Southwestern Louisiana with his daughters. In this 1931 photograph are, from left to right, Mrs. Stephens, Aubert Talbot, Lucille Talbot, Jo Talbot, Jane Talbot, Betty Talbot, and Dr. Stephens. (Courtesy of Edith Dupre Library, University of University of Louisiana at Lafayette.)

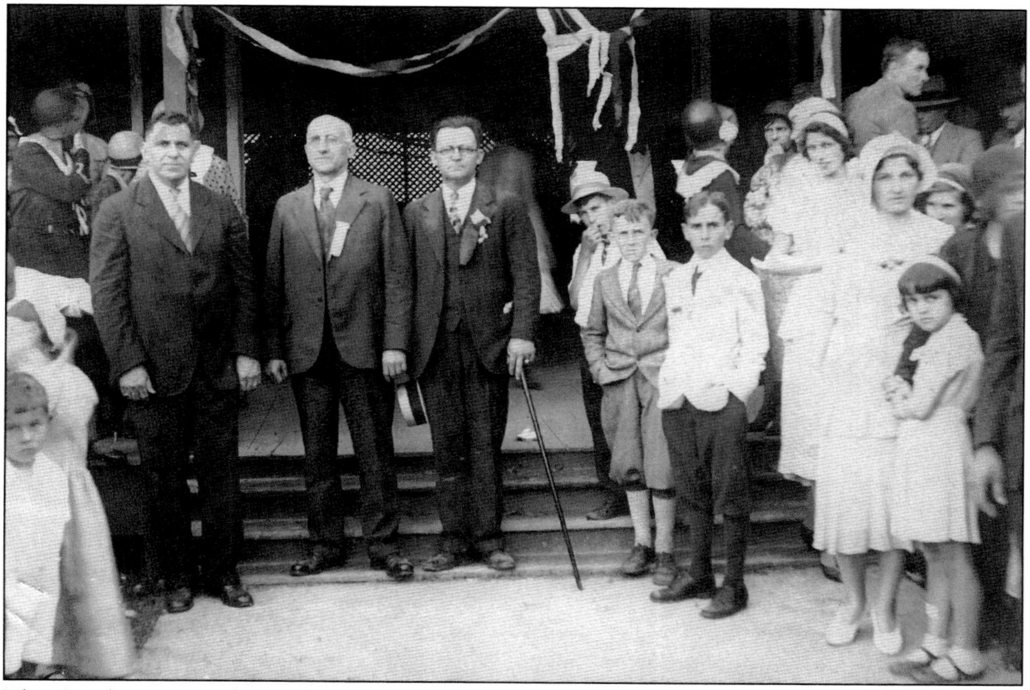

The Acadians visited Napoleonville in the early 1930s. Judge Sam LeBlanc hosted the event. (Courtesy of Cecile M. LeBlanc.)

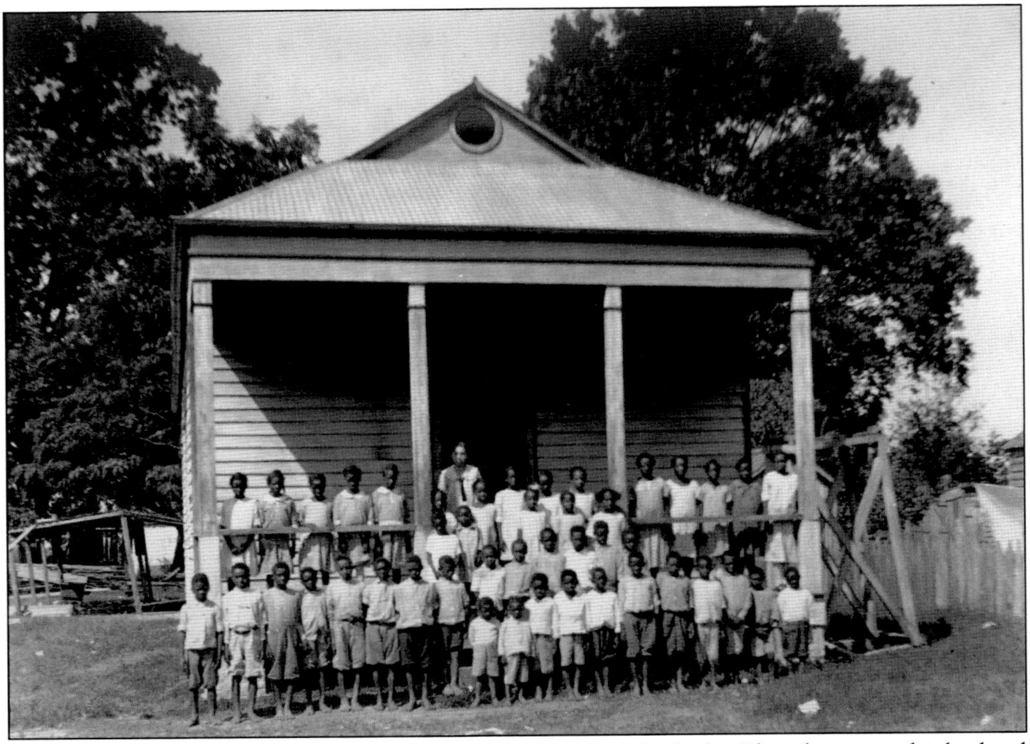

Following the establishment of the St. Benedict the Moor Catholic Church, a parochial school was incorporated into the church parish. This photograph was taken of the students in front of their school in 1922. (Courtesy of St. Benedict the Moor Catholic Church.)

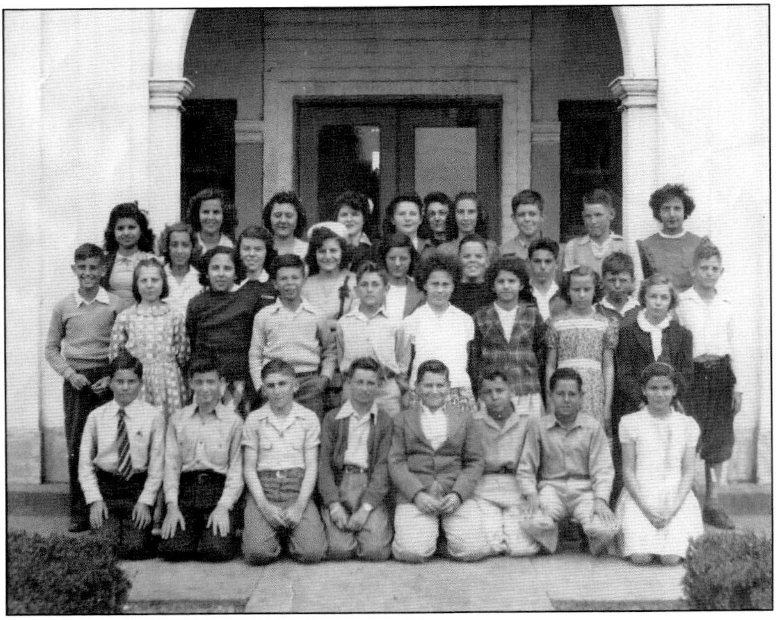

This is a sixth-grade class from Napoleonville Elementary School taken in the mid-1940s. The teacher at the time was Thelma Talbot LeBlanc. (Courtesy of Cecile M. LeBlanc.)

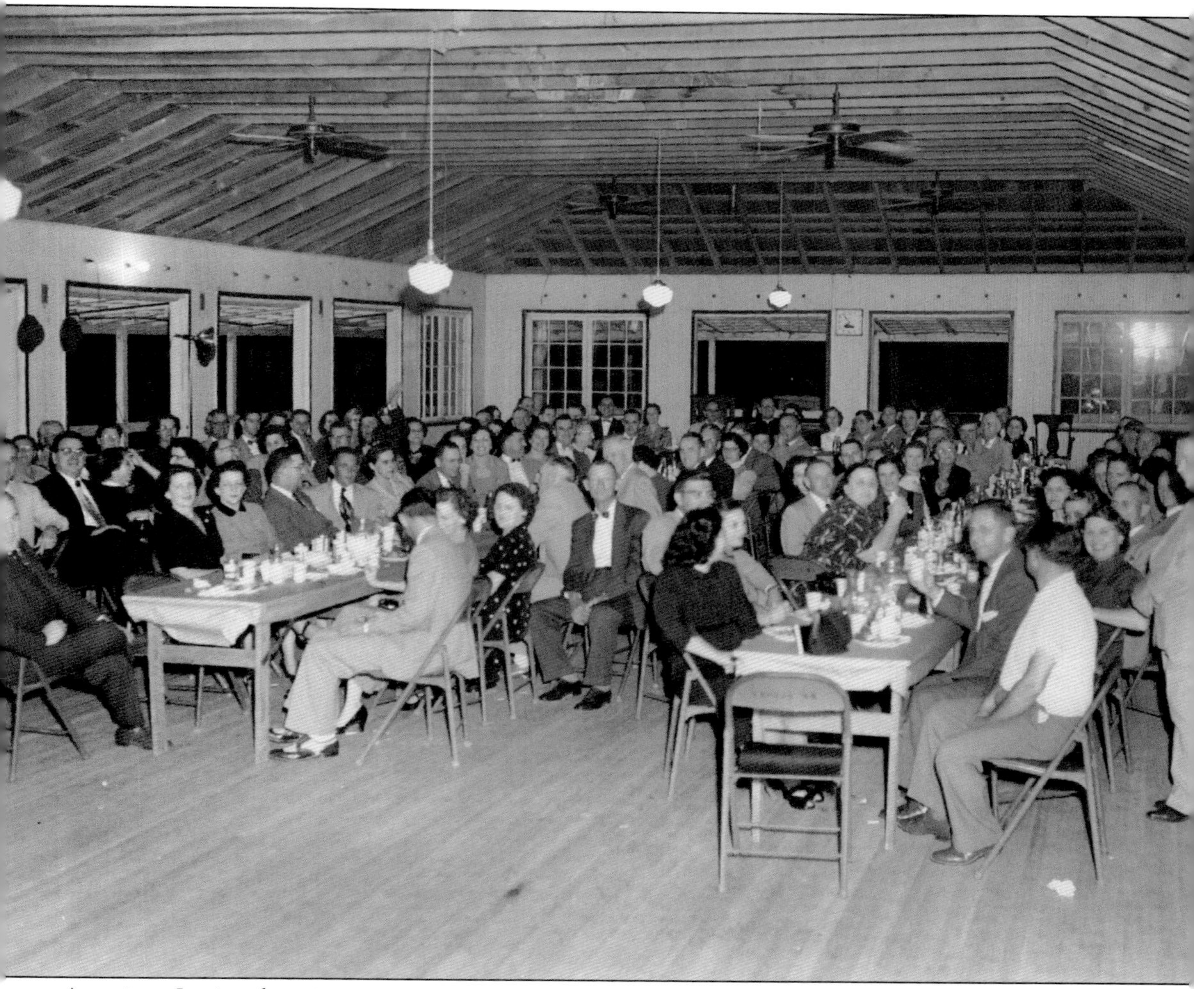

American Legion functions were common community events held in the mid-1950s. Social and civic organizations like these strengthened and united the fiber of the community. (Courtesy of the Gerald and Olivia Chenevert family.)

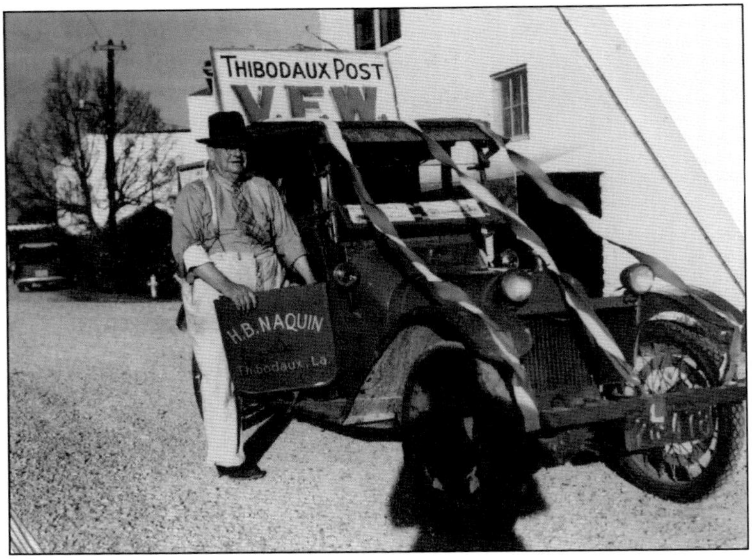

Henry B. Naquin's Wood's Mobilette came from France by way of Chicago in 1909 and was a parade staple from that time through at least 1963. (Courtesy of William Littlejohn Martin Collection, Archives and Special Collections, Nicholls State University, Thibodaux, Louisiana.)

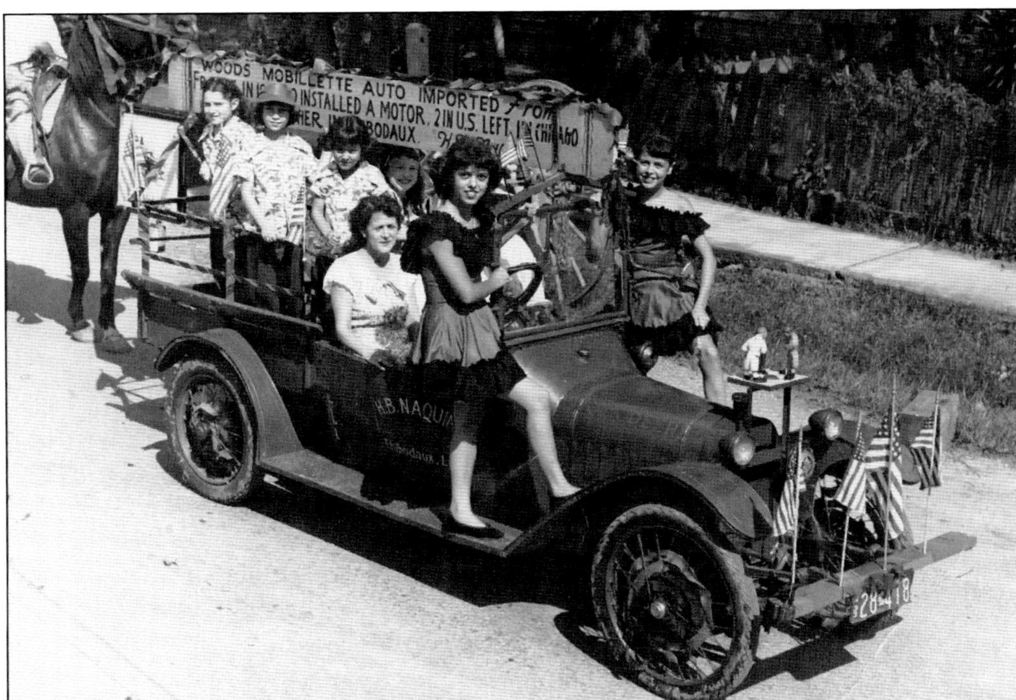

Charles Bergeron drives Naquin's Wood's Mobilette in an Assumption parade in the early 1950s. Bergeron would often drive Naquin's special vehicle in parades. (Courtesy of Yvette B. Winston.)

The men in this picture are part of a 1955 group of firefighters attempting to subdue the Glenwood fire. The fire burned the plantation home owned by the Munson family. (Courtesy of the Gerald and Olivia Chenevert family.)

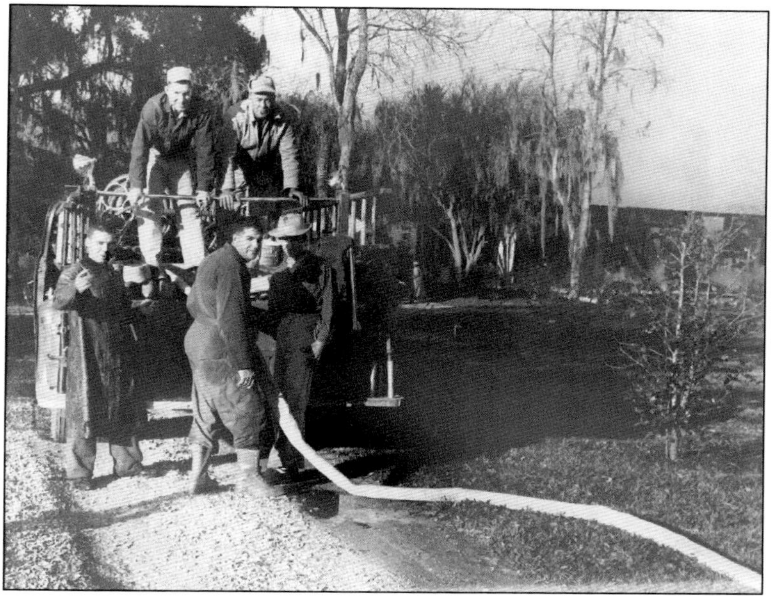

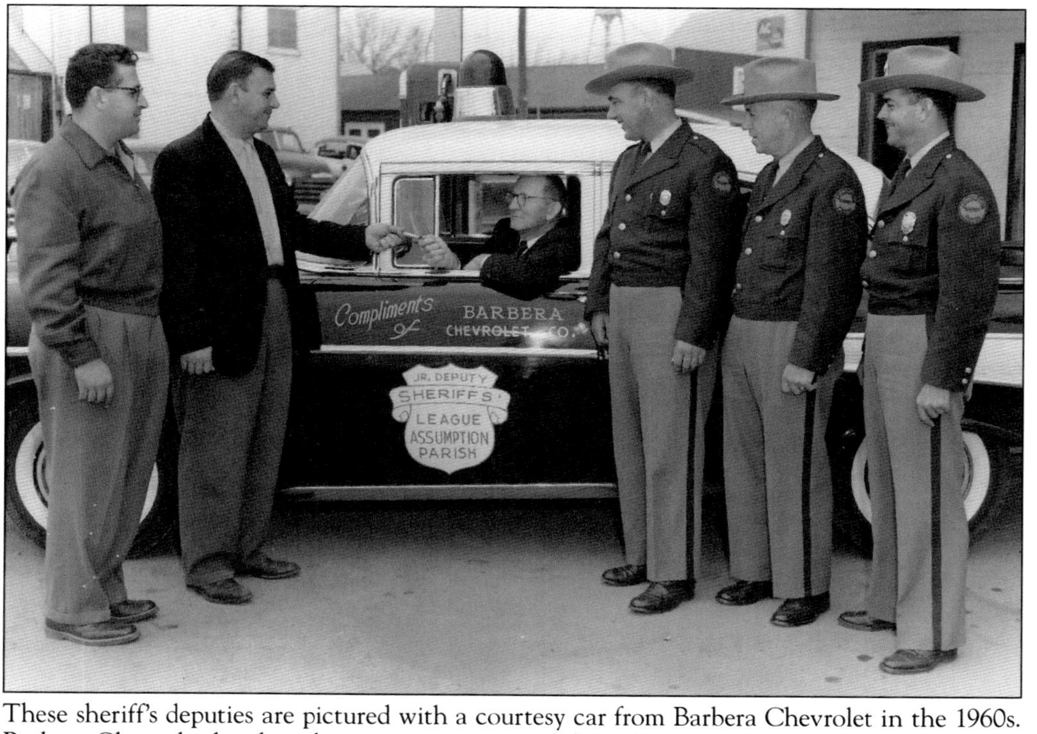

These sheriff's deputies are pictured with a courtesy car from Barbera Chevrolet in the 1960s. Barbera Chevrolet has long been a community staple and is operated by Bobby Barbera, son of Jerome Barbera. Pictured here from left to right are Jerome Barbera, Sam Barbera, Sheriff Dominique, "Boo" Caballero, Gaston Gros, and Murray Landry. (Courtesy of the Gerald and Olivia Chenevert family.)

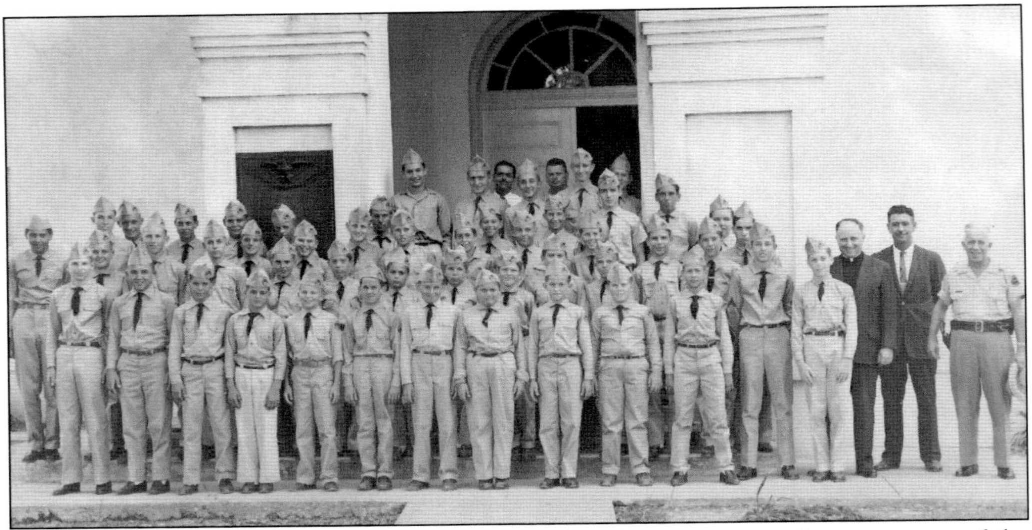

The Junior Sheriffs league of the 1960s was a popular civic organization for young men of the parish. Joining the league meant that the young men were committed to uphold the law and support civic causes. (Courtesy of the Gerald and Olivia Chenevert family.)

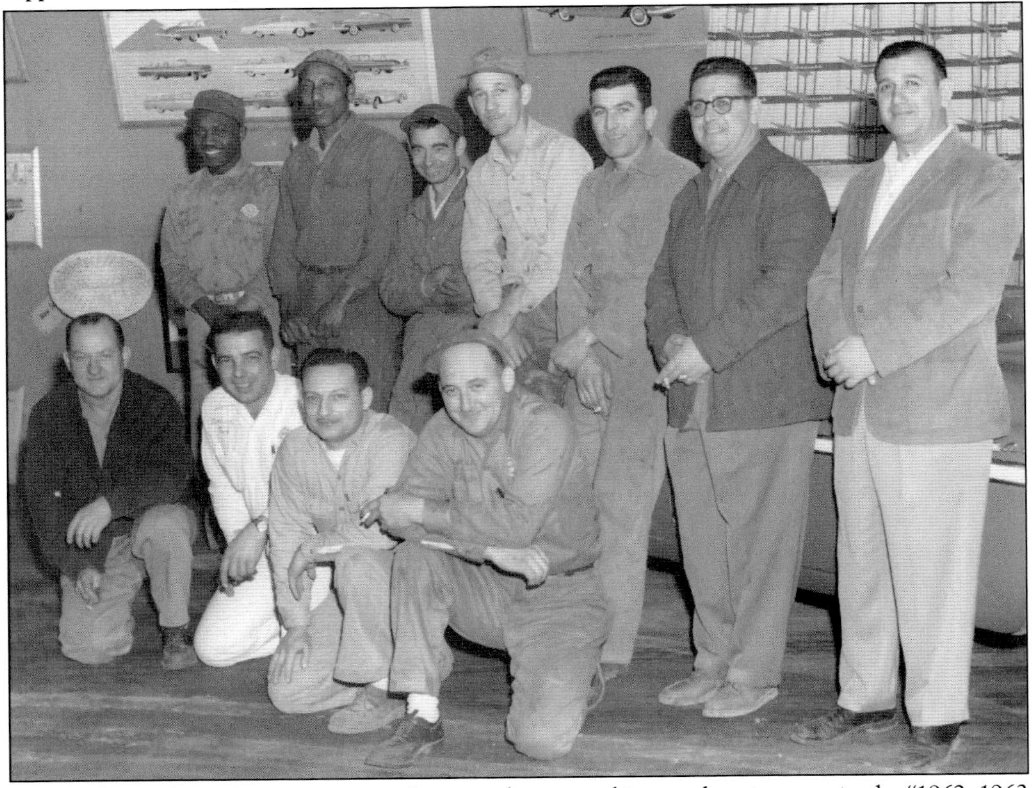

This Barbera Chevrolet service crew photograph was used in an advertisement in the "1962–1963 Assumption Parish Civic and Social Calendar" sponsored by the Napoleonville Mothers' Club. The advertisement states, "Your Chevrolet Dealer since 1926." (Courtesy of the Gerald and Olivia Chenevert family.)

Sam A. LeBlanc served as associate justice of the Louisiana State Supreme Court from 1949 to 1954, becoming a Knight of St. Gregory in 1958. He served as judge of the 23rd Judicial District Court from 1921 to 1928. LeBlanc was chair of the Chief Justice Edward Douglass White Memorial Association and the first president of the Bayouside Golf course. He was married to Elmire M. Lafaye. (Courtesy of Cecile M. LeBlanc.)

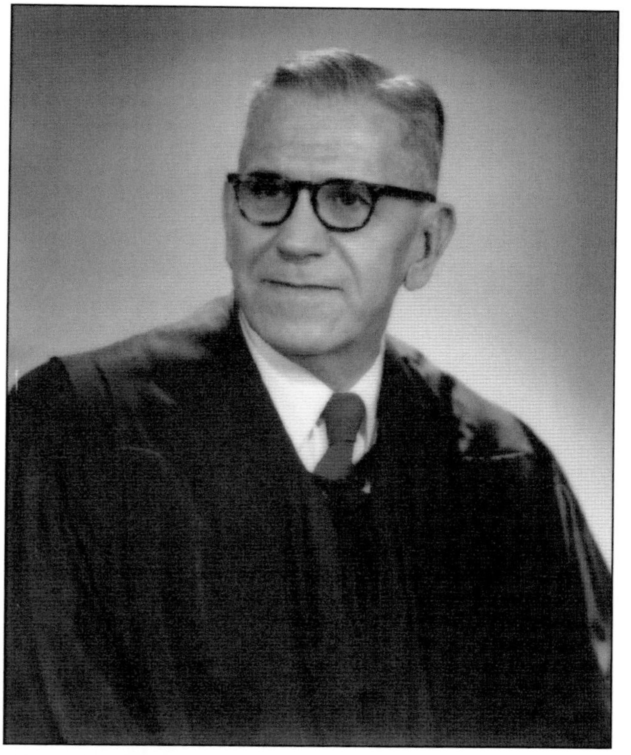

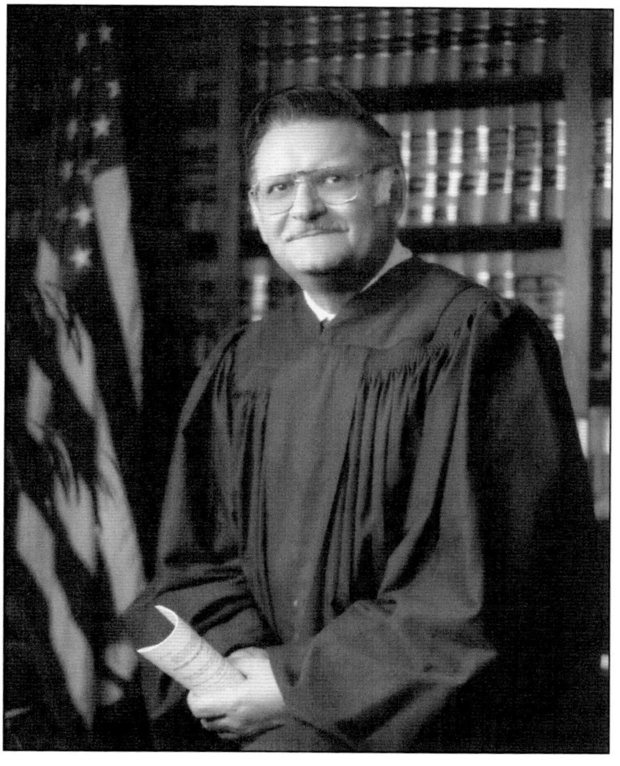

Pres. Jimmy Carter appointed Napoleonville native Henry A. Politz to the Fifth Circuit Court of Appeals in 1979. Judge Politz became the first Louisiana native to become chief judge of the Fifth Circuit in 1992, serving until 1999. A proud veteran of the Korean War from 1951 to 1955, he was in the US Air Force prior to his legal career. (Courtesy of the United States Fifth Federal Circuit and Judge Politz's family.)

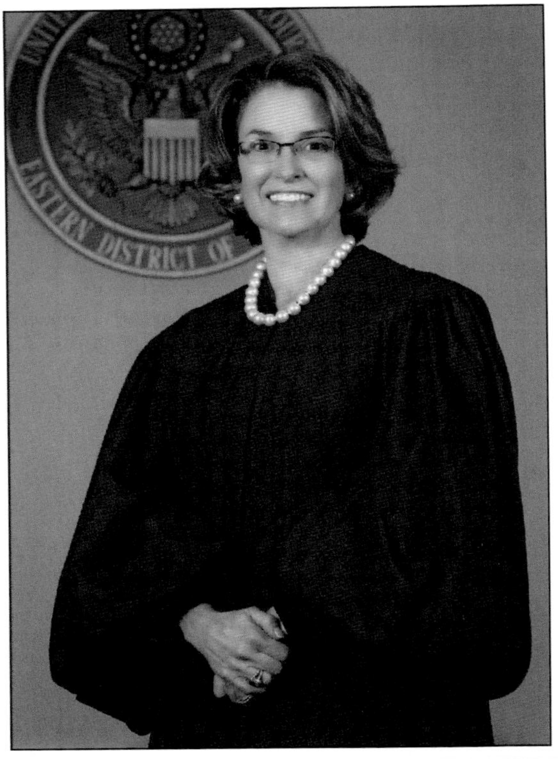

Jane Triche-Milazzo, judge of the 23rd Judicial District Court Division D, was appointed to the federal bench of Louisiana's Eastern District by Pres. Barack Obama in 2011. The 1992 graduate of Louisiana State University's (LSU) Paul M. Hebert Law Center serves on the board of trustees. She practiced law with her father, Risley "Pappy" Triche, and brother Martin Triche prior to her judicial service. (Courtesy of Judge Jane Triche-Milazzo.)

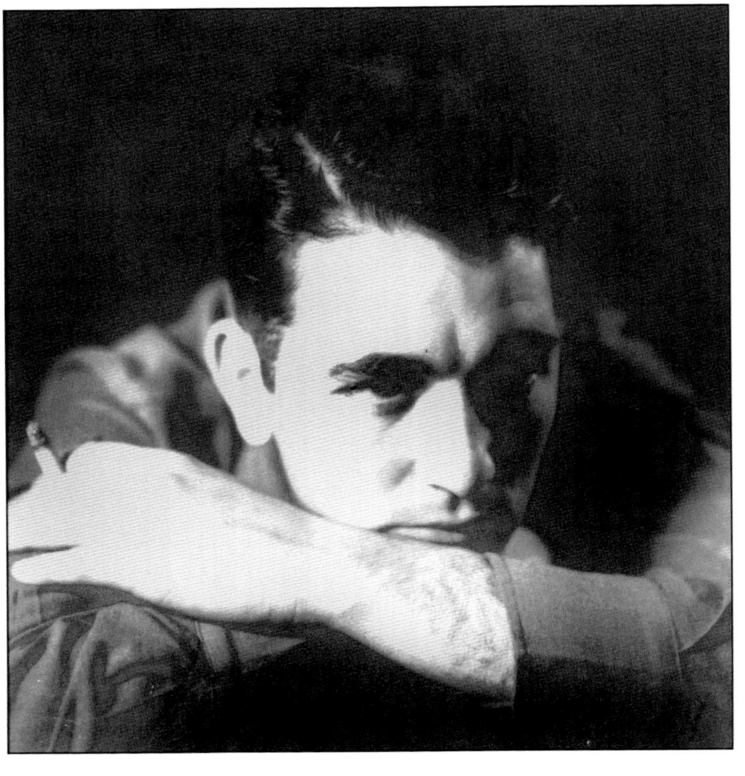

Risley "Pappy" Triche, a 2010 Louisiana Political Hall of Fame inductee, served Napoleonville as mayor from 1954 to 1955. Elected to the Louisiana House of Representatives in 1956, Triche served four terms under Gov. Jimmie Davis and Gov. Edwin Edwards. He championed two job-discrimination bills protecting racial minorities in 1972. These efforts launched a turn in Louisiana's racial political sentiment. Triche served as defense team leader in many high-profile cases. (Courtesy of Martin "Marty" Triche.)

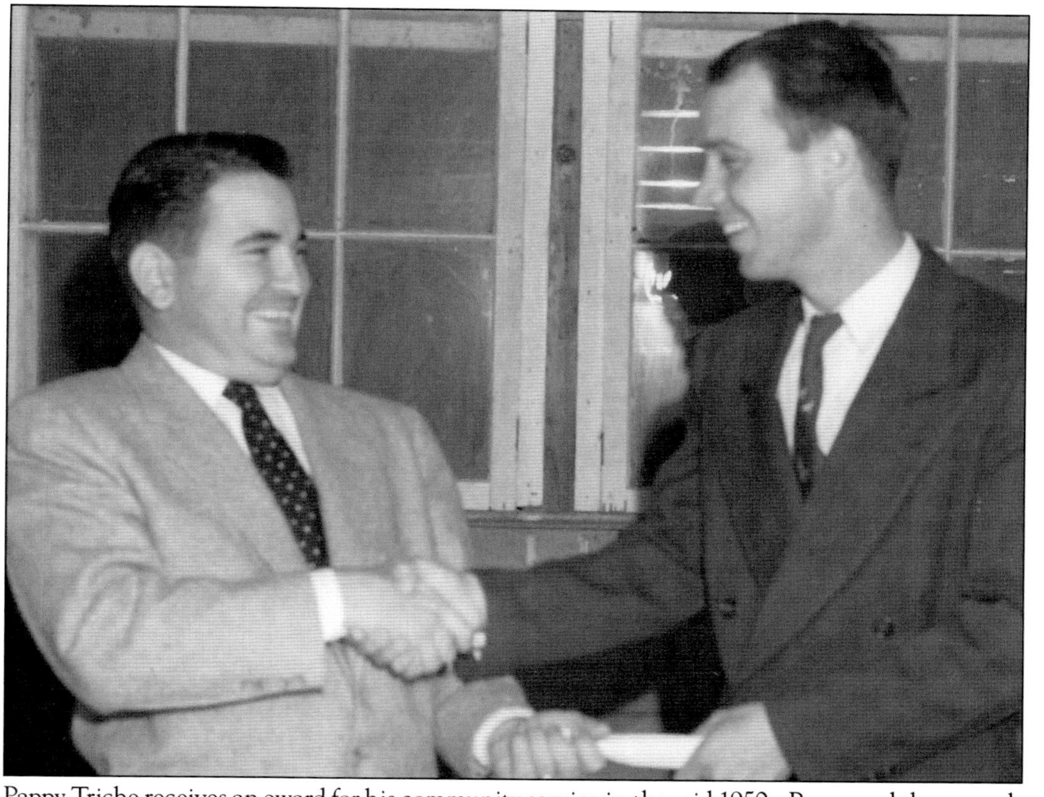

Pappy Triche receives an award for his community service in the mid-1950s. Pappy and the seventh child of Pappy and Clara Caballero Triche, Marty, who currently serves as parish president, are pictured here. (Courtesy of the Gerald and Olivia Chenevert family.)

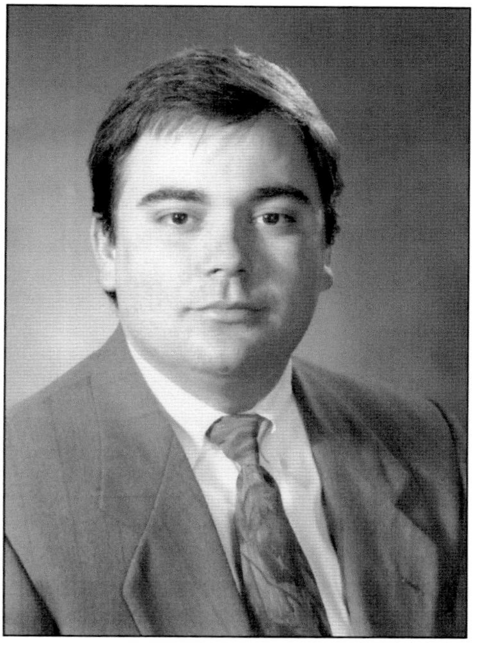

As president of the Assumption Parish Police Jury, Martin "Marty" Triche has assumed responsibility for actions and decisions made by the Assumption Parish Police Jury since 1991. Under his tenure, the Assumption Parish Office of Emergency Preparedness was established and the Local Emergency Planning Committee (LEPC) reactivated. Triche subsequently received the Dedication Award from the Louisiana Emergency Preparedness Association (LEPA). Helping clear the way to secure Community Development Block Grant funds for a new governmental building, Triche looks forward to the parish having adequate telecommunications and electrical systems in a facility allowing government to remain running following storms. He and his wife, Anissa Blanchard, have three sons. (Courtesy of Martin "Marty" Triche.)

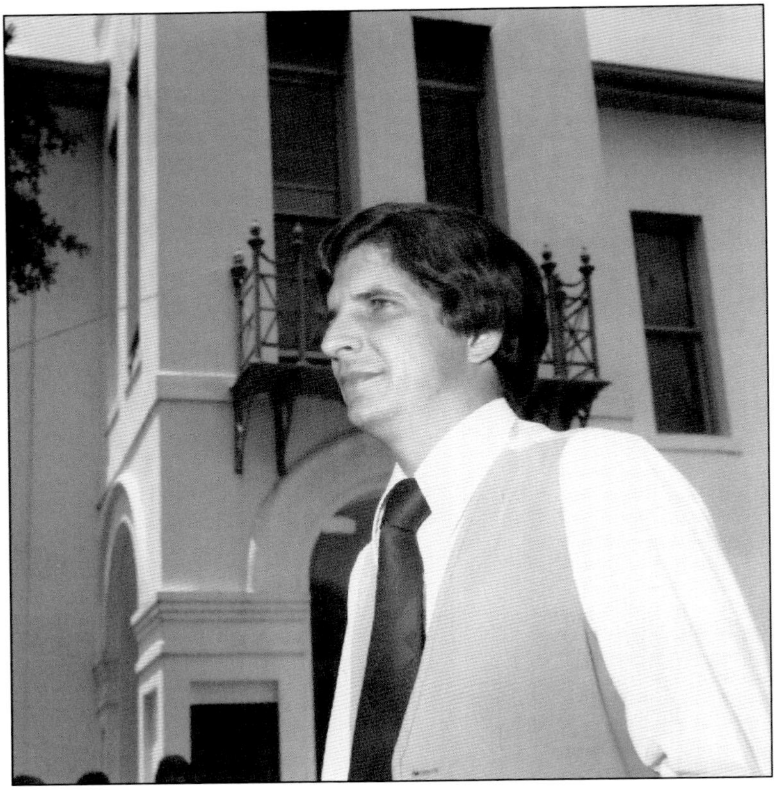

Anthony Falterman served multiple terms as both Sheriff of Assumption Parish and district attorney of the 23rd Judicial District. Falterman currently serves on the Louisiana State University Board of Supervisors. (Courtesy of the Gerald and Olivia Chenevert family.)

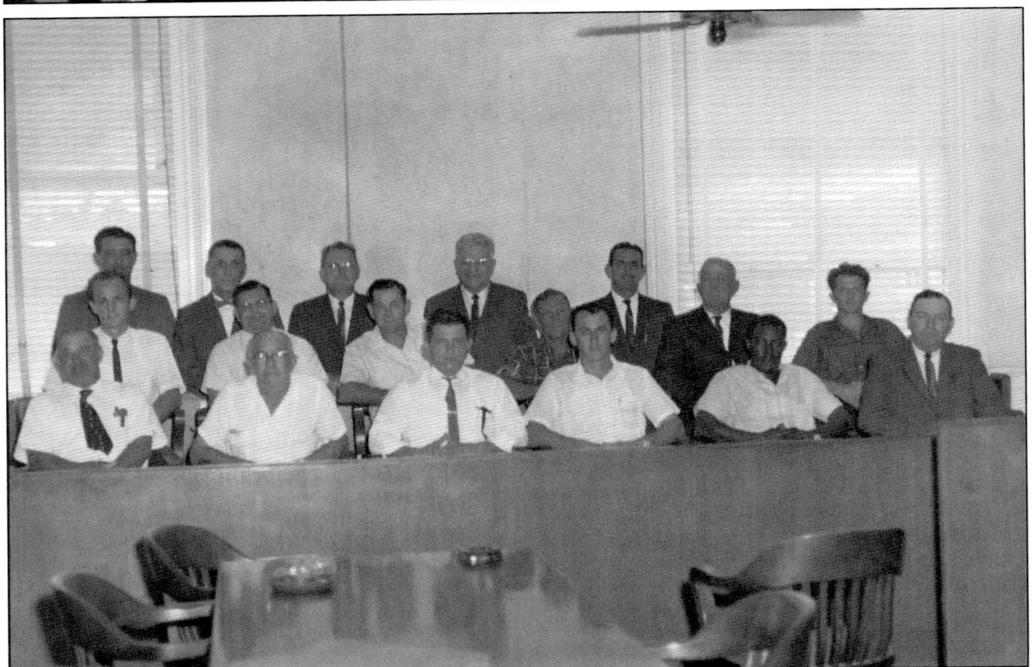

Parish officials are sequestered in the jury box of the Assumption Courthouse for this late-1960s photograph. (Courtesy of the Gerald and Olivia Chenevert family.)

The Assumption Parish Police of the late 1960s and early 1970s are pictured here. Many of the jurors served on multiple municipal and state civic associations throughout their lifetimes, as well as in political service. (Courtesy of the Gerald and Olivia Chenevert family.)

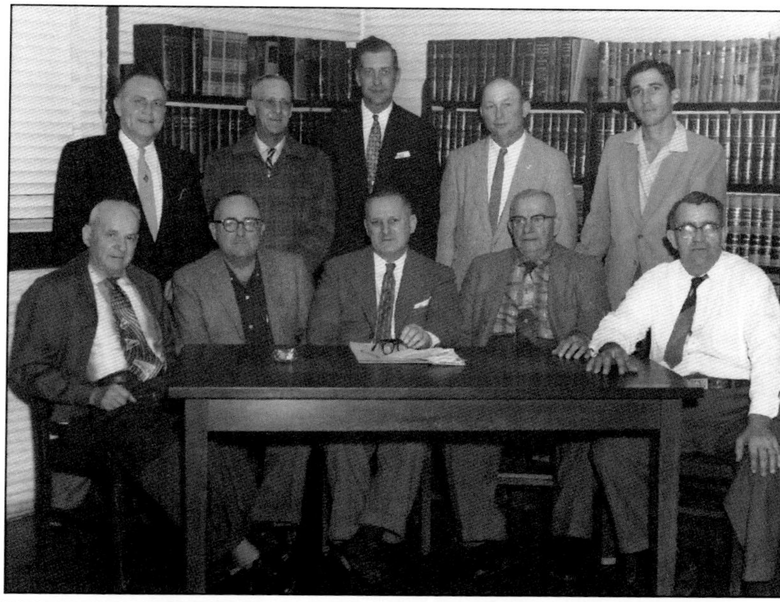

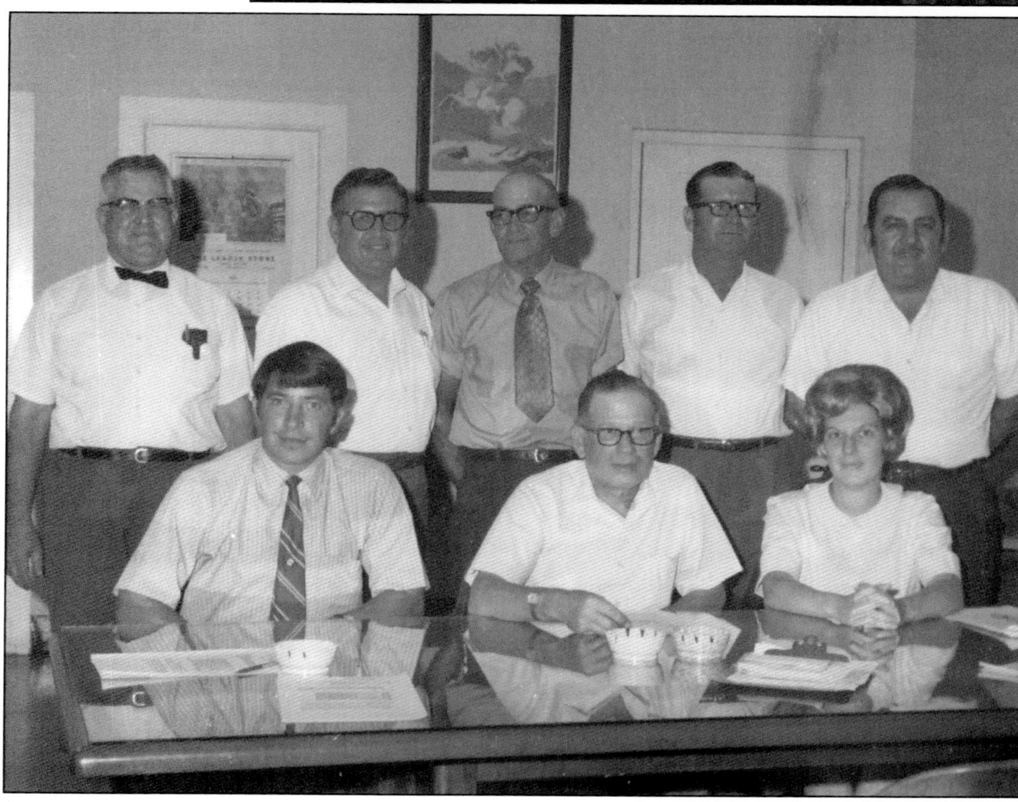

This group of Napoleonville Town Council members served in the late 1960s. The framed art on the wall is a print of Jacques Louis David's *Napoleon Crossing the Alps*. The town's namesake is believed to be derived from a soldier who fought under Napoleon, not the general himself. (Courtesy of the Gerald and Olivia Chenevert family.)

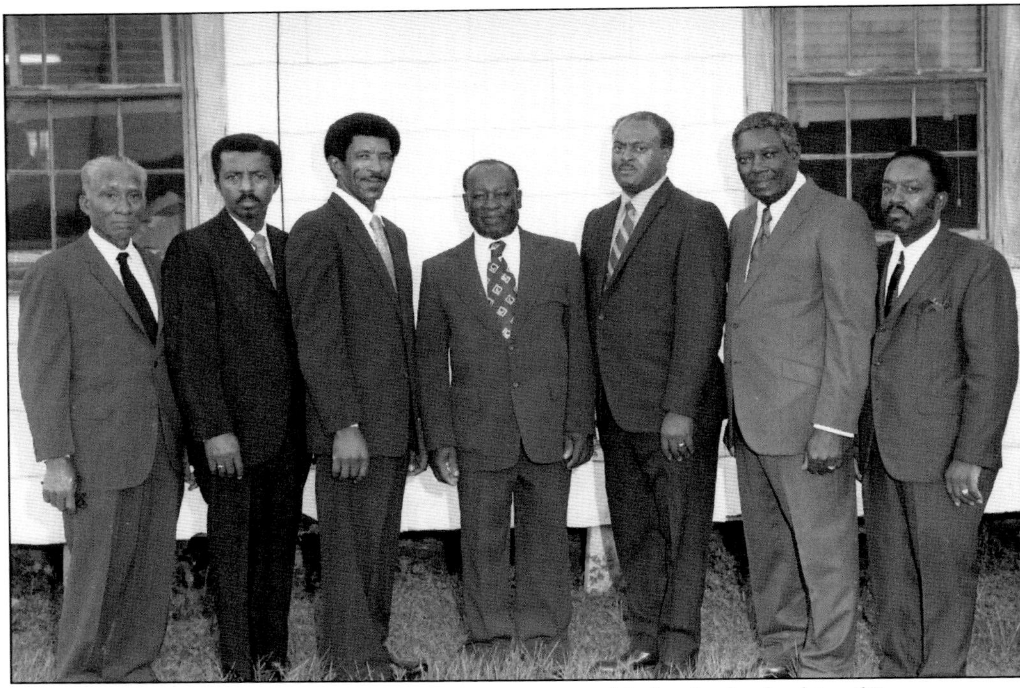

Under the leadership of Prosper Johnson, the New Belmont Building Committee administered the construction of the current building pictured. Seen here in front among the group are Edward Duplantis, Roland Harris, Spurgeon Holly Jr., Walter Jones, Lawrence Robinson, and Alvin Sylvester (third from the right). (Courtesy of Mildred Sylvester.)

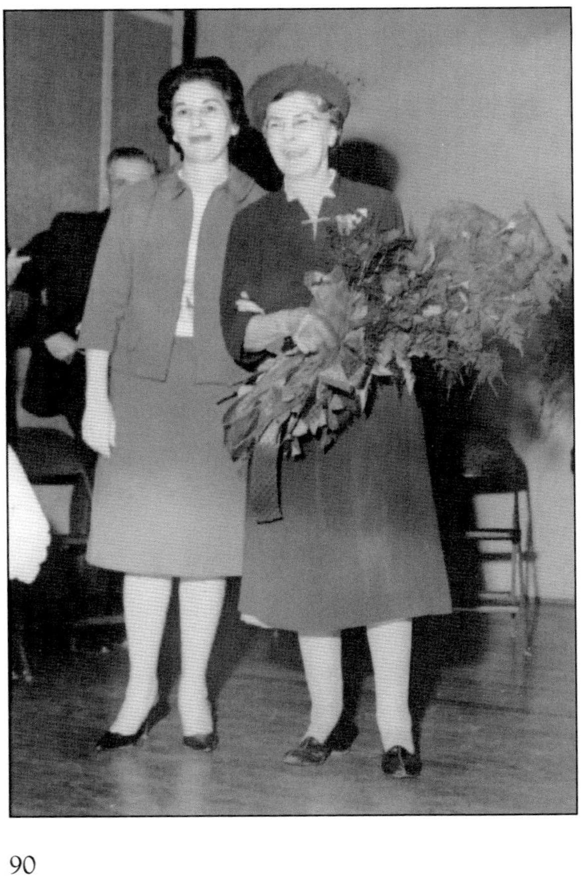

Rose Simmons (left) celebrates at the St. Anne Church hall with Enola Corde, who received the highest award the Vatican bestows on laity, Pro-Ecclesia et Pontifice, in 1963. (Courtesy of the Gerald and Olivia Chenevert family.)

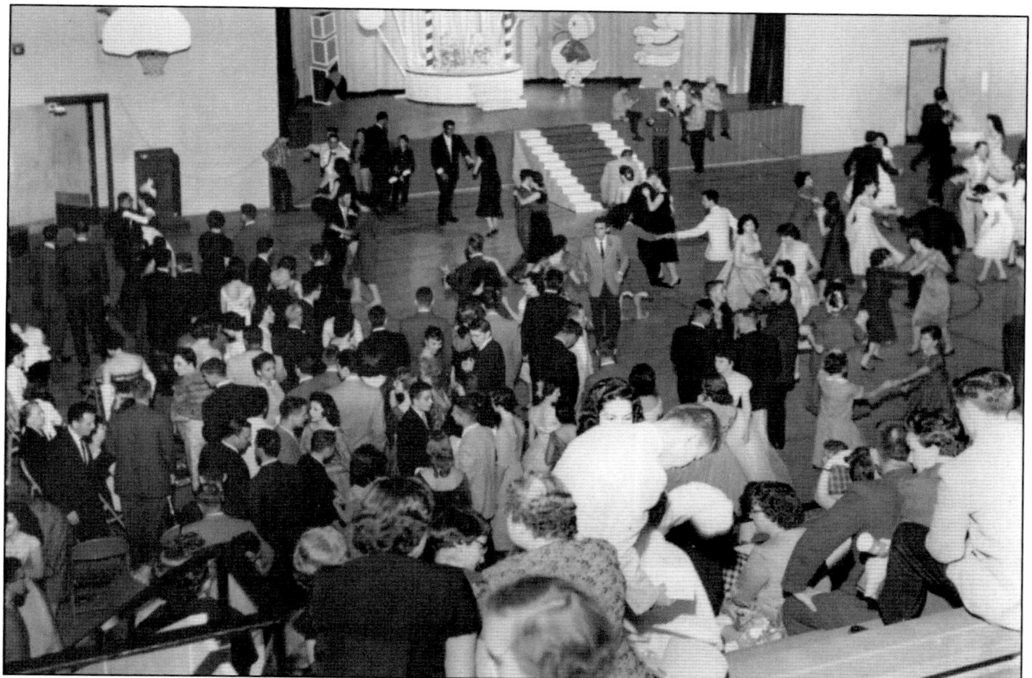

This late-1950s Assumption High dance was held at the present Assumption High School gym. (Courtesy of the Gerald and Olivia Chenevert family.)

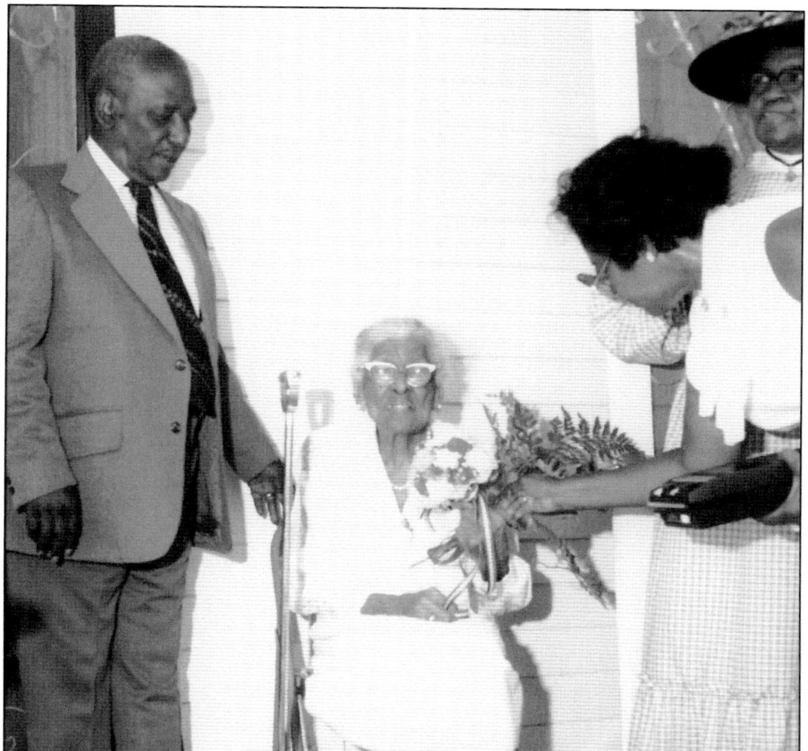

In 1973, the Council on Aging purchased a house from the widow of former police jury member Philip Kern to be its headquarters. The facility moved to its current location on Highway 1008 in Napoleonville in 2010. (Courtesy of the Gerald and Olivia Chenevert family.)

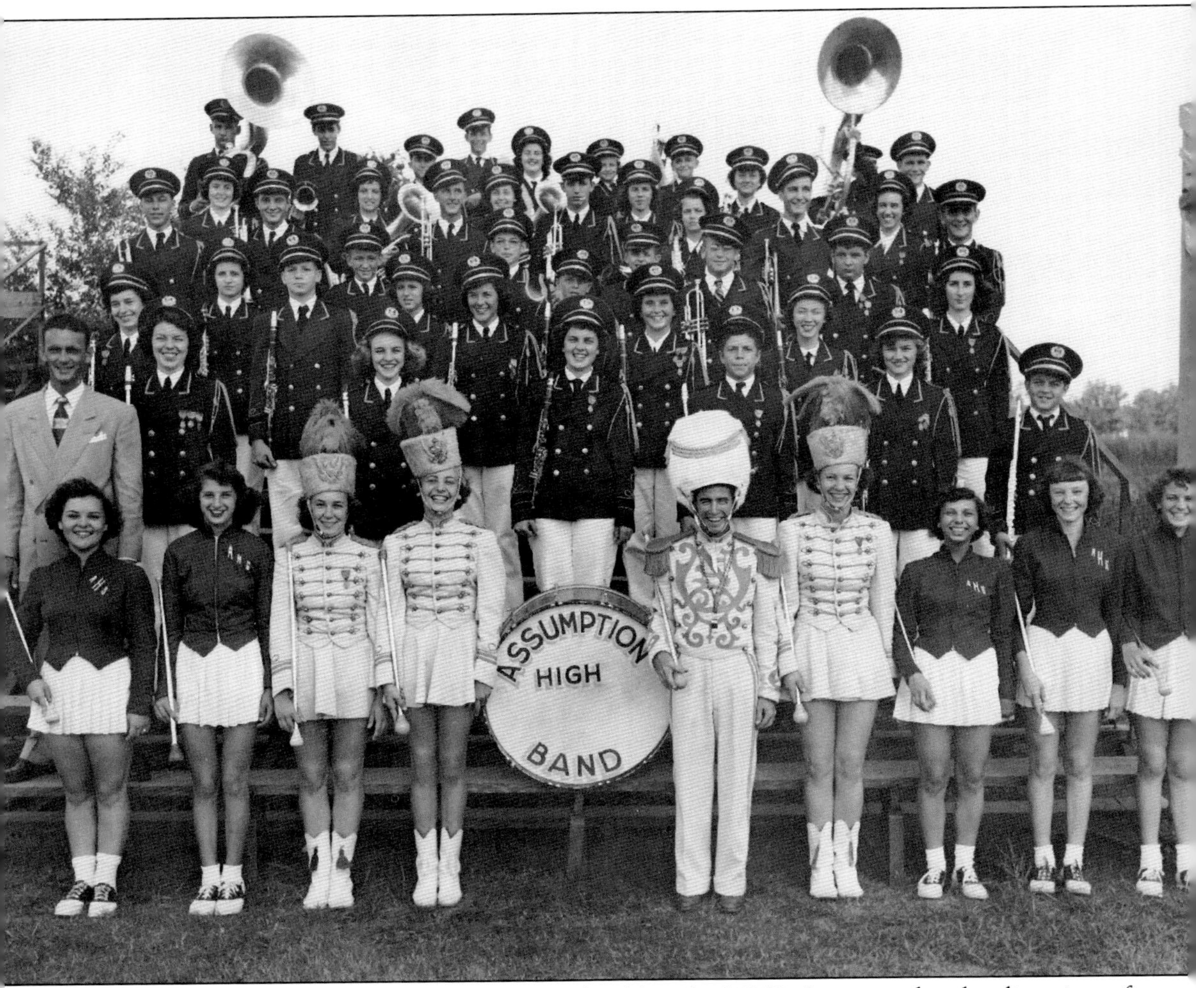

Pictured here is the Assumption High School band of 1952. It was under the direction of Gaston Waguespack, who was also a popular local musician. (Courtesy of the Gerald and Olivia Chenevert family.)

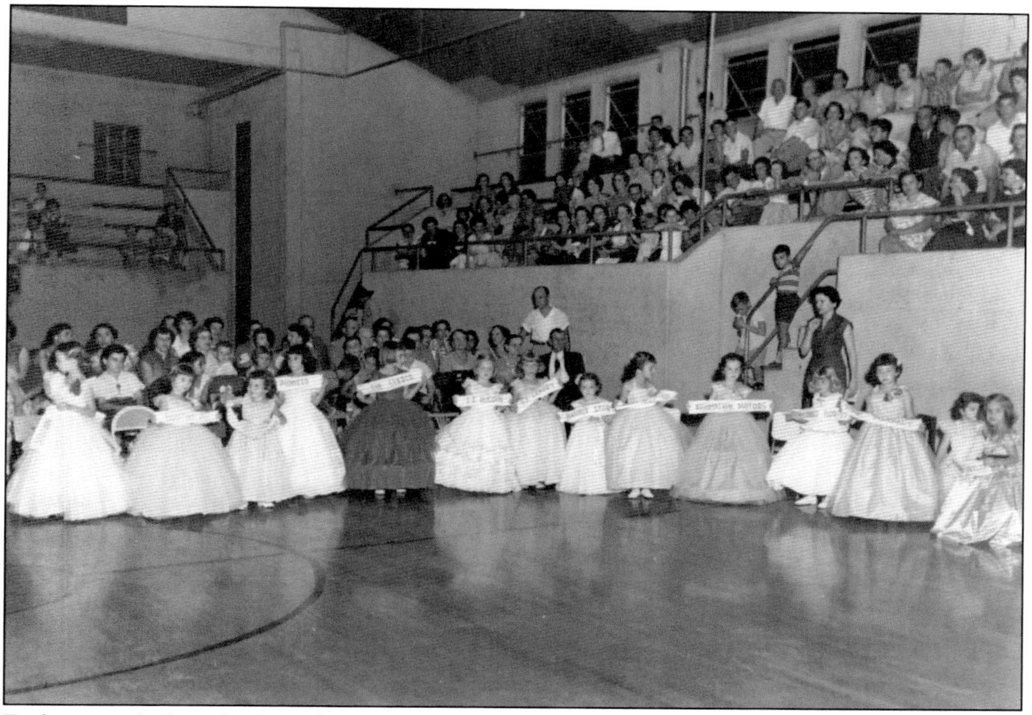

Each spring before the formal Miss Assumption Pageant, the pageant would have a little Miss Assumption procession. In these two photographs, future beauties hone their skills in preparation for the day when they can participate in the big pageant. (Courtesy of the Gerald and Olivia Chenevert family.)

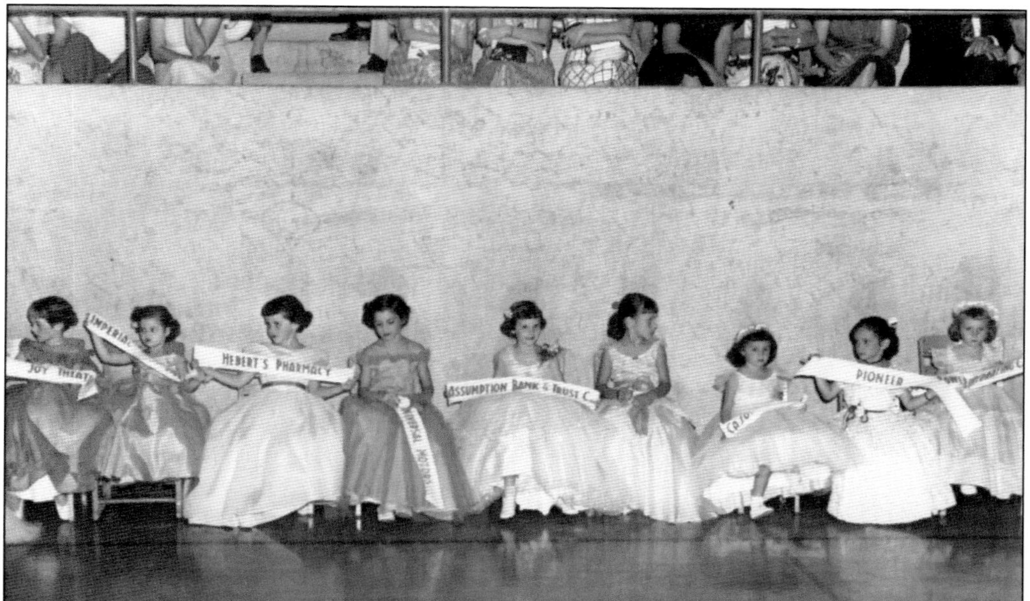

Little Miss Assumption contestants proudly display their sponsorship banners in this early-1950s photograph. (Courtesy of the Gerald and Olivia Chenevert family.)

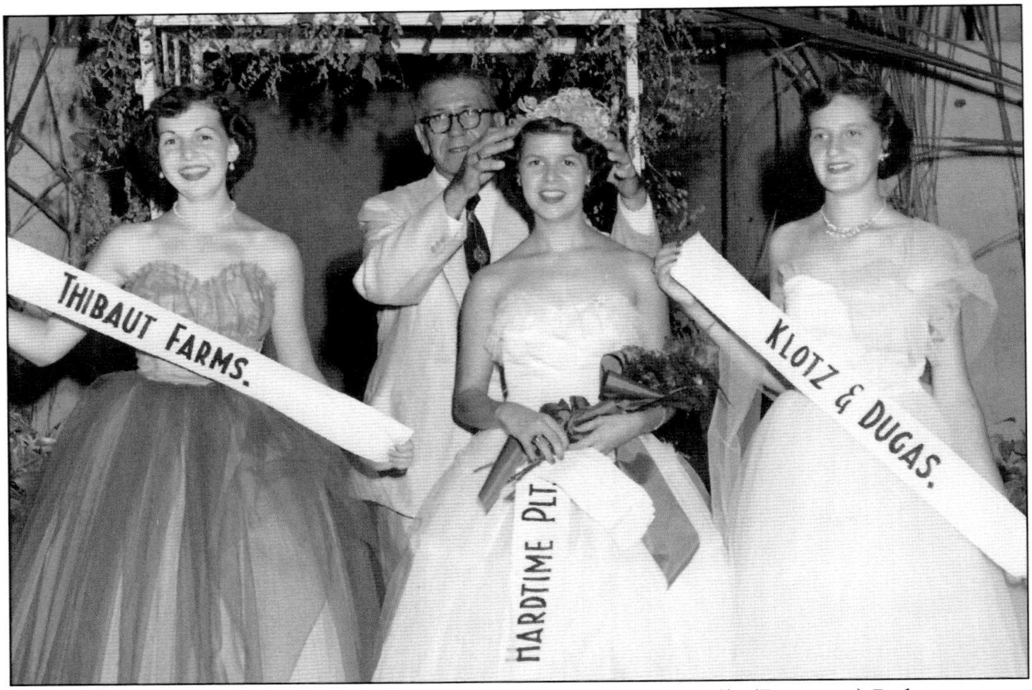

Sally (Bergeron) Padgett accepts her Miss Assumption title from Judge Sam LeBlanc, with pageant maids Barbara (Blanchard) Hidalgo (left) and Audrey (Aucoin) LeBlanc. (Courtesy of the Gerald and Olivia Chenevert family.)

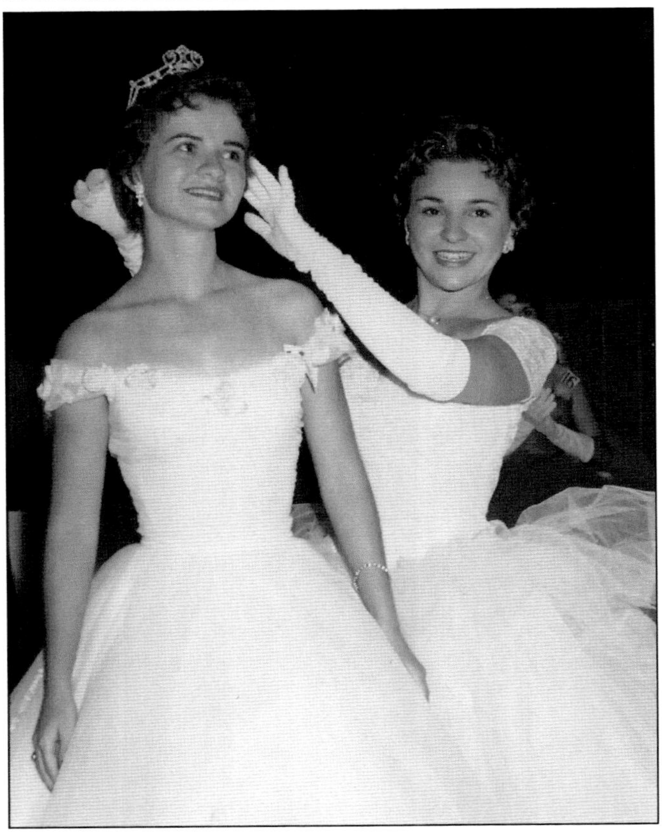

Sophie (Fernandez) Bergeron passes the title of Miss Assumption to her successor, Gloria Allemand, in this 1958 Miss Assumption crowning. (Courtesy of the Gerald and Olivia Chenevert family.)

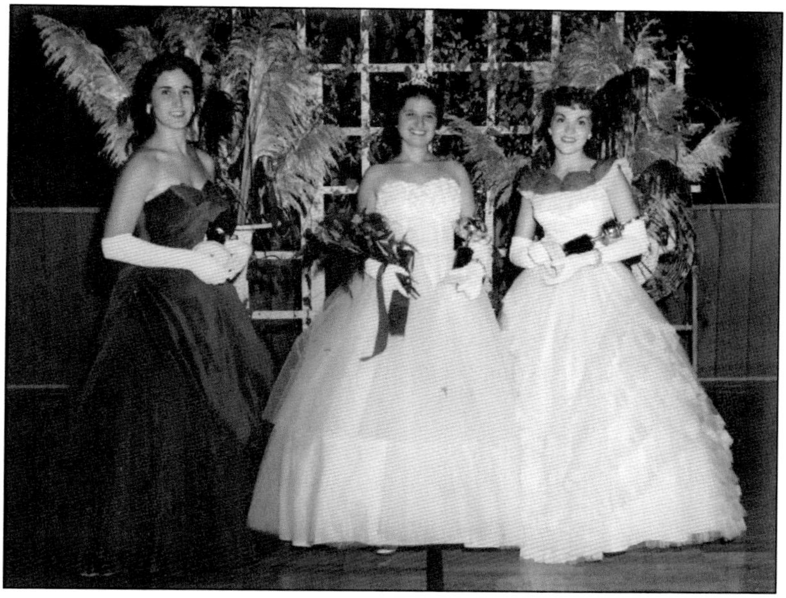

Sue Marquette Sternfels poses for her first official photograph after becoming Miss Assumption with maids Kitty Kern (left) and Joan Lauland. (Courtesy of the Gerald and Olivia Chenevert family.)

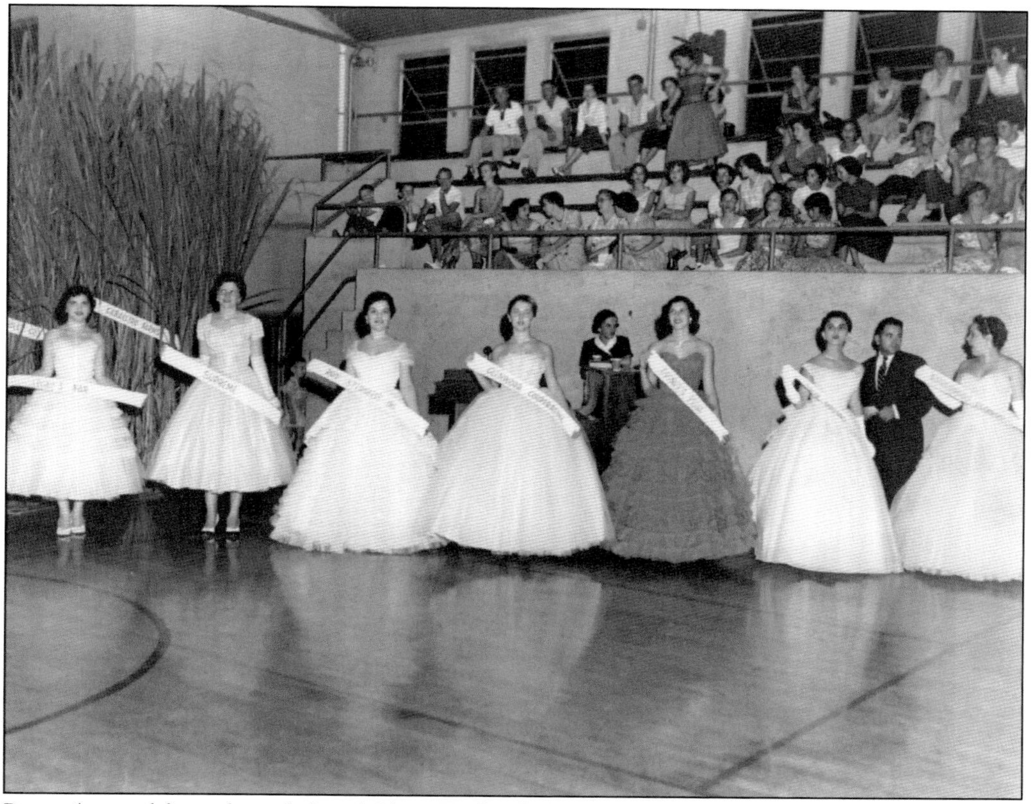

Pappy (second from the right) and Clara Triche (behind contestants) are seen serving as masters of ceremony for this Miss Assumption pageant held in the mid-1950s. (Courtesy of the Gerald and Olivia Chenevert family.)

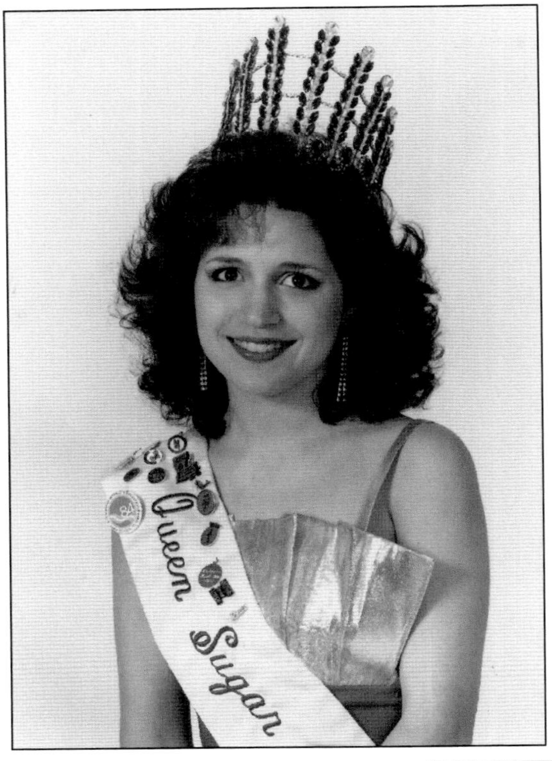

Amy B. Roth served as Louisiana's Sugar Queen while pursuing her degree from LSU, where she graduated summa cum laude in 1985 with a bachelor of interior design and minors in business and fine arts. She used her education as a springboard to start her own business in Thibodaux. It is one of the most sought-after interior design firms in south Louisiana, creating commercial and residential interior spaces. (Courtesy of Amy Bergeron Roth.)

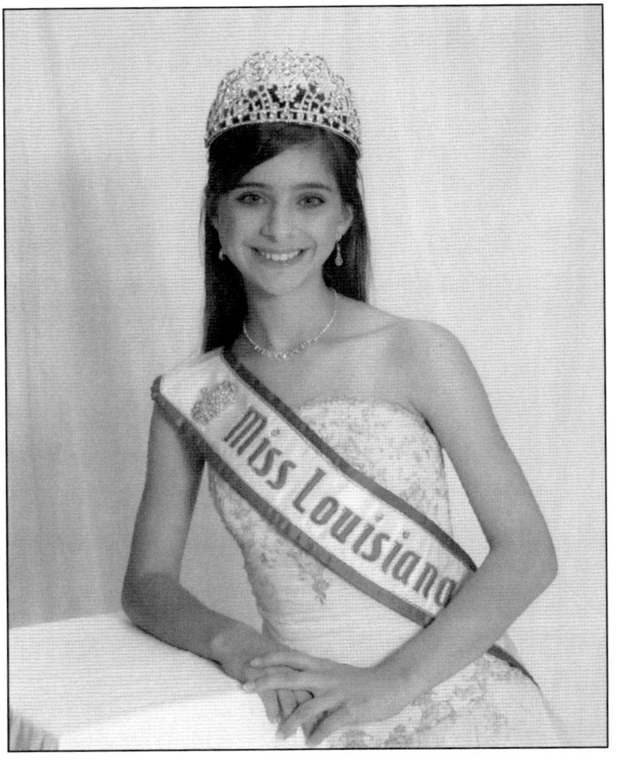

Kaitlyn Blanchard represented Louisiana as the 2006–2007 National American Miss Louisiana Preteen. The daughter of Richard and Stacey Blanchard, Kaitlyn competed with 84 other contestants for her national title. In addition to her crown, Blanchard also received awards for most promising model, casual-wear model winner, and best-resume winner. (Courtesy of Donald and Billie Eris Blanchard.)

Mignon Folse Gillen first danced professionally with the Metropolitan Opera Ballet at Lincoln Center in 1987. The Napoleonville native fulfilled a lifelong dream of dancing in an international contemporary dance company when she became principal dancer with Jennifer Muller in *The Works*, a show that Jennifer Muller produced. Currently codirector of the Omega Dance Company, Gillen has found her choreographic voice in a leading sacred and liturgical dance company. (Courtesy of Mignon Folse Gillen.)

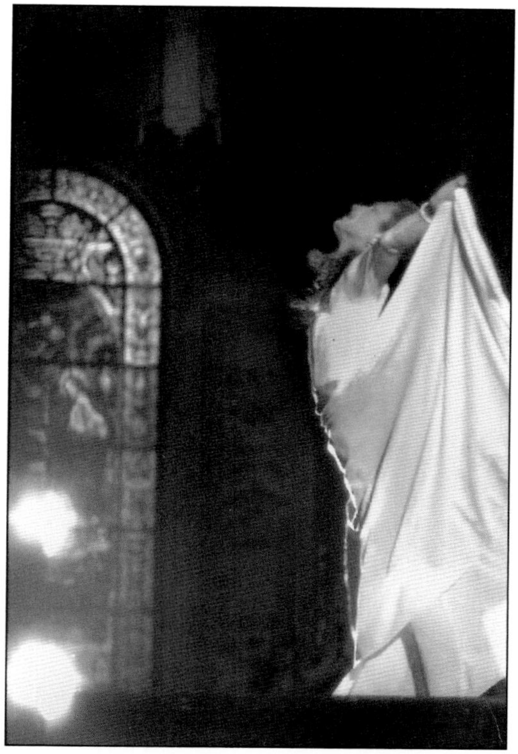

Gaston Waguespack sits at the piano as Barbara Talbot and other guests listen to the evening's speaker at this dinner at the St. Anne Church hall. Church hall dinners were a common community activity during the late 1950s and were often functions of the Knights of Columbus. (Courtesy of the Gerald and Olivia Chenevert family.)

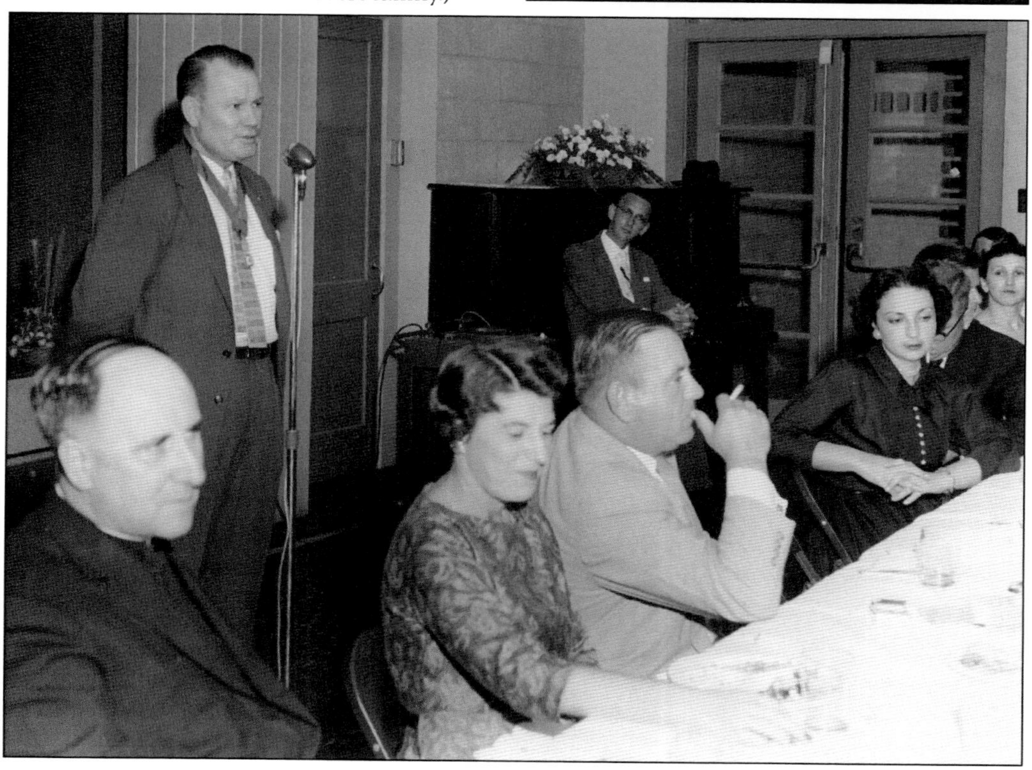

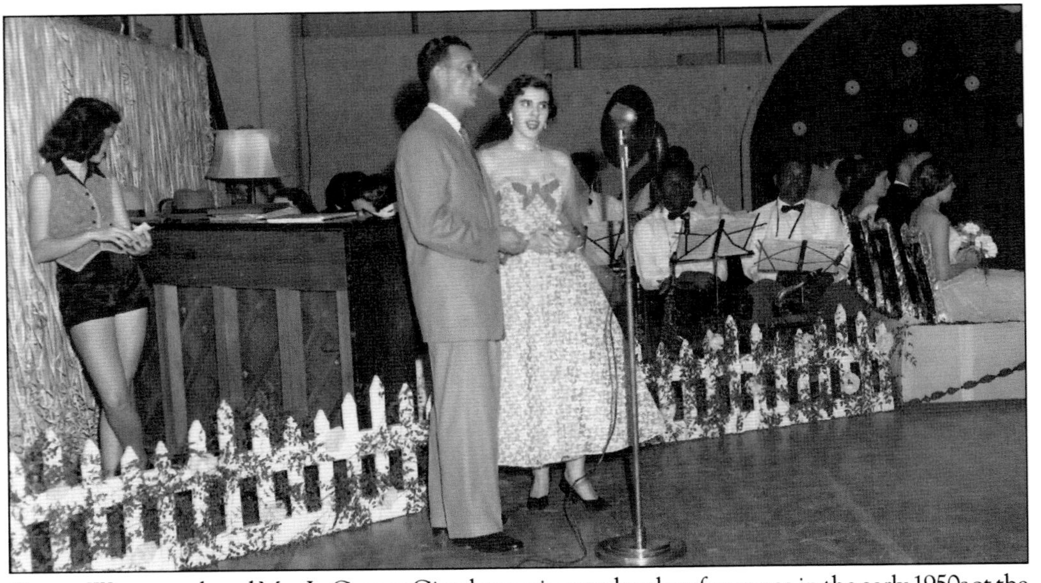

Gaston Waguespack and May LaGrange Giambrone sing at a local performance in the early 1950s at the Assumption High School gymnasium. (Courtesy of the Gerald and Olivia Chenevert family.)

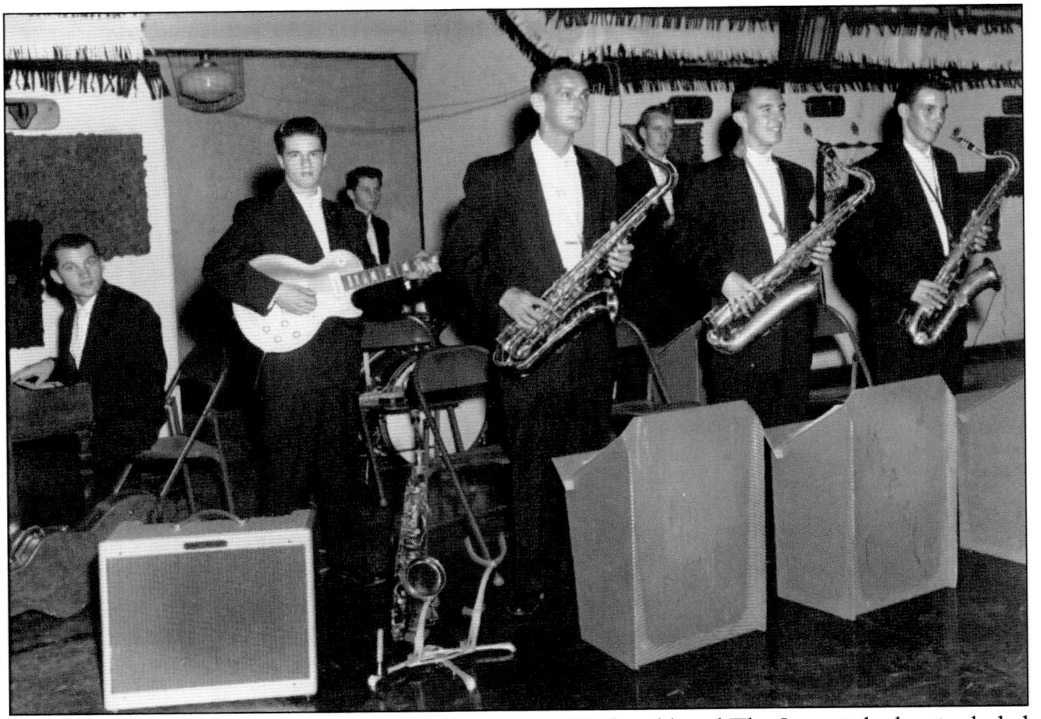

Gaston Waguespack plays music with the popular 1950s local band The Imperials that included Perry Blanchard, Gerald Clause, Billy Arcement, Larry Arcement, Marcel Clause, and Freddy St. Germain. (Courtesy of the Gerald and Olivia Chenevert family.)

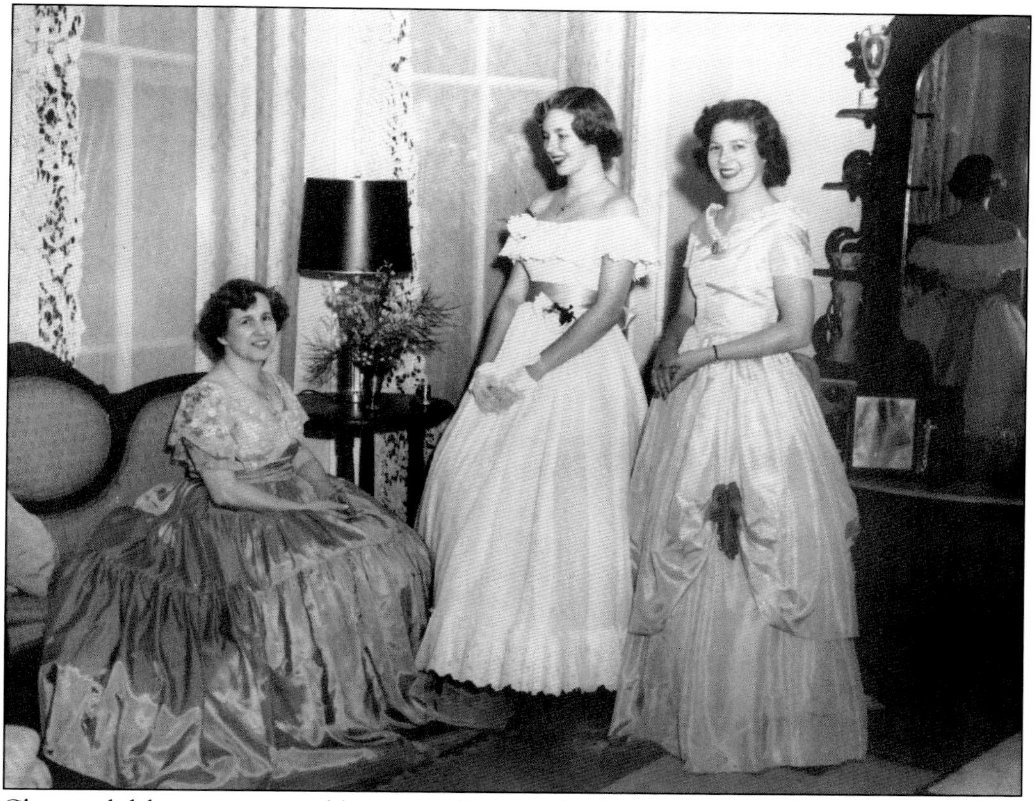

Glenwood debutants, pictured here in 1955, would be the last to enjoy the home prior to the annual spring festival. The house would succumb to fire shortly after this photograph was taken. (Courtesy of the Gerald and Olivia Chenevert family.)

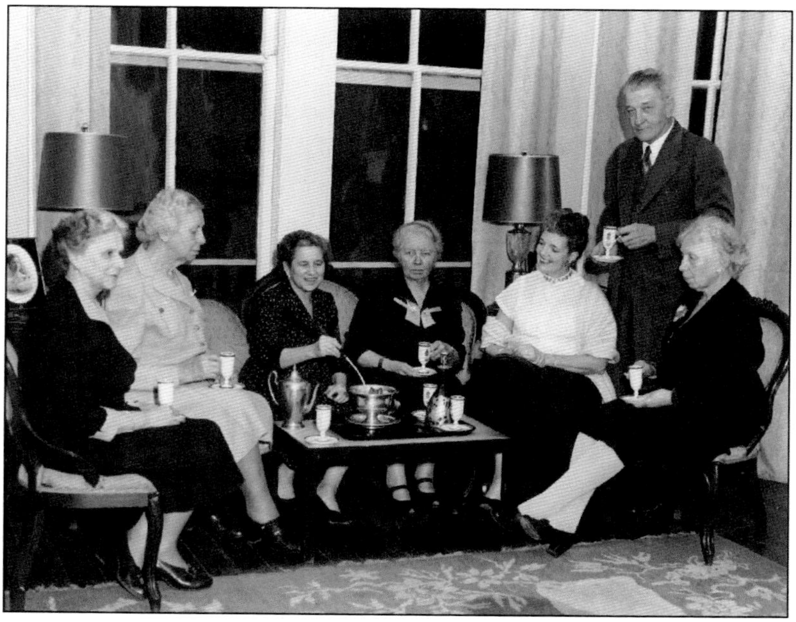

Ladies at Glenwood enjoy afternoon coffee. (Courtesy of the Gerald and Olivia Chenevert family.)

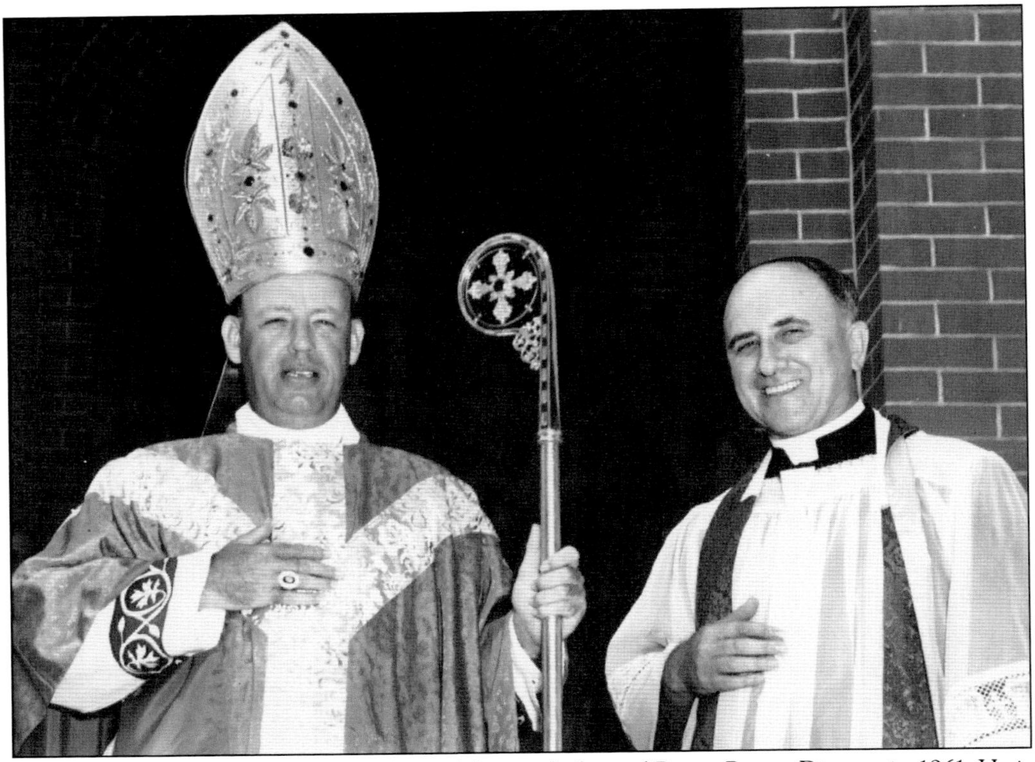

Robert E. Tracy became the first bishop of the newly formed Baton Rouge Diocese in 1961. He is pictured here with Msgr. Paul Landsmann, who served as pastor of the deanery from 1950 until 1980. (Courtesy of the Gerald and Olivia Chenevert family.)

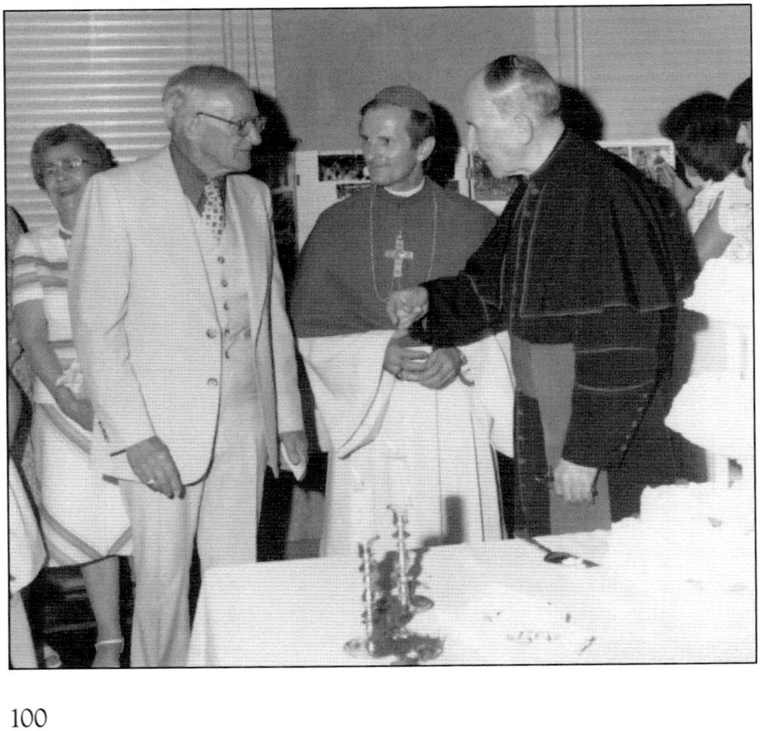

Bishop Ott enjoys a moment of celebration with Roy Himel and Msgr. Paul Landsmann in this 1978 photograph at the St. Anne Church hall. (Courtesy of the Gerald and Olivia Chenevert family.)

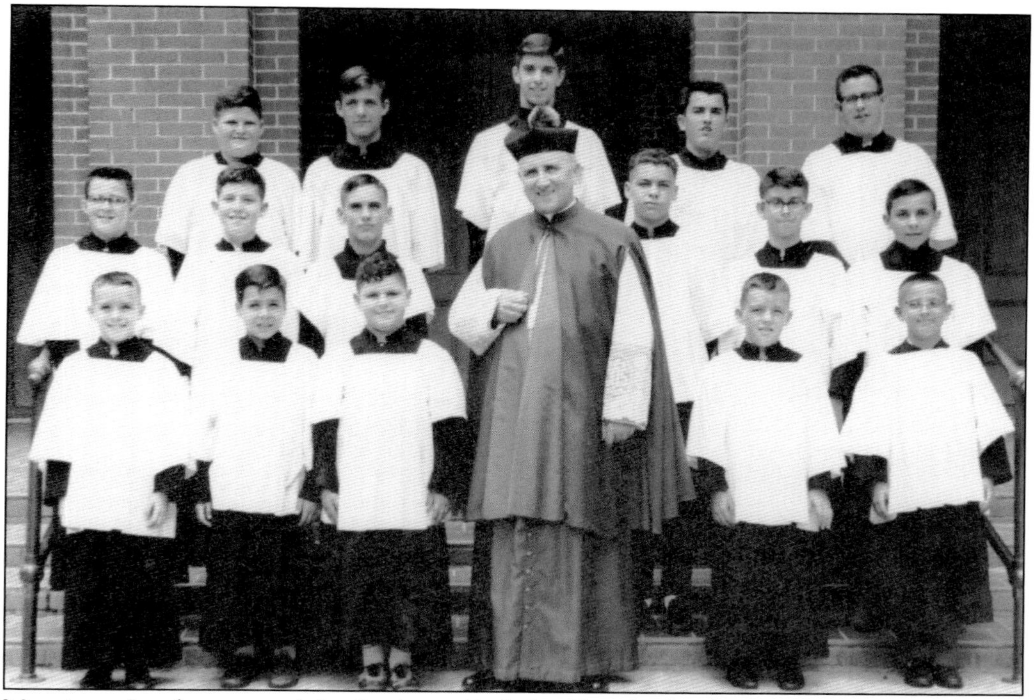

Monsignor Landsmann and the St. Anne Catholic Church altar boys pose for this early-1960s photograph. (Courtesy of the Gerald and Olivia Chenevert family.)

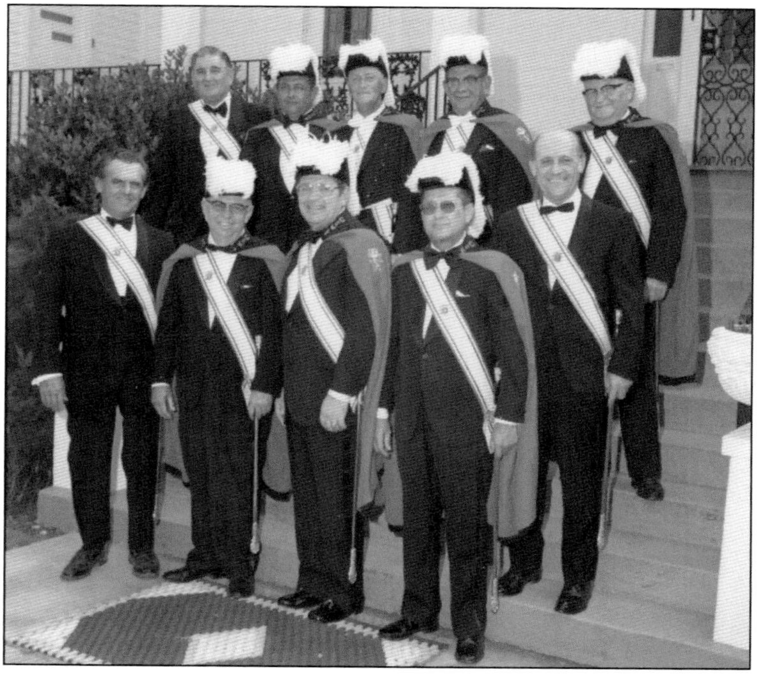

The Knights of Columbus Fourth Degree is the patriotic arm of the organization. Members coordinate service projects, donating flags to schools and public organizations. They present patriotic awards to outstanding high school seniors, deserving junior Reserve Officer's Training Corps (ROTC) students, law-enforcement officers, and fire-department personnel. (Courtesy of the Gerald and Olivia Chenevert family.)

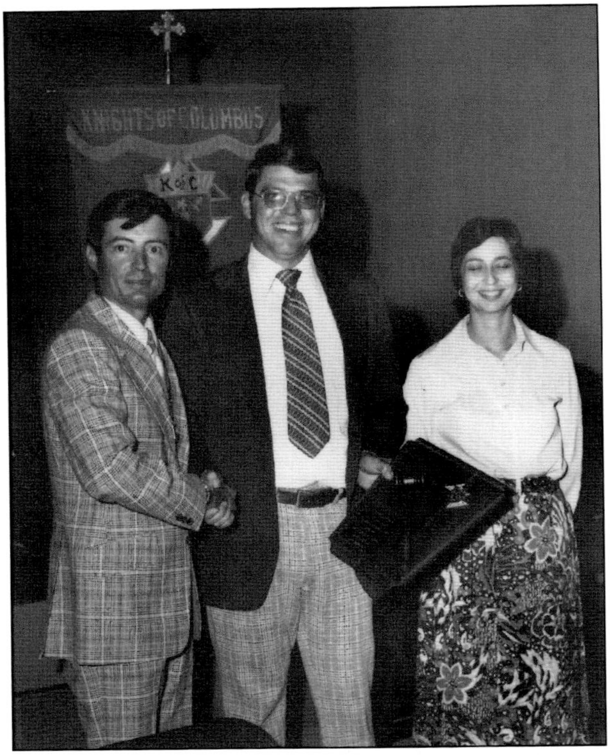

Henry Adolph presents a Knights of Columbus gavel plaque to Ronald Blanchard, pictured here with his wife Carolyn in the late 1970s. The plaque was awarded to Blanchard for his service to the organization as grand knight. (Courtesy of the Gerald and Olivia Chenevert family.)

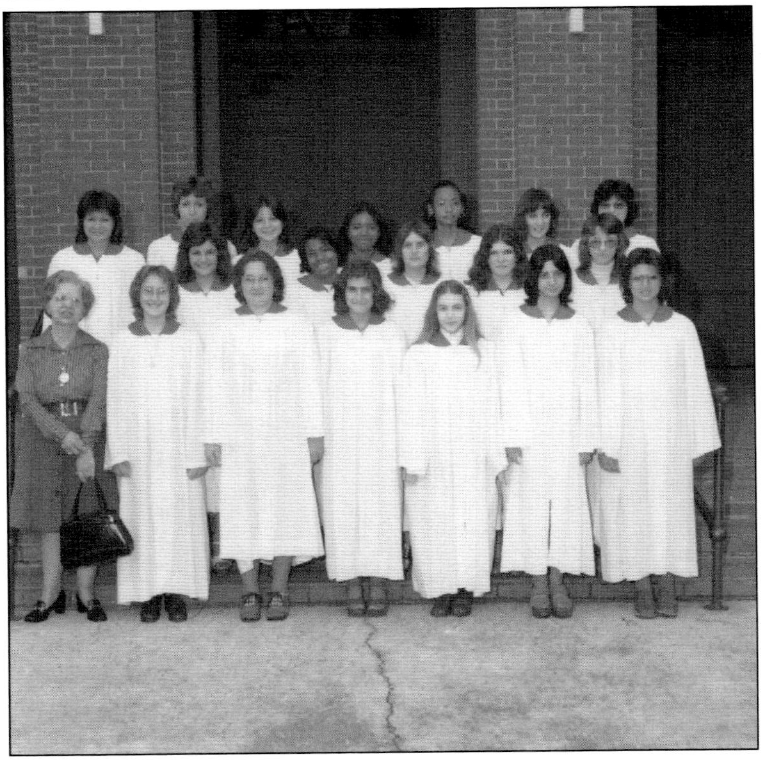

This early-1980s St. Anne confirmation class was taught by Eva Bergeron. Bergeron was the wife of Sam Bergeron of Wildwood and taught catechism to St. Anne's children for over 40 years. (Courtesy of the Gerald and Olivia Chenevert family.)

Via Sicilian immigrants, the St. Joseph altar came to New Orleans in the late 19th century. The altar provided the church community opportunities to share blessings with others and was part of this St. Anne Church's late-1980s St. Joseph Feast Day celebration. (Courtesy of the Gerald and Olivia Chenevert family.)

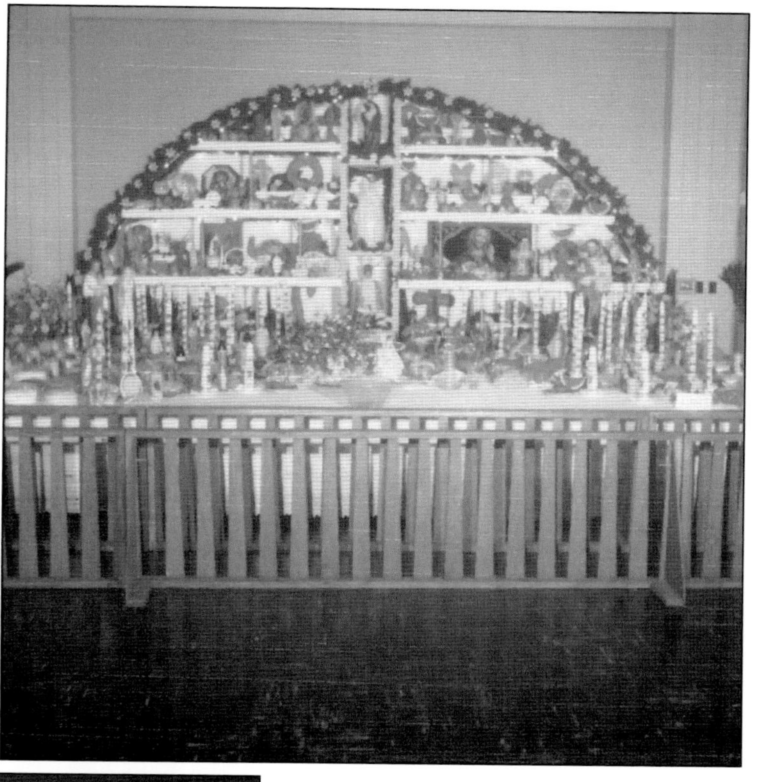

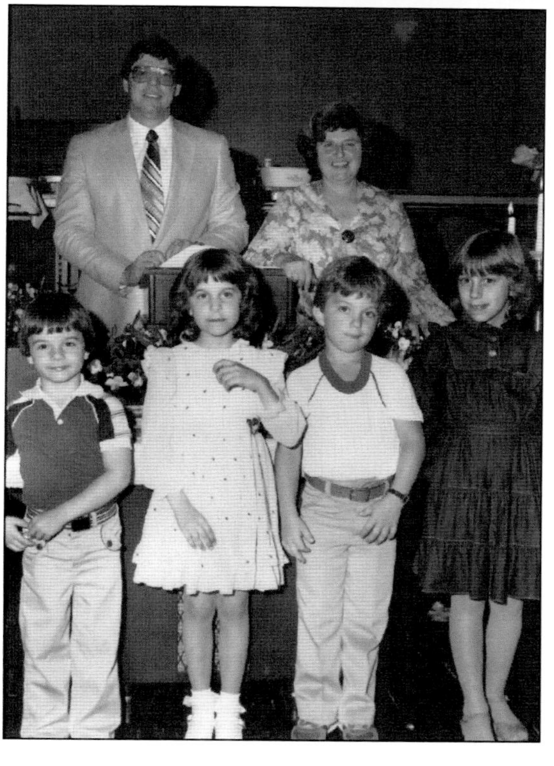

Ronald Blanchard and Olivia Chenevert recognize communion candidates at this Knights of Columbus event at the St. Anne Church hall in the late 1970s. (Courtesy of the Gerald and Olivia Chenevert family.)

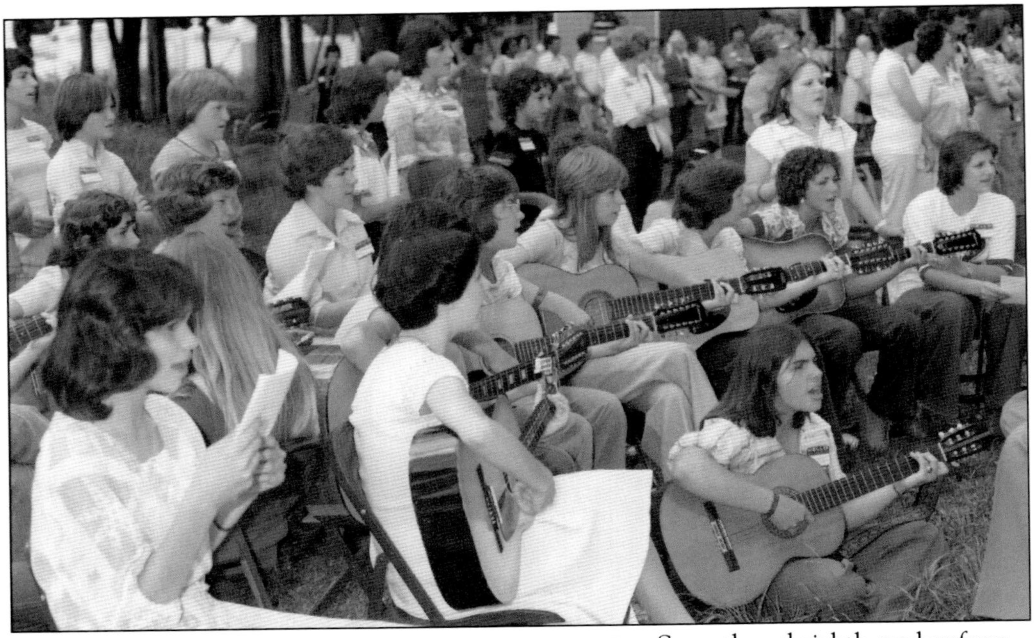

Seventh and eighth graders from St. Elizabeth School were given the opportunity to learn how to play guitar and practiced to perform weekly at the school's Friday morning guitar mass. These guitarists are playing for a mid-1970s church celebration. (Courtesy of Diane LeBlanc.)

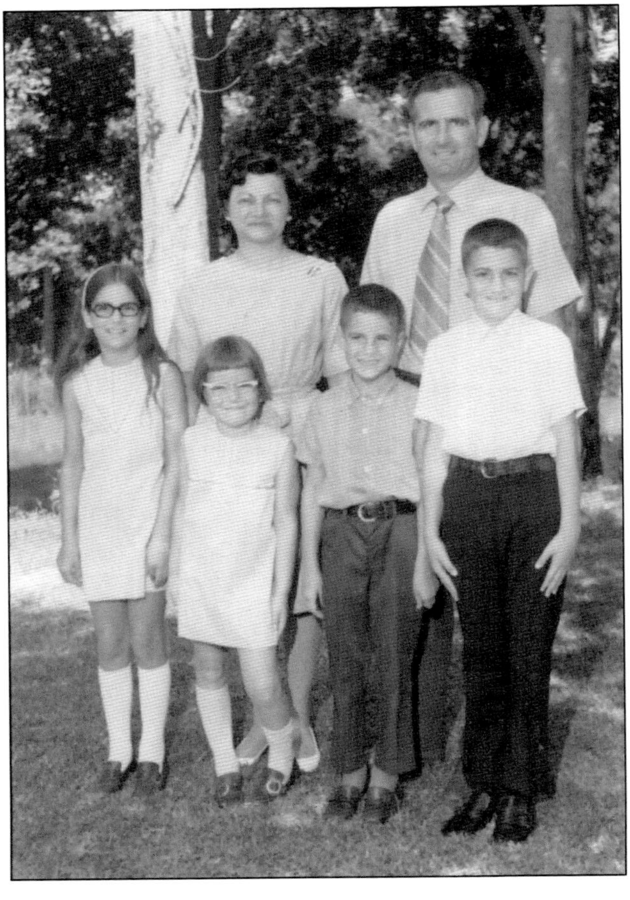

James Hubbell, a Vacherie native, moved to Napoleonville in 1969. Faith and family are, and have been, central to his life and drive his service. A retired agriculture teacher from Assumption High School, "Jimmy" has always been active in community events as a parishioner of St. Anne Church and member of the Knights of Columbus, Bayou Right to Life, Assumption Retired Teachers Association, and the Bayouland Young Farmers. (Courtesy of Lee Hubbell.)

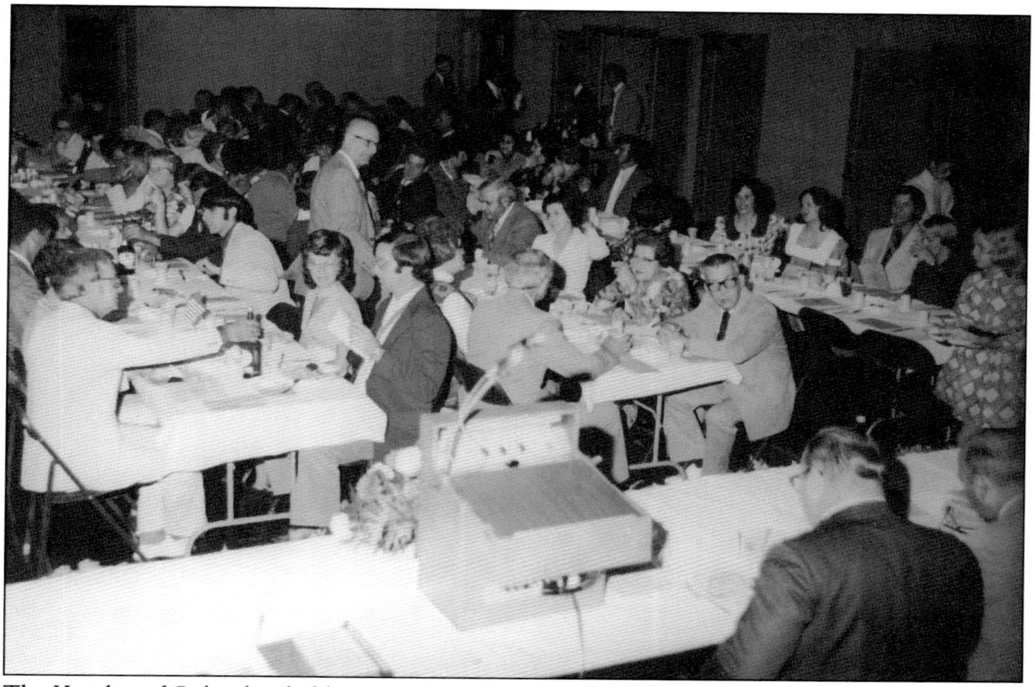

The Knights of Columbus held events throughout the church year. These St. Anne parishioners enjoy food and fellowship at a mid-1970s supper. (Courtesy of the Gerald and Olivia Chenevert family.)

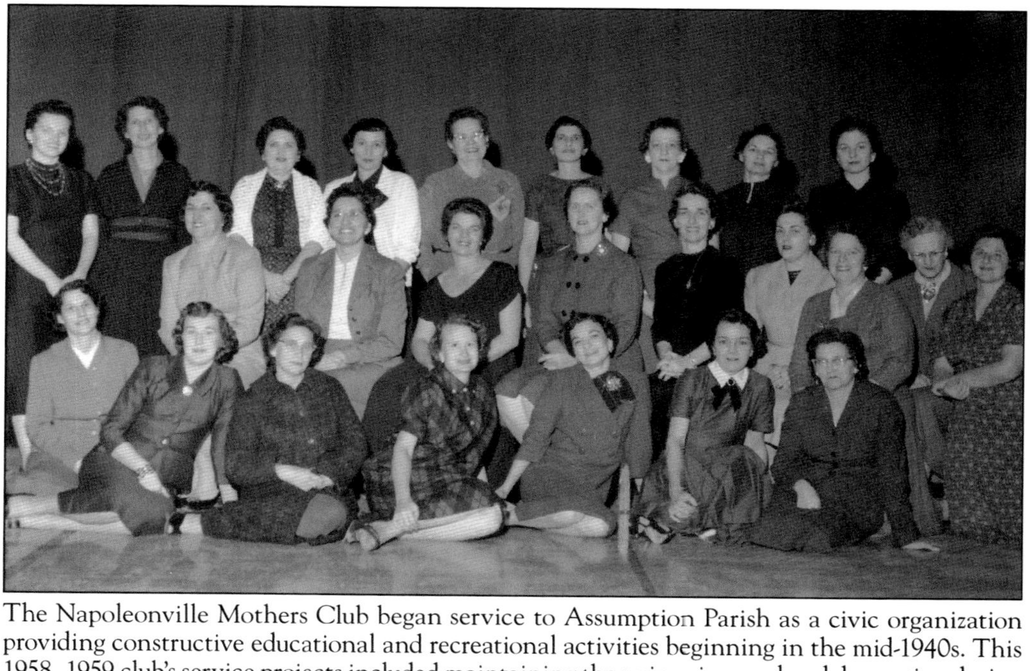

The Napoleonville Mothers Club began service to Assumption Parish as a civic organization providing constructive educational and recreational activities beginning in the mid-1940s. This 1958–1959 club's service projects included maintaining the swimming pool and decorating during the Christmas season. Members published an annual parish-wide civic and social calendar. (Courtesy of the Gerald and Olivia Chenevert family.)

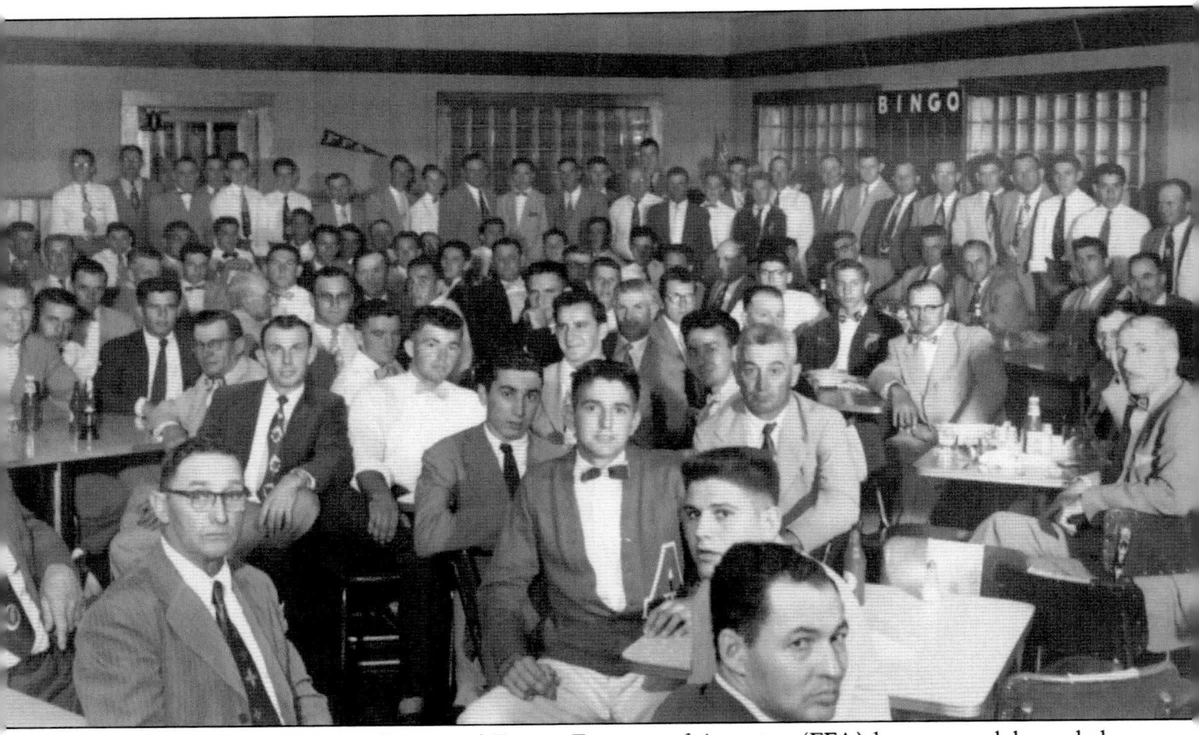

Assumption High School's annual Future Farmers of America (FFA) banquet celebrated the accomplishments of members participating in projects that support agricultural industries. This Oncale-Solar Post FFA event took place in the early 1950s. (Courtesy of the Gerald and Olivia Chenevert family.)

Pat Kinniff relaxes with the crew of the Southern Pacific Railroad station of Napoleonville in 1955. At this time, the rail line ran lumber and freight through the parish. This railroad depot was located near the Napoleonville Lumber Company. (Courtesy of the Gerald and Olivia Chenevert family.)

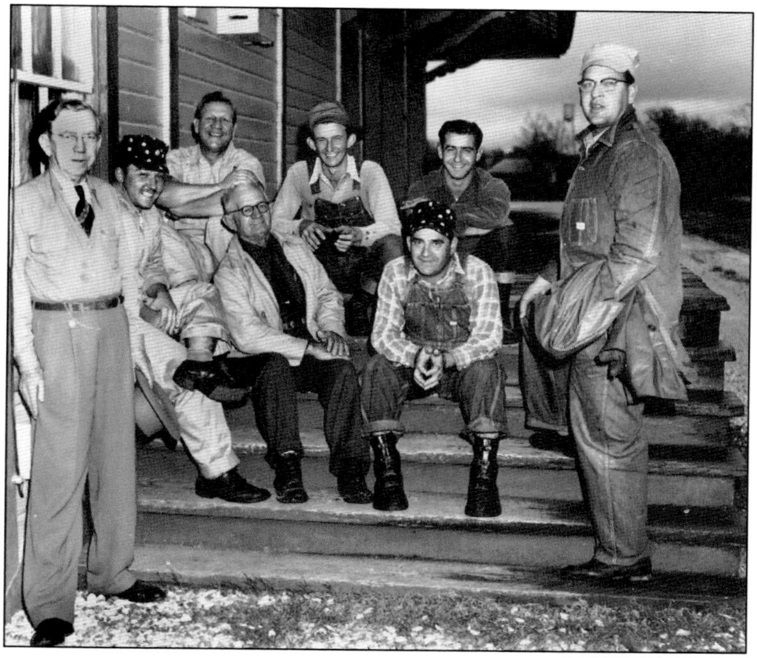

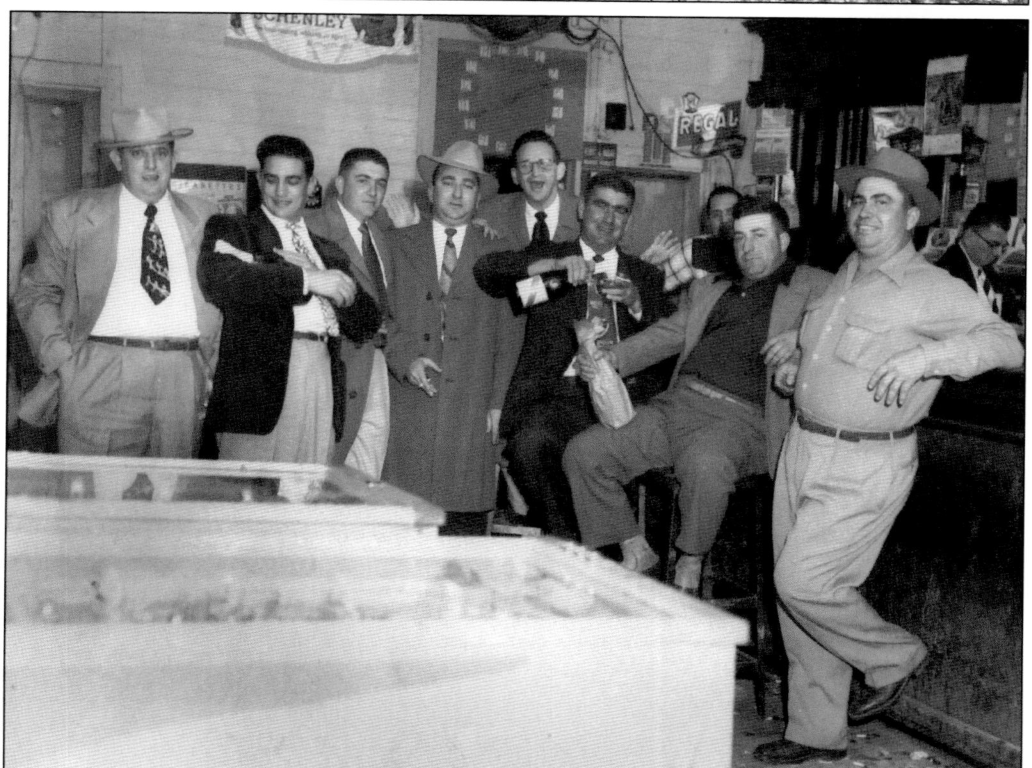

These fellows are celebrating with champagne in the 1950s. Perhaps the reason for the celebration is the birth of a new child, depicted by the cradling gesture of one of the revelers. (Courtesy of the Gerald and Olivia Chenevert family.)

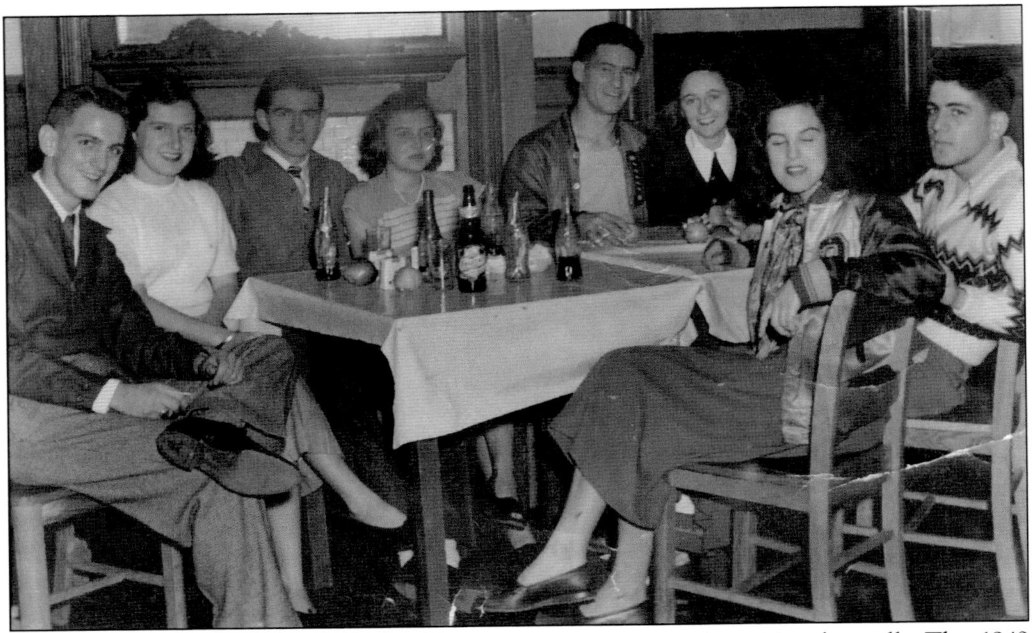

The Oaks was a venue on Highway 1 just north of Barbera Chevrolet in Napoleonville. This 1949 photograph shows a group of local high school students enjoying date night at the restaurant. (Courtesy of the Gerald and Olivia Chenevert family.)

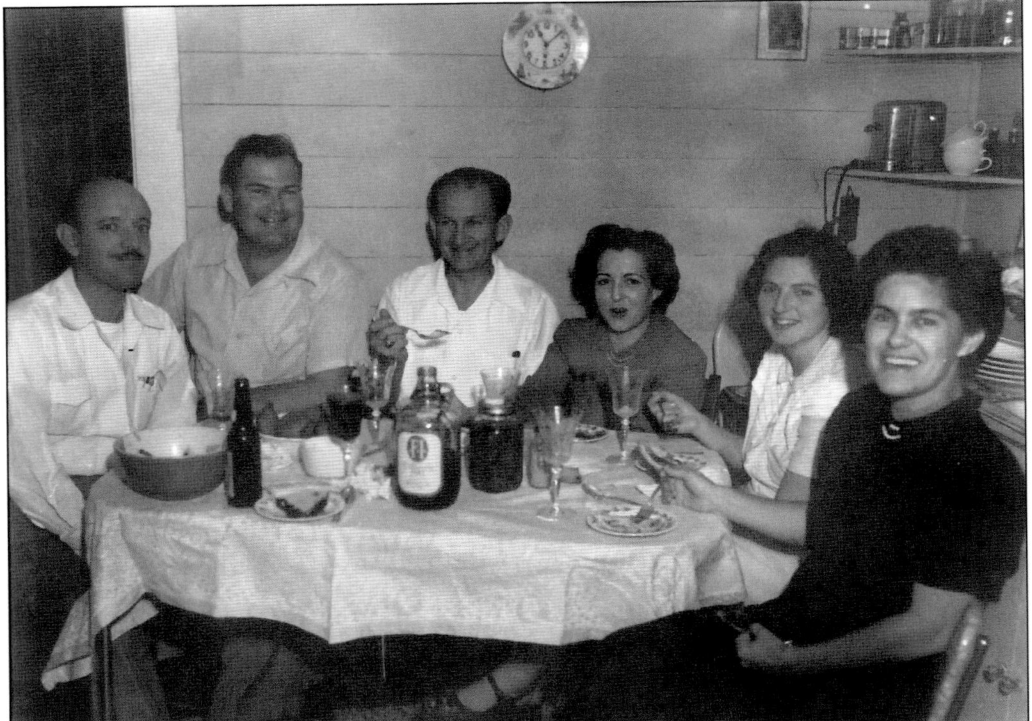

Dinner parties were popular among young couples in the parish in the 1950s. This group of friends enjoys wine with their pie. (Courtesy of the Gerald and Olivia Chenevert family.)

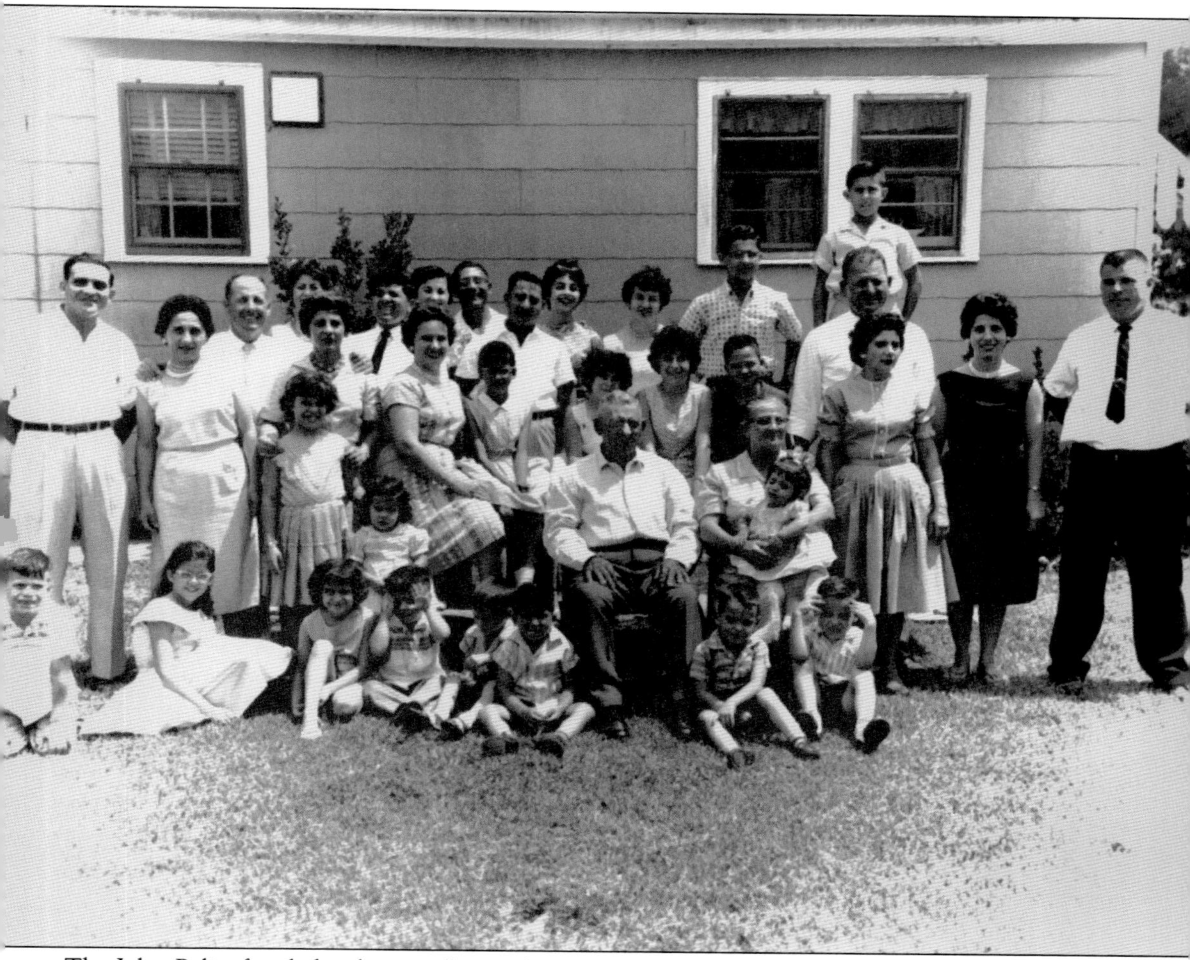

The John Politz family has been influential in Assumption Parish for generations. Their family restaurant and bar, Politz's, has been owned and run by family members for more than 50 years. (Courtesy of the Gerald and Olivia Chenevert family.)

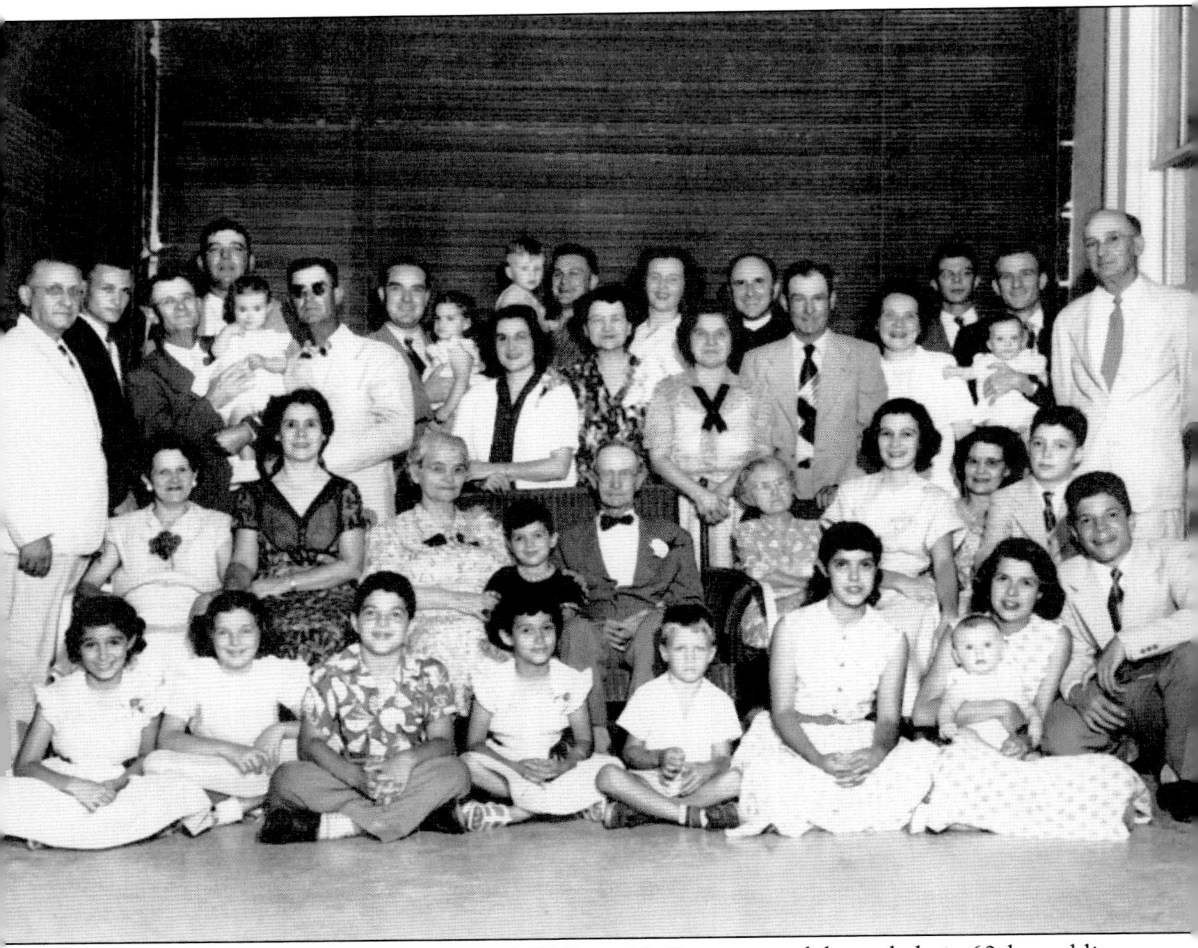

Corinne (Boudreaux) Bergeron and William N. Bergeron celebrated their 60th wedding anniversary in the mid-1950s. William became overseer of Little Texas Plantation in 1894, eventually becoming co-owner. All six of their children were born at Little Texas. (Courtesy of Don and Diane Bergeron.)

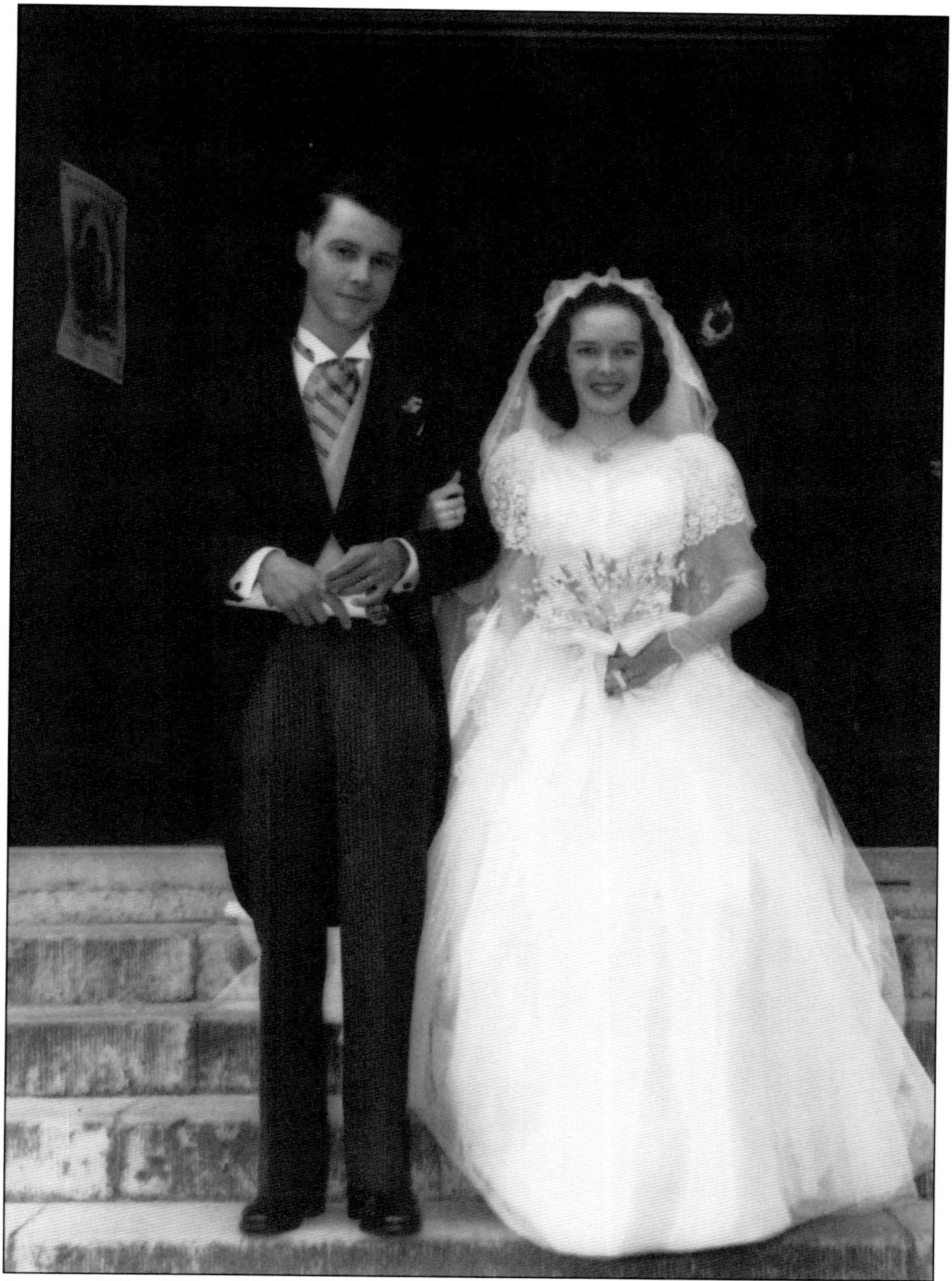

Sonny and Tini Wilbert Thibaut are all smiles on their wedding day in 1949. They became active in the community, where Tini was a Boy Scout den mother, president of St. Elizabeth School Mother's club, and an organist at St. Anne and Assumption Catholic Churches, with over 25 years of service. (Courtesy of John "Sonny" and Carolyn "Tini" Thibaut estate.)

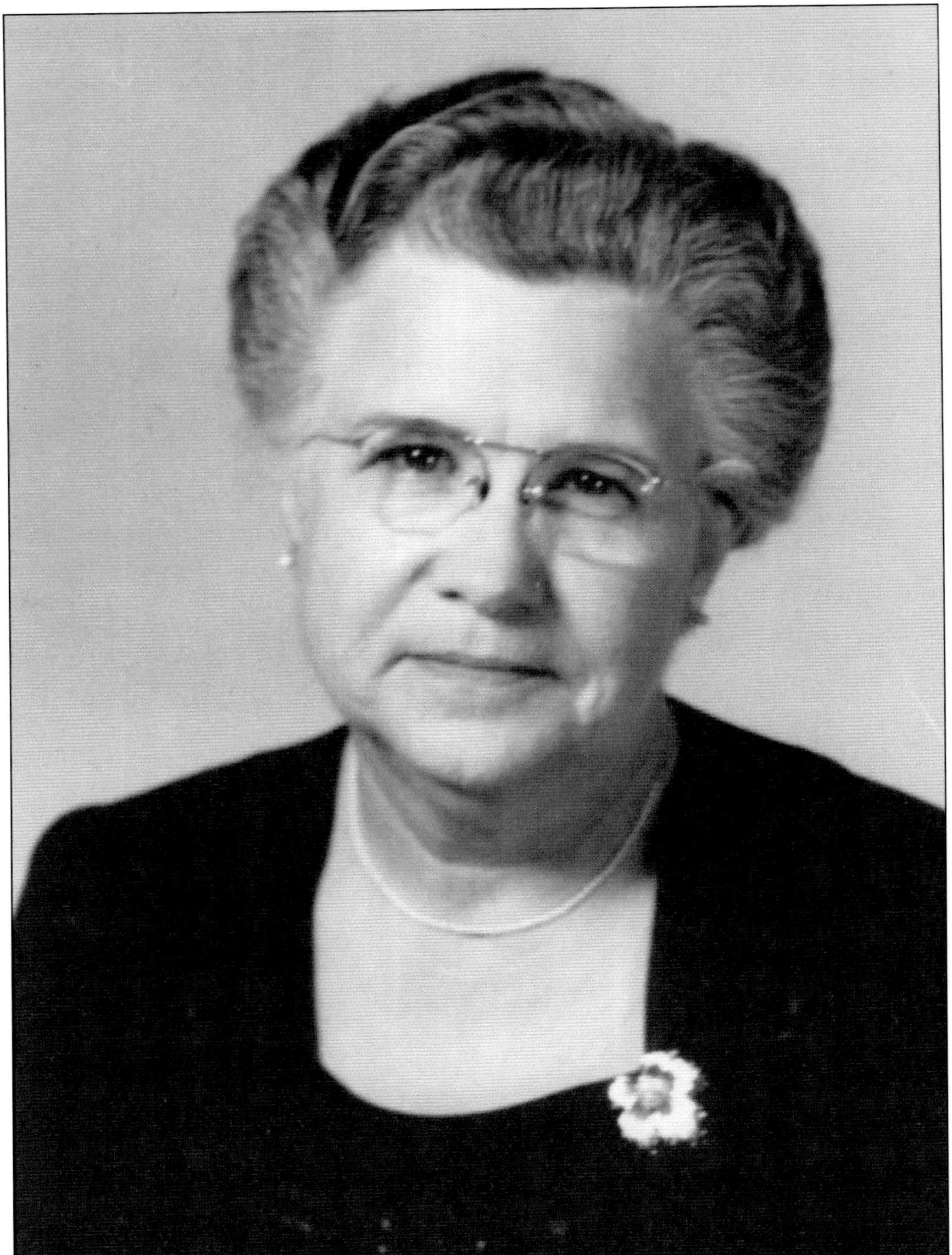

Josephine Elmina Thibaut influenced thousands of parish residents with over 45 years of service as an English teacher, assistant principal, school librarian, and counselor. She became one of five founding members of the Louisiana Library Association in 1937. (Courtesy of John "Sonny" and Carolyn "Tini" Thibaut estate.)

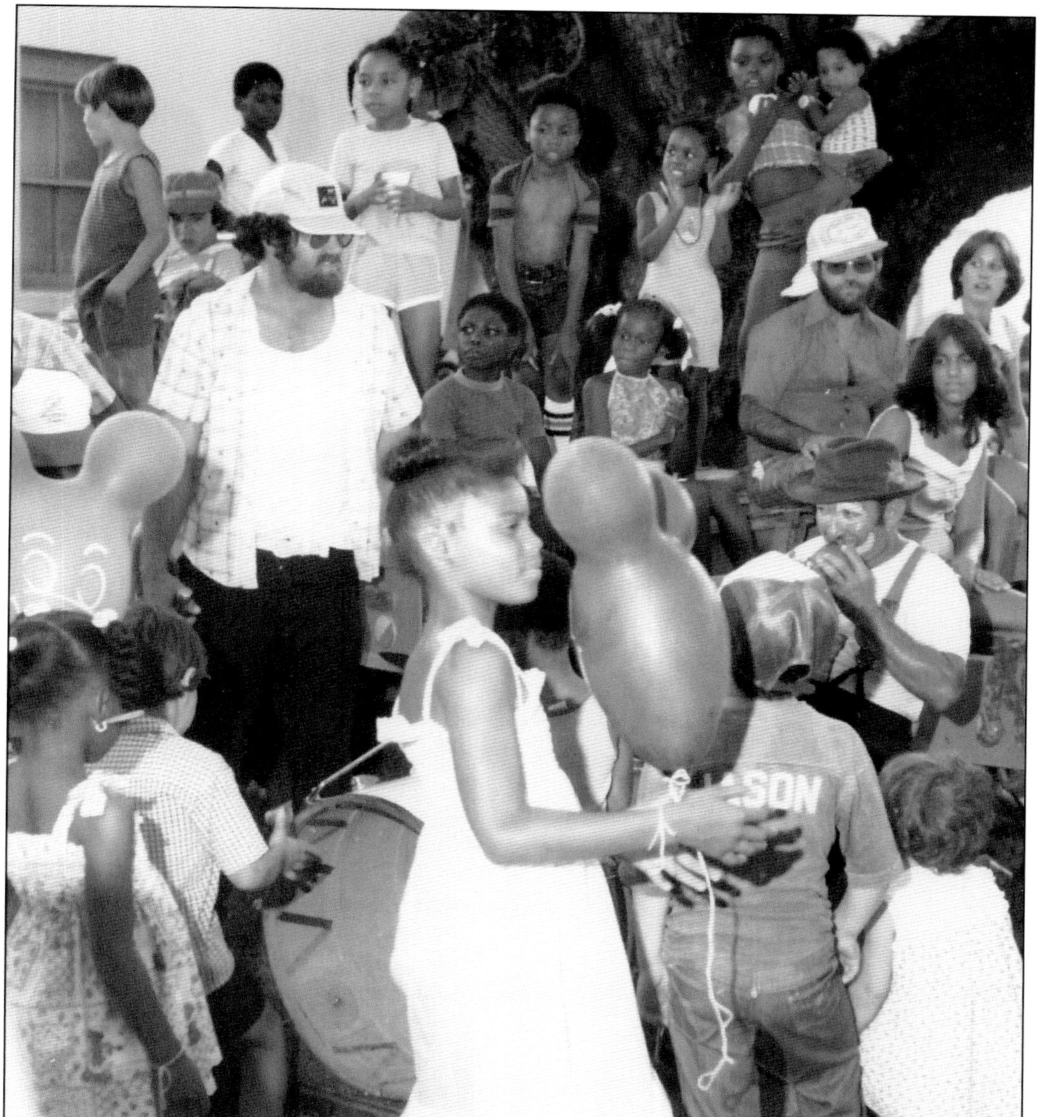

Children are happy to wait their turn to receive an animal-shaped balloon at this late-1970s Napoleonville Festival. (Courtesy of the Gerald and Olivia Chenevert family.)

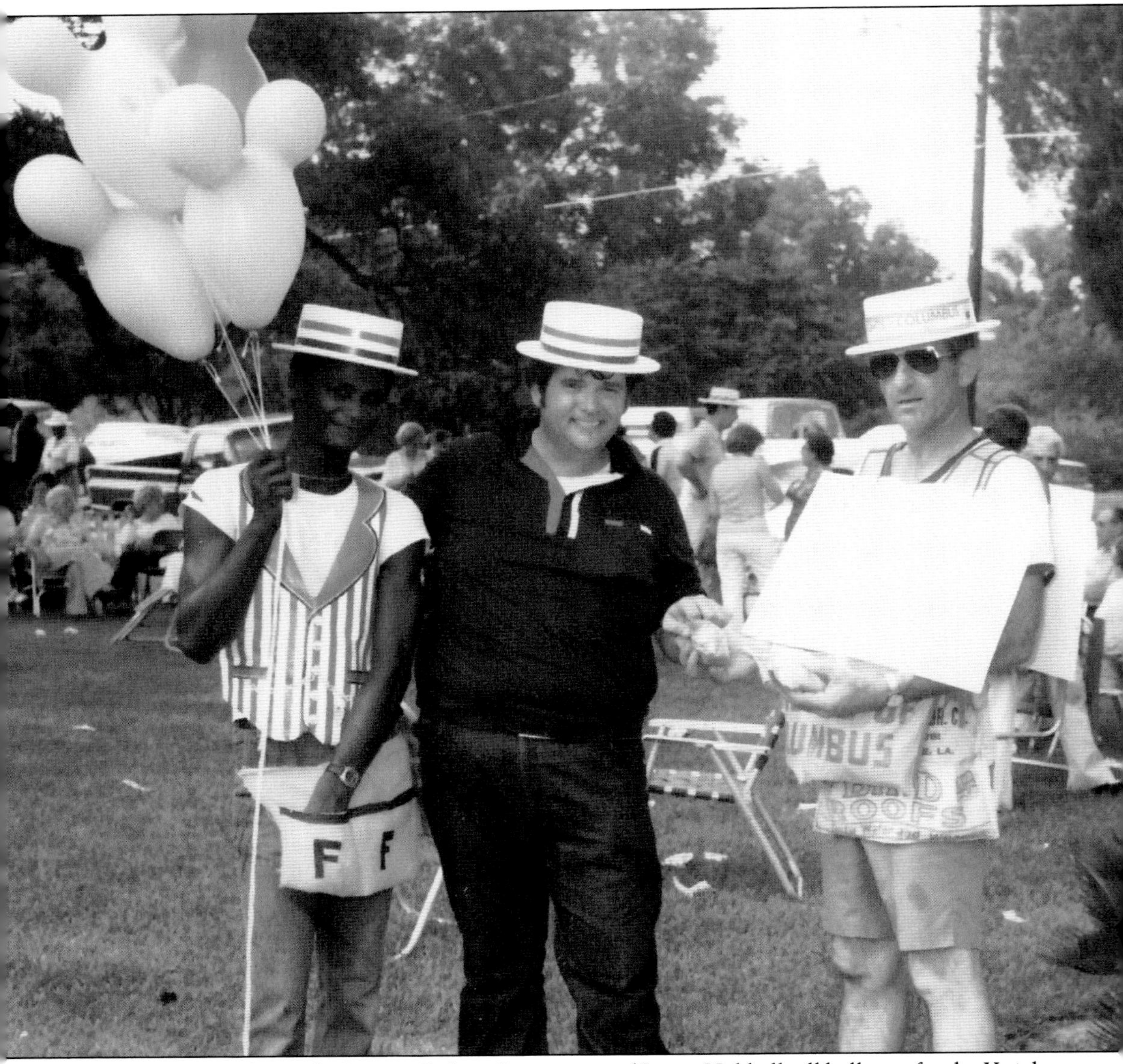

From left to right, Ricky Breaux, Robert Simmons, and James Hubbell sell balloons for the Knights of Columbus at a late-1970s Napoleonville Festival. The Knights of Columbus participated in many community-related activities throughout its history in the parish, beginning in 1906. (Courtesy of the Gerald and Olivia Chenevert family.)

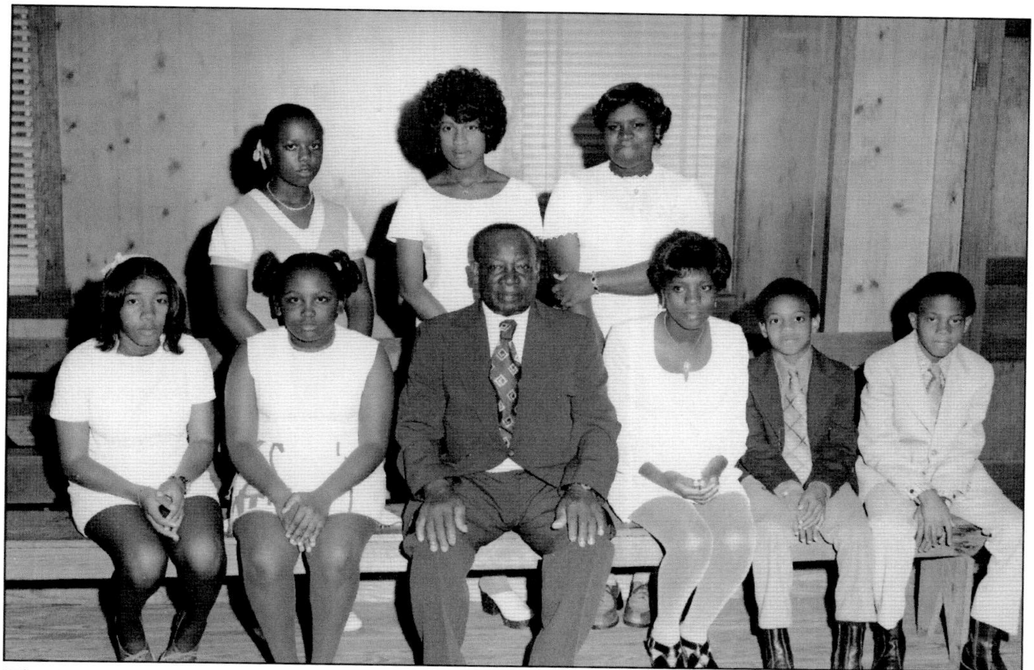

The New Belmont youth choir of 1974 enjoyed the comforts of their newest church building, completed the same year. The church congregation is one of the parish's oldest, with more than 140 years of continual commitment to the Lord and community. (Courtesy of Mildred Sylvester.)

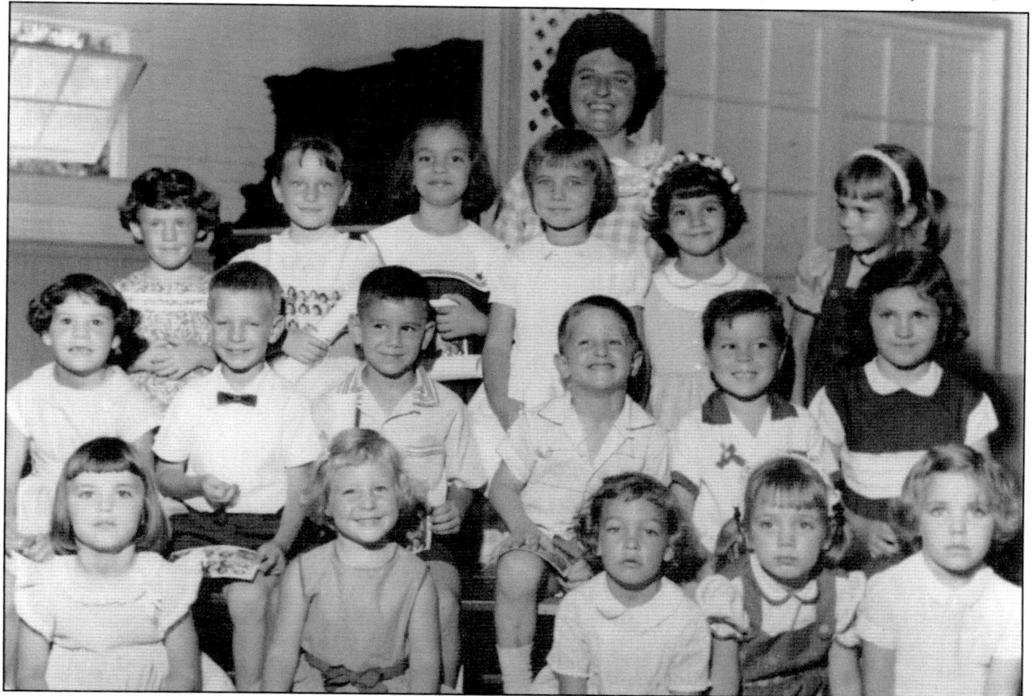

Olivia Chenevert's preschool was an entertaining way for local children to ease into the rigors of education. (Courtesy of the Gerald and Olivia Chenevert family.)

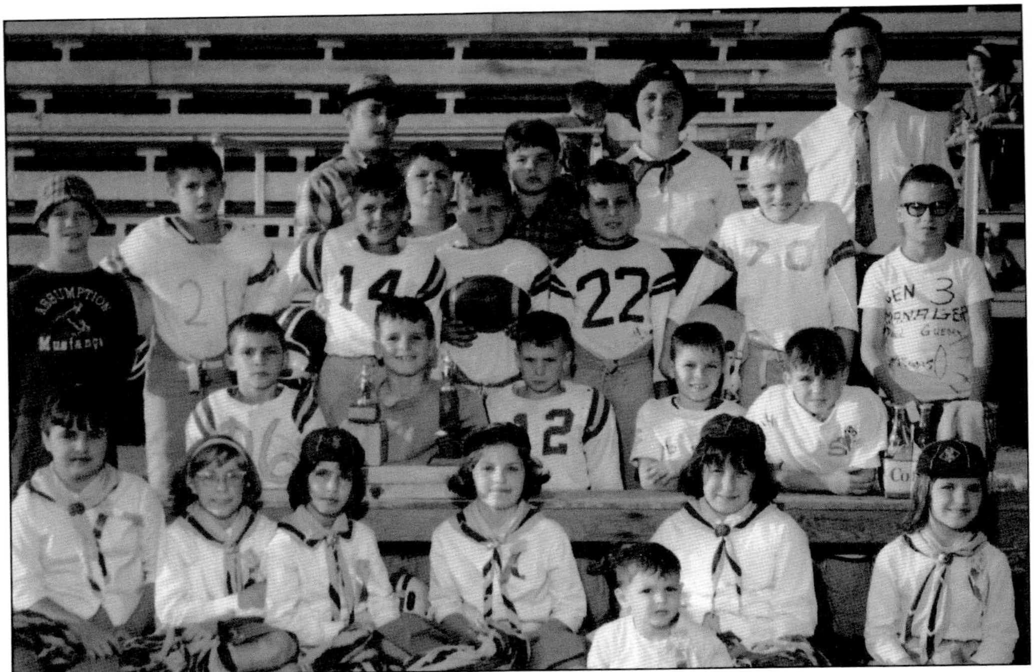

This Boy Scouts football team from the early 1960s combined the integrity of the Boy Scouts with the competitive advantage taught by little-league sports. (Courtesy of the Gerald and Olivia Chenevert family.)

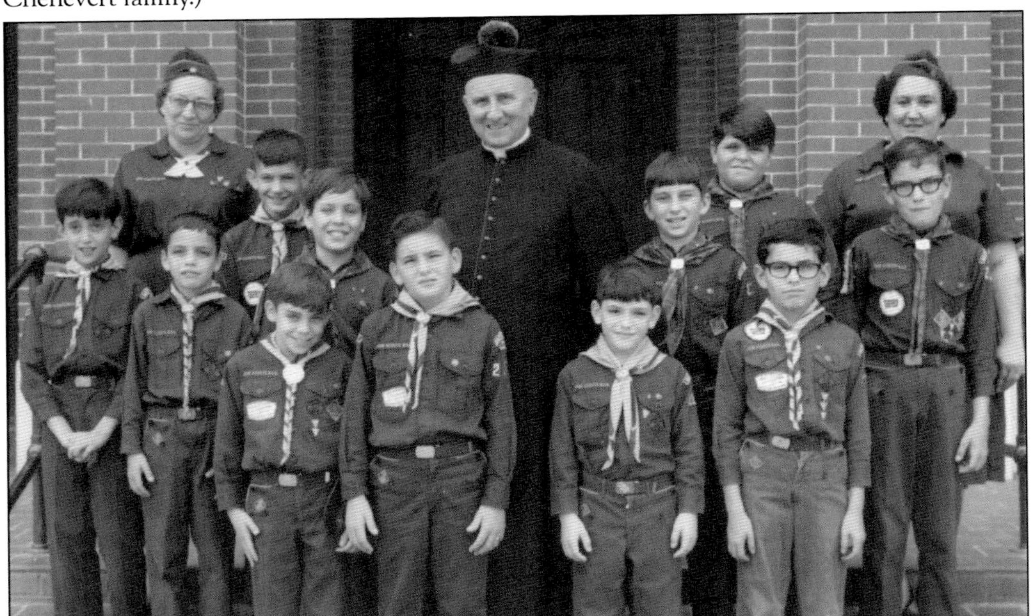

Here, early-1960s Boy Scouts pose with then Fr. Paul Landsmann. Landsmann was the first pastor of the deanery of Napoleonville, appointed in 1961 by Bishop Robert E. Tracy under the Baton Rouge Diocese. He also served as pastor from 1950 until his subsequent appointment under the New Orleans Diocese. (Courtesy of the Gerald and Olivia Chenevert family.)

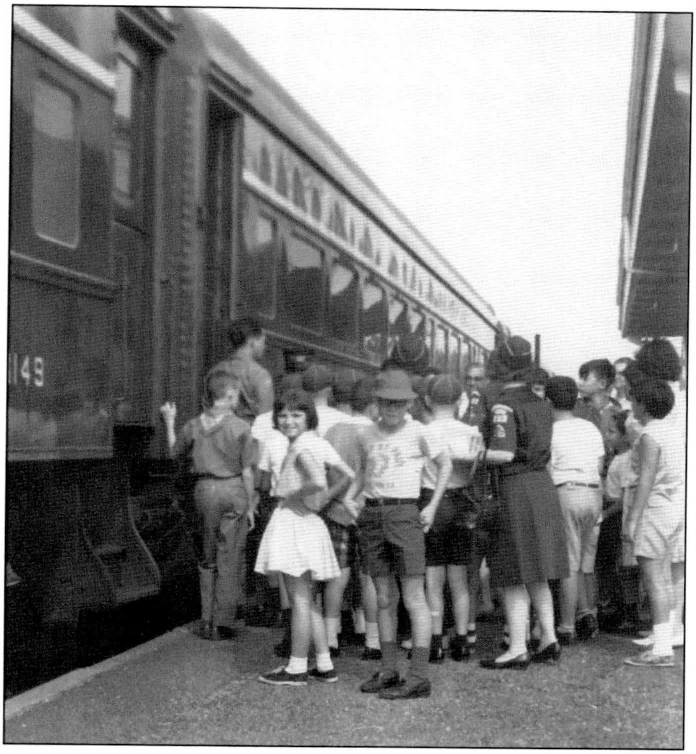

Edith Boudreaux and Olivia Chenevert organized and chaperoned this 1960s Boy Scout field trip. In the photograph below, the scouts wait in anticipation for their train to depart. (Both, courtesy of the Gerald and Olivia Chenevert family.)

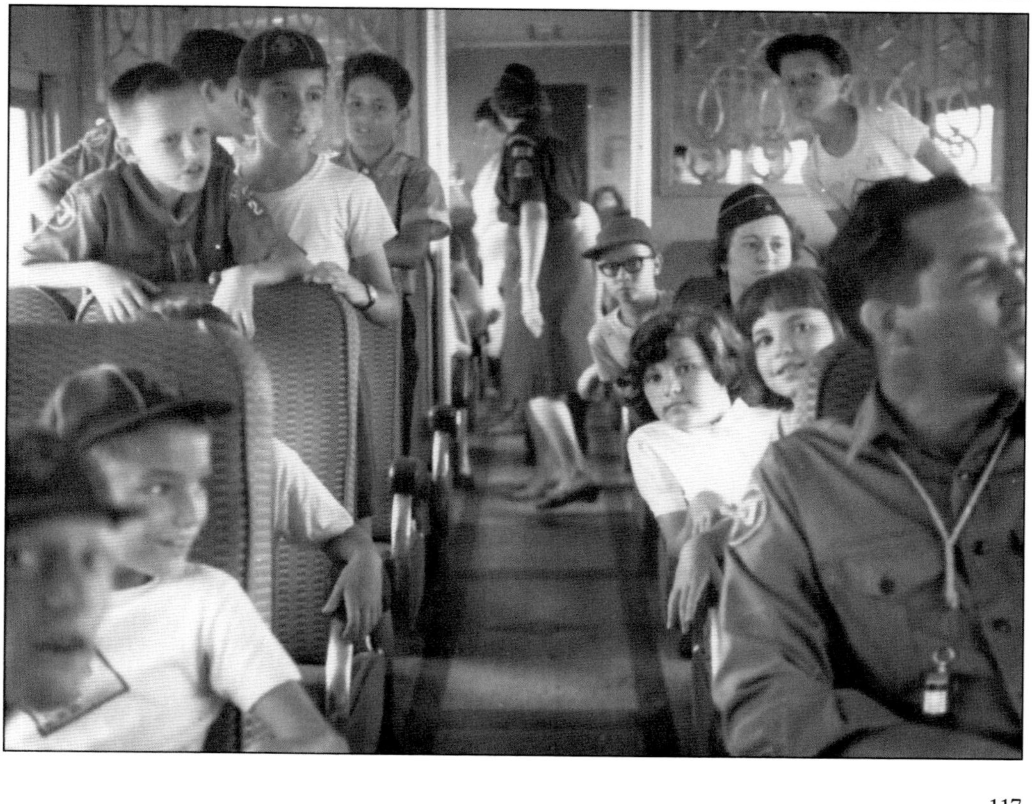

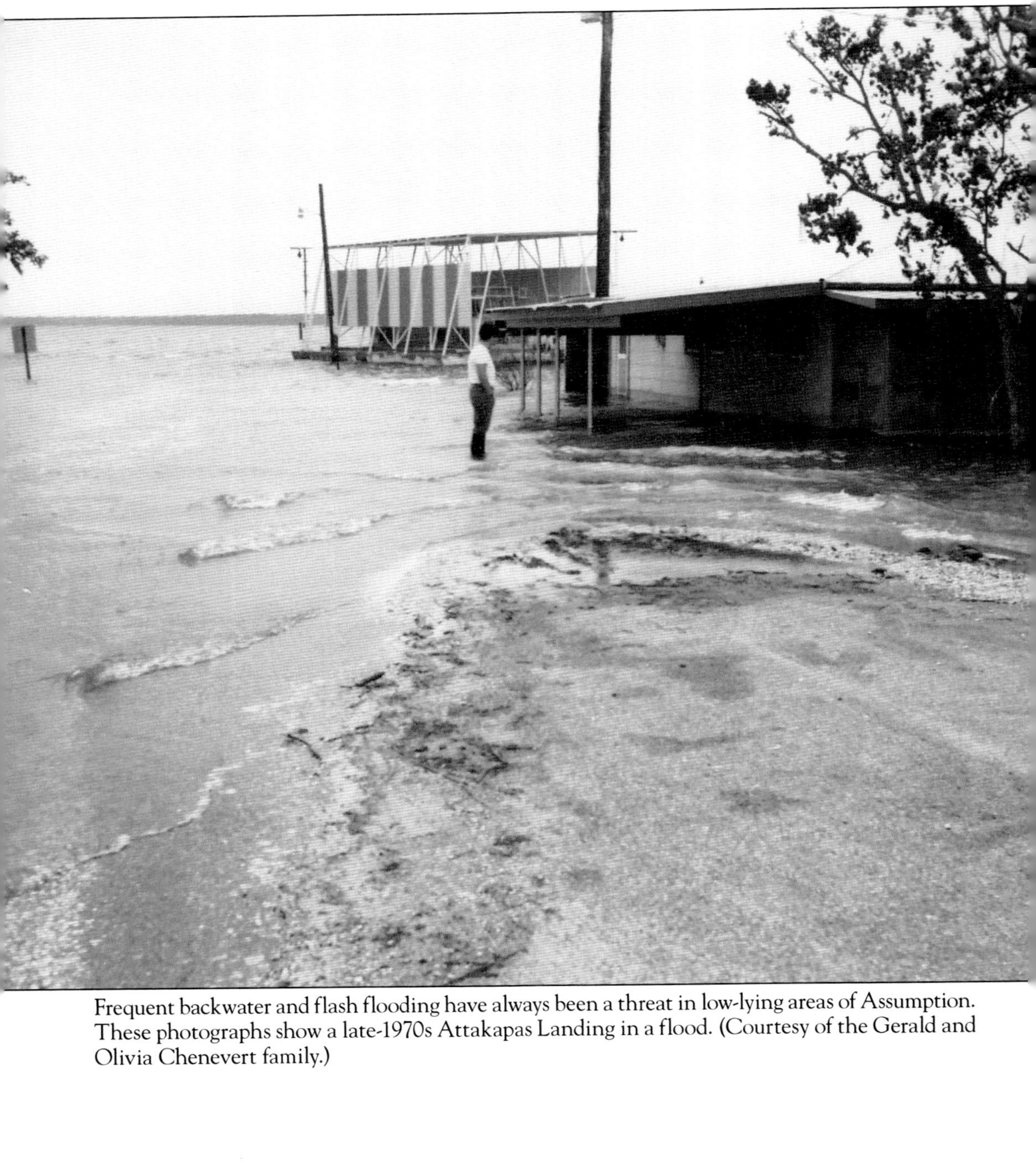

Frequent backwater and flash flooding have always been a threat in low-lying areas of Assumption. These photographs show a late-1970s Attakapas Landing in a flood. (Courtesy of the Gerald and Olivia Chenevert family.)

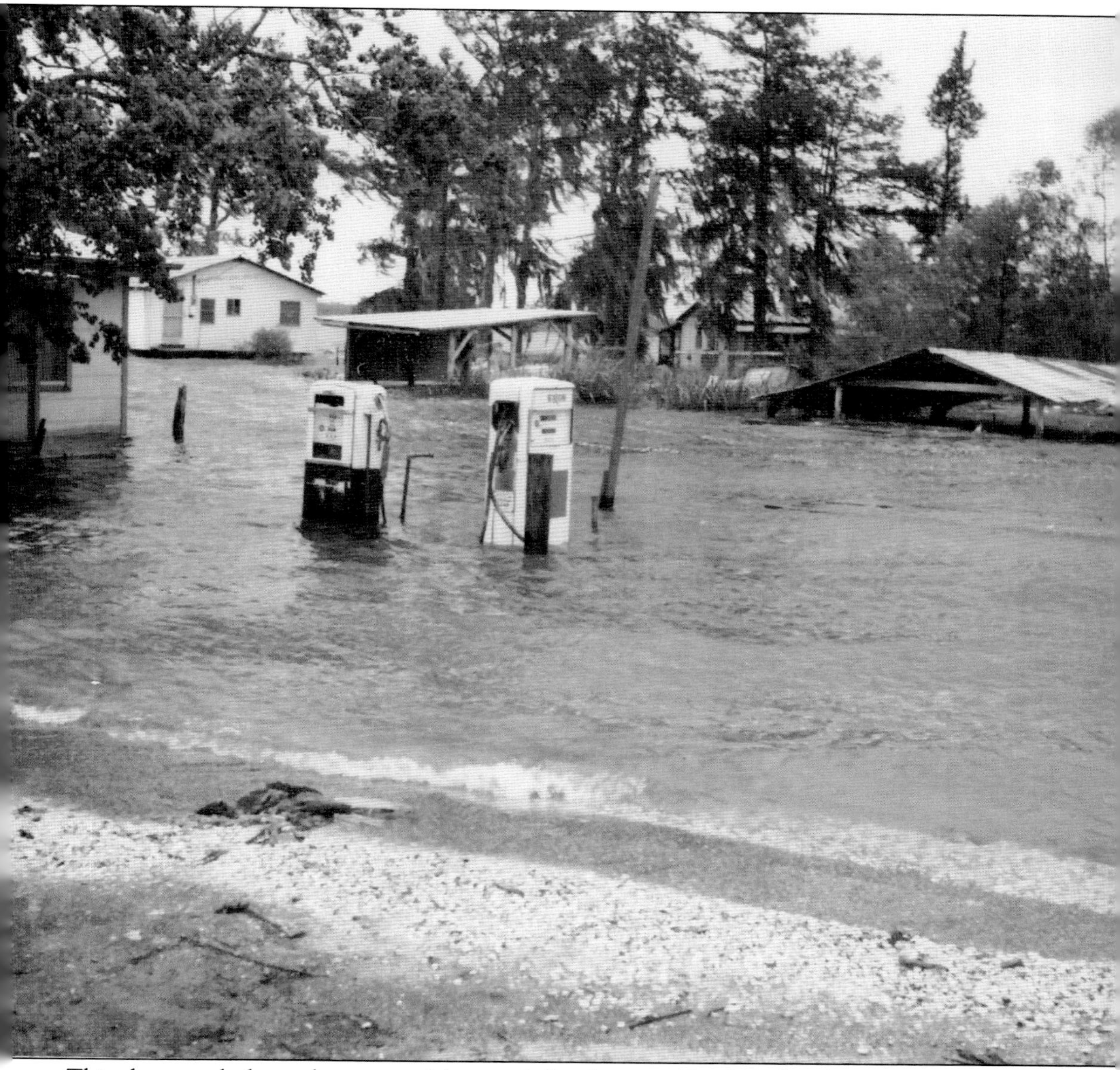

This photograph shows the extent of that year's flooding near Frank Bailey's home and business. (Courtesy of the Gerald and Olivia Chenevert family.)

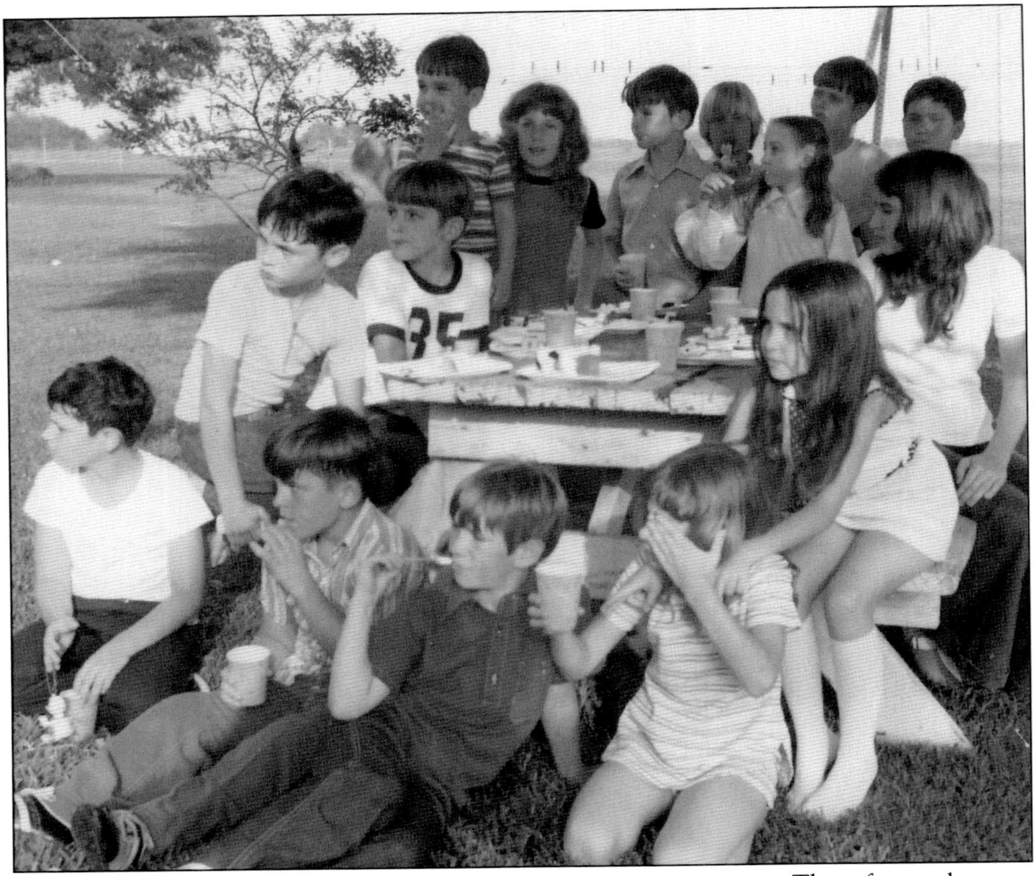

These future class of 1980 Assumption High School graduates enjoy a birthday party for one of their classmates. (Courtesy of the Gerald and Olivia Chenevert family.)

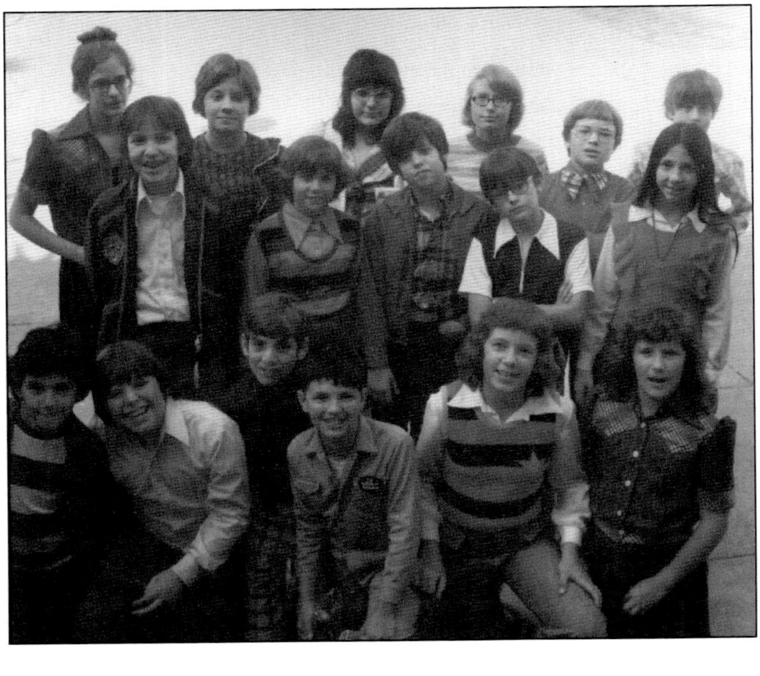

This photograph of Assumption High School students was taken in the late 1970s. (Courtesy of the Gerald and Olivia Chenevert family.)

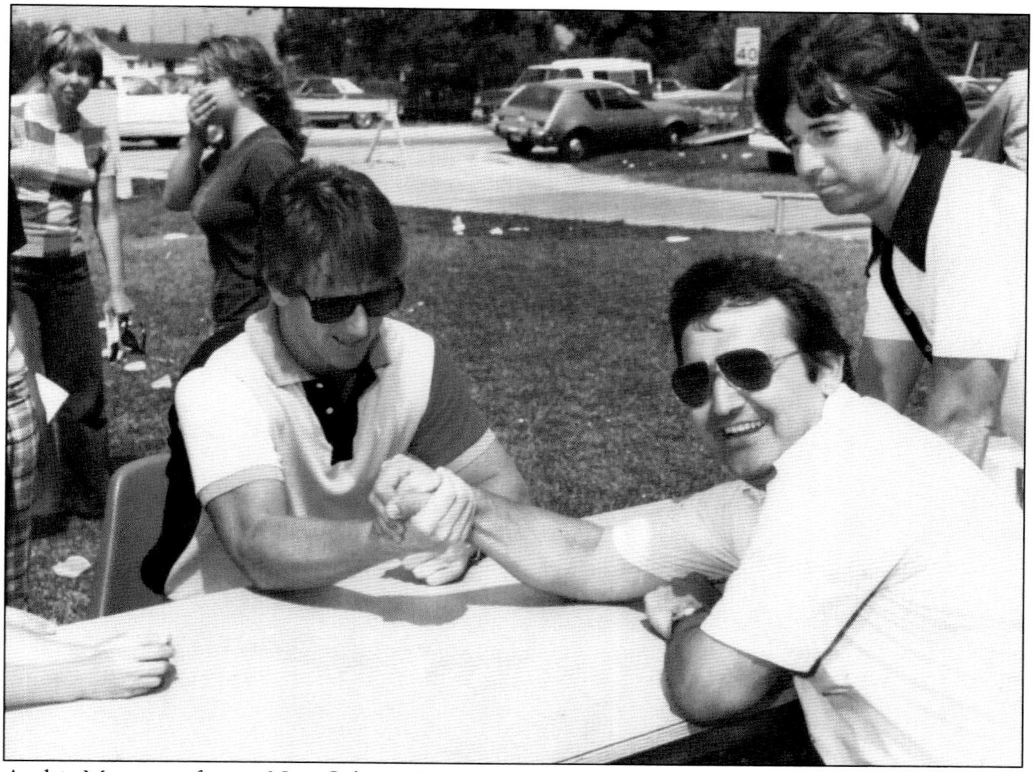

Archie Manning, former New Orleans Saints quarterback and father of National Football League quarterbacks Peyton and Eli Manning, gets pinned by Donald Blanchard in this arm-wrestling match as his brother Kenneth officiates. (Courtesy of Nick and Loretta Carrier.)

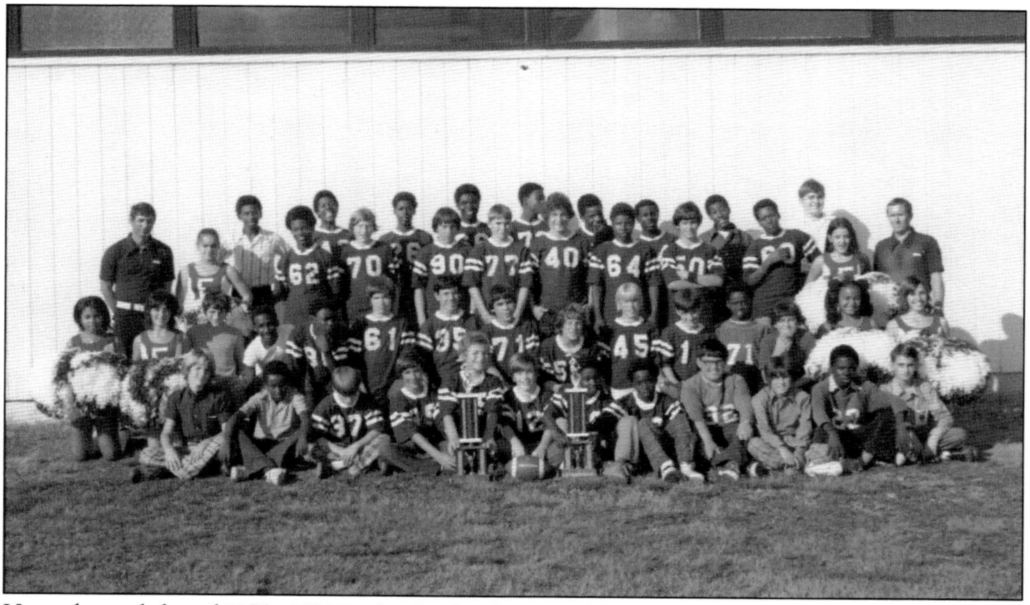

Here, the undefeated 1973–1974 Eagles display their regular-season and title-game trophies. Rodney Paul LeBlanc and Bobby Crochet coached this winning team. (Courtesy of Kent Templet.)

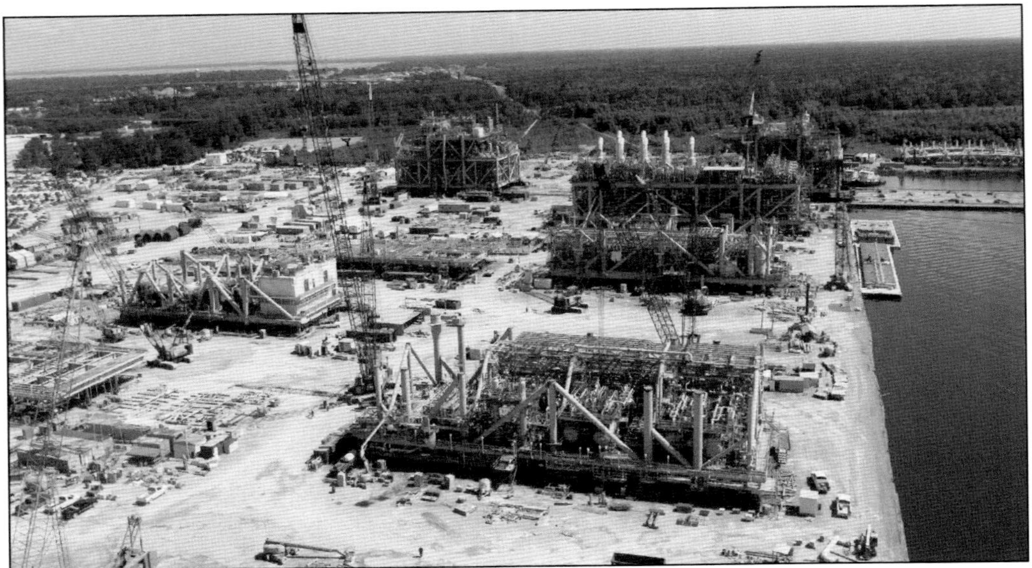

McDermott's Morgan City facility in Bayou L'Ourse is a fabrication yard with over 300 acres. From this facility, the company expanded its construction capabilities worldwide. As the yard and offshore oil and gas support industry developed throughout local parishes, the area became an energy infrastructure fabrication hub. Recently, McDermott played a key role in protecting the community, providing one of its very large launch barges to act as a temporary dam across Bayou Chene, averting potential flooding. McDermott is active in oil and gas operating regions worldwide. Its success is credited to locally focused and globally integrated resources. It has over 14,000 employees, a diversified fleet of marine vessels, fabrication facilities, and engineering offices worldwide. (Courtesy of McDermott International.)

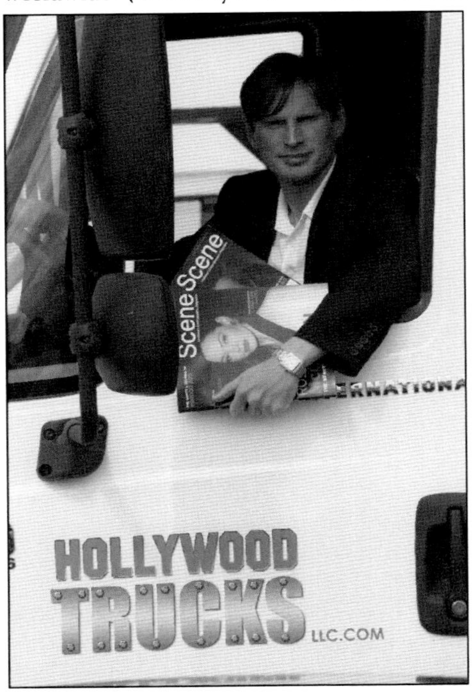

The *Greater Baton Rouge Business Report* asserts that Napoleonville native Andre J. Champagne's company Hollywood Trucks has had a hand in 95 percent of all films made in Louisiana since 2007; it is the largest entertainment transportation trucking company in the southeastern United States. In 2007, Champagne founded the state's premier entertainment magazine, *Scene Magazine*. He plans the production of two feature films per year beginning in 2012 and serves as vice president of the Louisiana Film and Entertainment Association. (Courtesy of Andre Champagne.)

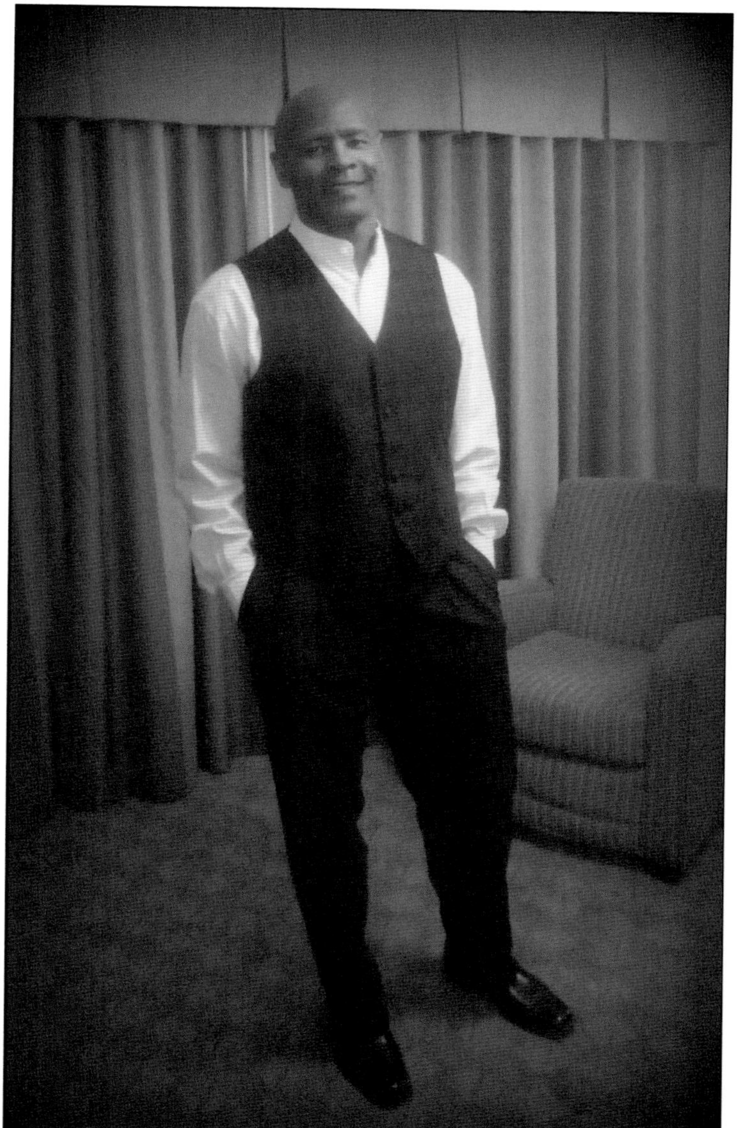

Johnny S. Meads has an eye for talent that has led him to become a scout for the Tennessee Titans and his receipt of the 2007 Fritz Pollard Alliance Award for the American Football Conference (AFC) Scout of the Year. He began his scouting career with the Green Bay Packers following a 13-year career with the Houston Oilers, where he was a third-round selection in the 1984 National Football League Draft. Baptized on August 17, 1969, at St. Mark Baptist Church in Freetown, Louisiana, the Labadieville native, son of Zack and Ethel Meads, began his football career in Labadieville playing in the Jaycee Football League. He played at Assumption High School, where his jersey no. 85 was retired. Inducted into the Nicholls State University Sports Hall of Fame, Meads was awarded a Certificate of Recognition from the Outstanding Alumni Committee. He was a Division I-AA All-American and second-leading tackler in Nicholls State University history. He received the key to the city on May 8, 1992. In 2005, he became a Tri-Parish (Lafourche-Terrebonne-Assumption) Hall of Fame inductee. He and wife, Darby, reside in Navarre, Florida, and are the parents of Jeremy, Brittney, and Andrea. (Courtesy of Johnny Meads.)

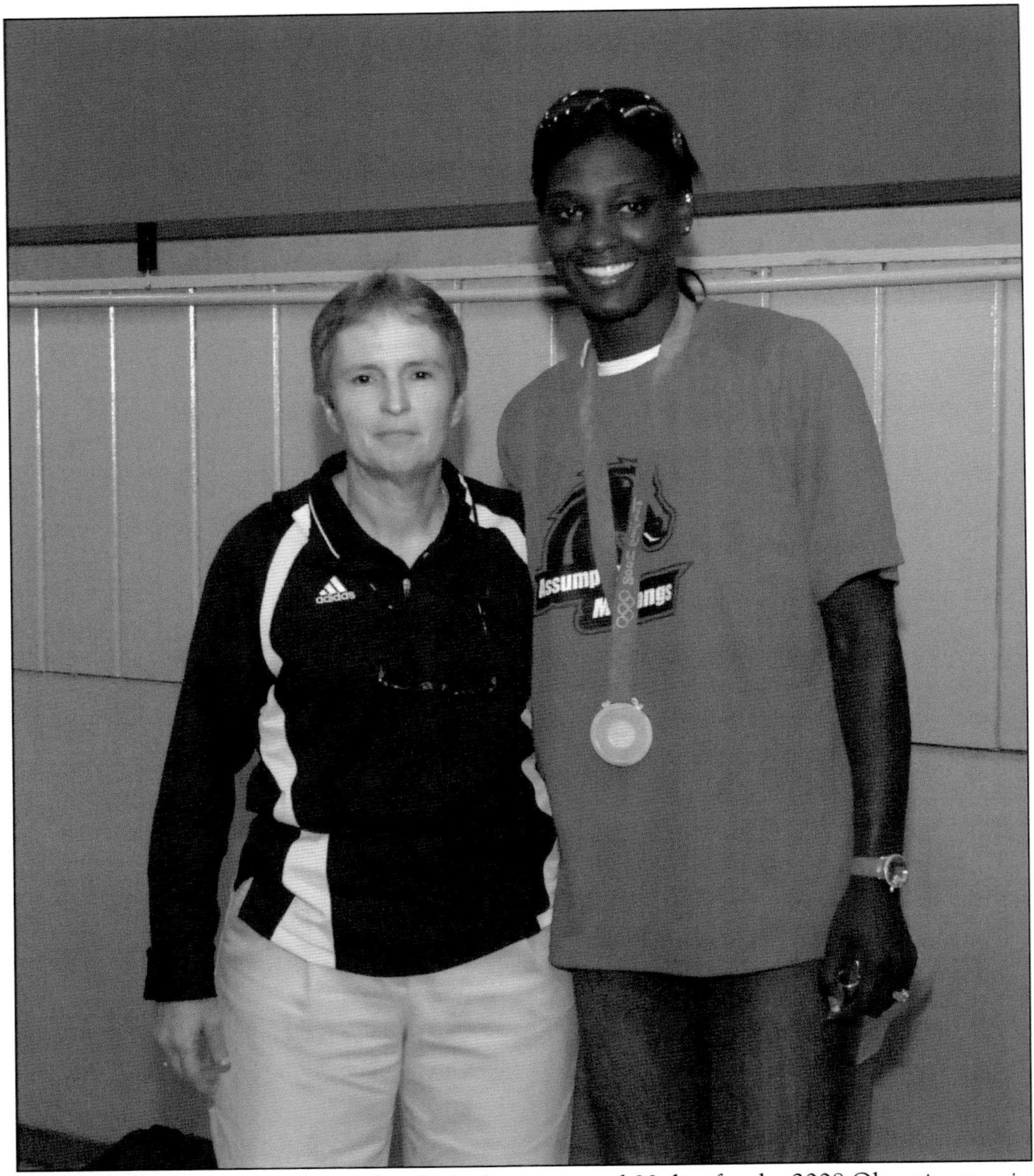

Kim Willoughby recorded 35 kills, a block, four aces, and 20 digs for the 2008 Olympic team in Beijing, returning home with a silver medal. Here, Kim stands with her Assumption High School volleyball coach, Sandy Bergeron Fussell. Fussell led Assumption High School to three state volleyball championships, where Kim was chosen the state's top player twice and earned a spot on the US Junior National team. After graduation in 2000, Willoughby continued her volleyball career at the University of Hawaii and became a three-time All-American before earning a place on the US Olympic Volleyball team. (Courtesy of Kim B. Comeaux.)

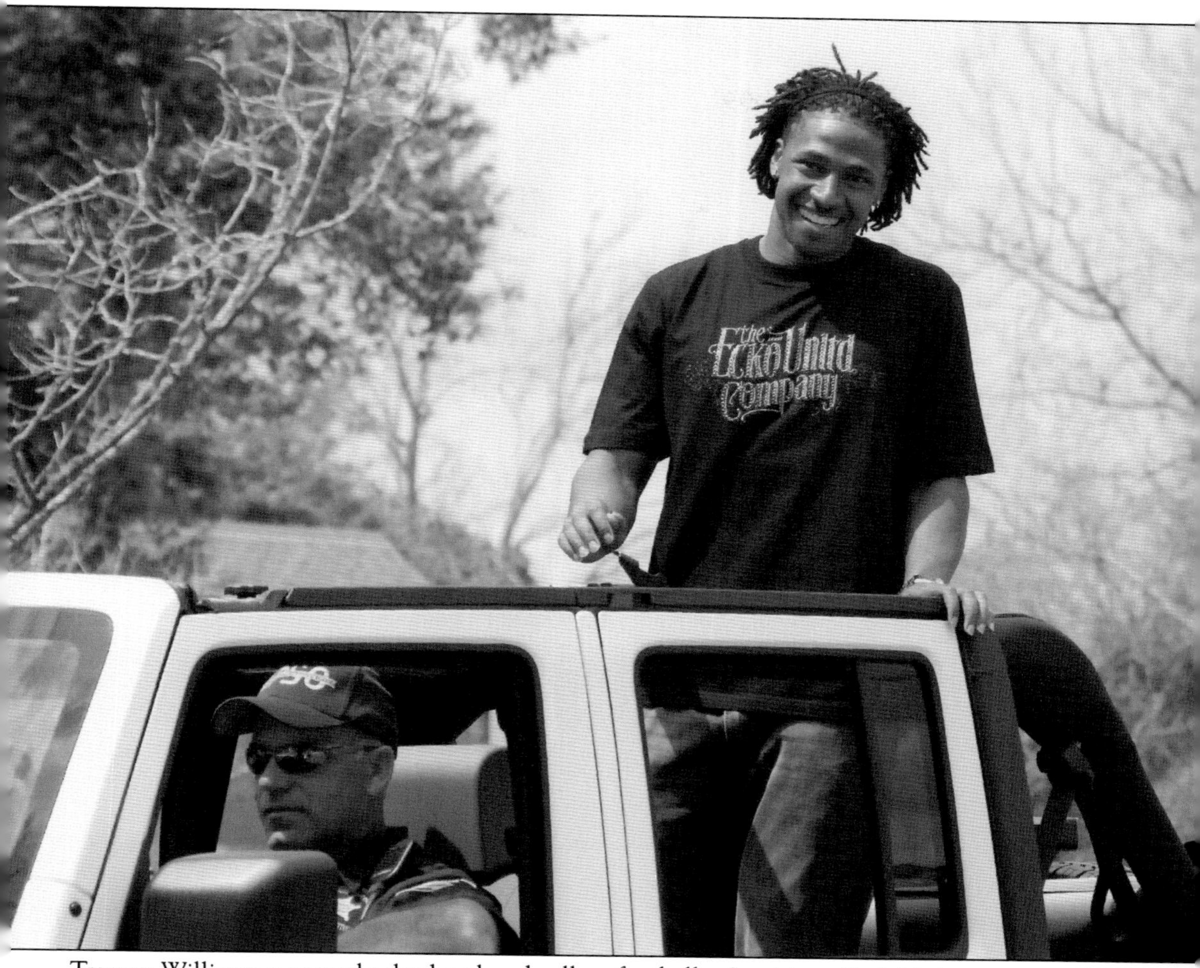

Tramon Williams, a cornerback who played college football at Louisiana Tech University, signed with the Green Bay Packers in 2006 after his debuting with the Houston Texans. Williams's highlights include being added as a reserve to the 2011 Pro Bowl roster; however, he did not play as he was part of Super Bowl XLV when the Packers defeated the Pittsburg Steelers, 31-25. He is a 2001 graduate of Assumption High School. (Courtesy of Kim B. Comeaux.)

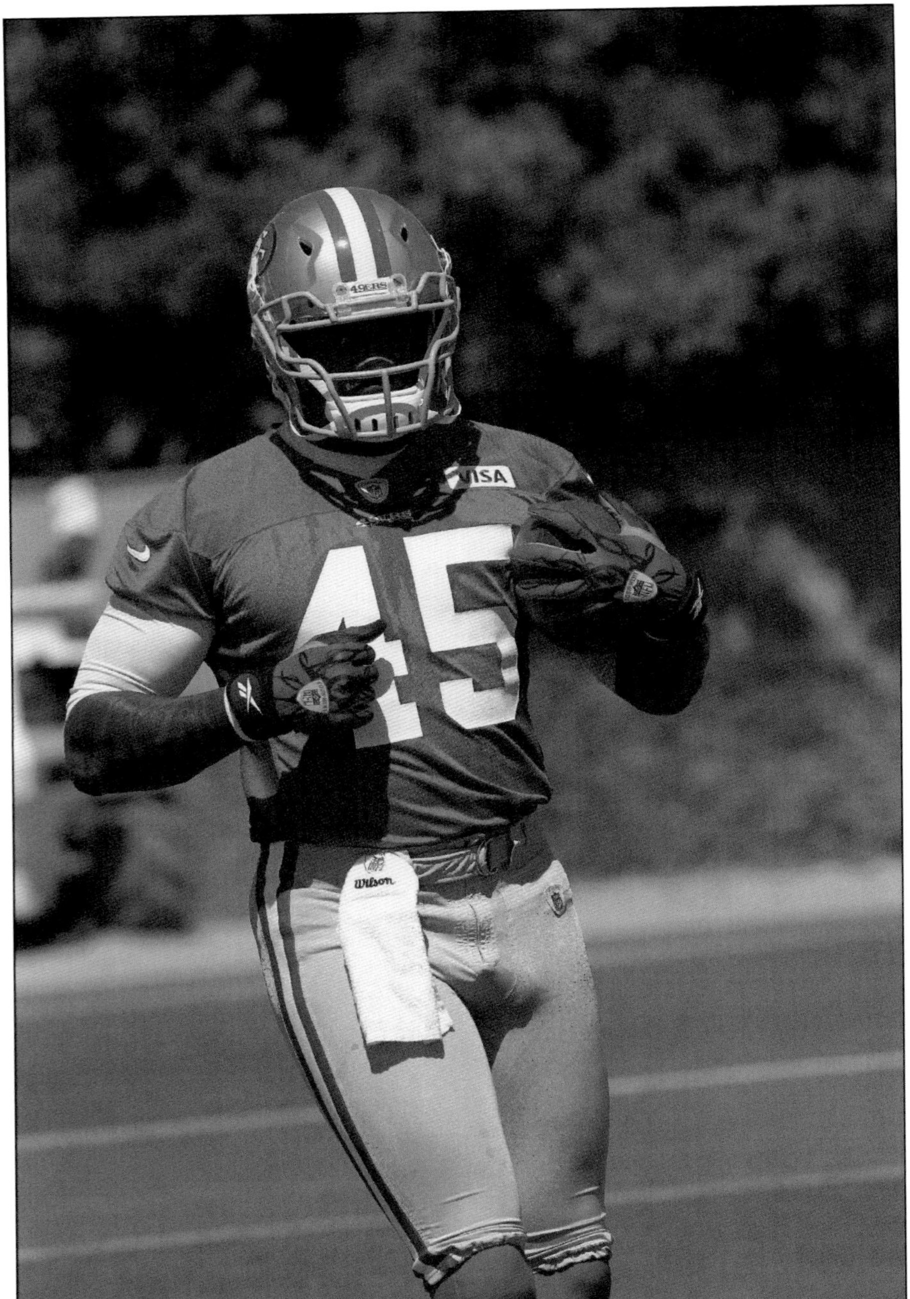

Brandon Jacobs holds the record for the most rushing touchdowns in Giants history. This 2001 Assumption High School graduate attended Coffeyville Community College in Kansas before transferring to the University of Auburn and then transferring to Southern Illinois University. There, he became a fourth-round draft choice for the New York Giants. On February 5, 2012, he played in Super Bowl XLVI and won the second Super Bowl ring of his career. A Fairleigh Dickinson University graduate with a bachelor's in sociology, Jacobs signed with the San Francisco 49ers on March 28, 2012. (Courtesy of the San Francisco 49ers.)

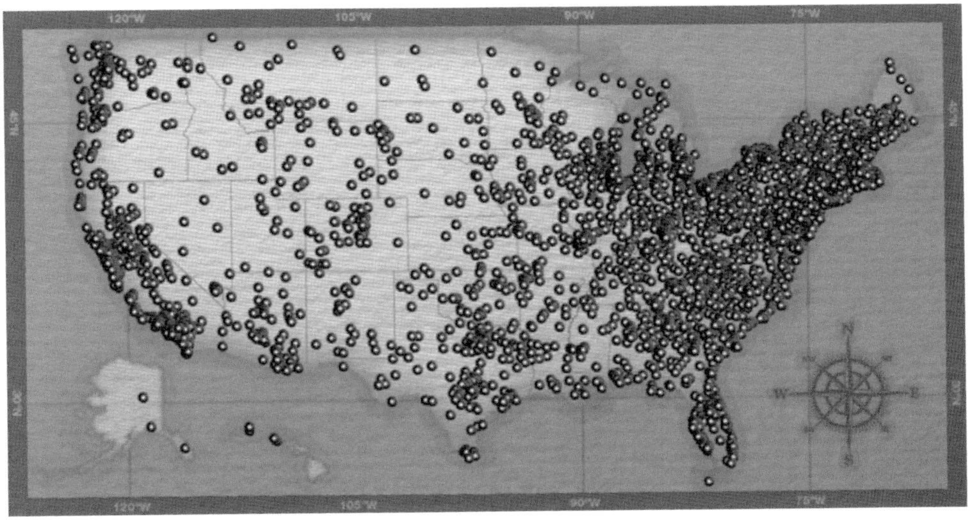

Bibliography

"Assumption Parish Civic and Social Calendar." Napoleonville Mothers Club, 1958–1959, 1962–1963.

Assumption Pioneer. 1850.

Bergeron, Eva Hidalgo, and Richard Rene Bergeron. *Wildwood Plantation*. Baton Rouge: Renee B. Richard, 1999.

Butler, W.E. *Down Among the Sugar Cane: The Story of Louisiana Sugar Plantations and Their Railroads*. Baton Rouge: Moran Publishing Corp., 1980.

Conrad, Glenn R., and Ray F. Lucas. *White Gold: A Brief History of the Louisiana Sugar Industry, 1795–1995*. Louisiana Life Series, no. 8. Lafayette, LA: University of Southwestern Louisiana, 1995.

"Down the Bayou." *Times-Picayune*, December 8, 1963.

Field, Martha R. *Louisiana Voyages: The Travel Writings of Catharine Cole*. Jackson, MS: University Press of Mississippi, 2006.

Holleman, Henry. *The Gem of Bayou Lafourche: A Short History of the Assumption Church in Plattenville, Louisiana*. New Orleans: Franklin Printing Co., 1948.

Howell, Roland Boatner Sr. *Louisiana Sugar Plantations, Mardi Gras, and Huey P. Long: Reminiscences of Roland Boatner Howell Sr.* Baton Rouge: Claitor's Publishing Div., 1969.

Leumas, Emilie G., and Renée B. Richard, *Roots of Faith: History of the Diocese of Baton Rouge*. Éditions du Signe, 2009.

Mariz, Linda French. *Dugas and Leblanc: A Case Study in Post-Reconstruction Sugar Cane Planting, 1880–1900*. A thesis presented to the faculty of Western Washington State College, 1973.

"Pugh (Thomas and Family) Papers," Mss. No. 4437. Louisiana and Lower Mississippi Valley Collections Special Collections, Hill Memorial Library, Louisiana State University Libraries, Baton Rouge.

Stahls, Paul F. *Plantation Homes of Lafouche Country*. Gretna, LA: Pelican Pub., 1976.

Taylor, Joe Gray. *Louisiana: A History*. New York: W.W. Norton & Co., 1976.